# New Proficiency PASSKEY

## Student's Book

**NICK KENNY**

with Peter Sunderland and Jane Barnes

# Contents Map

|  | Vocabulary | Grammar Focus | Help Sections | Exam Focus |
|---|---|---|---|---|
| **UNIT ONE** *Sign of the Times* 1 | | | | |
| Food<br>Health | Definitions<br>Phrasal verbs with 'out'<br>Prefixes<br>Prepositions<br>Word stress<br><br>Spelling: silent *e* (WB) | Past tense review<br>Linking words and phrases<br>Causatives<br><br><br><br>Full stops and capital<br>  letters (WB) | Help with writing: articles<br>Help with cloze passages | **Paper 1**: Multiple-choice questions<br>**Paper 2**: Descriptive writing<br>**Paper 3**: Comprehension questions<br>          Summary skills<br>**Paper 4**: Matching task<br>          Sentence completion task<br>**Paper 5**: Expressing opinions<br>          Talking together about a visual prompt<br>          Negotiating and selecting |
| **UNIT TWO** *Call of the Wild* 22 | | | | |
| Animals<br>Conservation<br>  issues | Idiomatic phrases<br>Phrasal verbs<br>Collocation<br><br>Spelling: double consonants (WB)<br>Word stress (WB) | Cause and result<br>Relative pronouns<br><br><br>Uses of the article (WB)<br>Commas (WB) | Help with gapped sentences<br>Help with listening:<br>  sentence completion tasks<br>Help with reading:<br>  gapped text tasks | **Paper 1**: Multiple-choice questions<br>          Lexical cloze task<br>**Paper 2**: Formal letters<br>**Paper 3**: Comprehension questions<br>          Cloze passage<br>**Paper 4**: Four-option multiple-choice questions<br>**Paper 5**: Talking together about a visual prompt<br>          Expressing opinions<br>          Discussing pros and cons |
| **UNIT THREE** *A Word in your Ear* 42 | | | | |
| Language<br>  learning<br>Books and<br>  reading | Collocation<br>Referencing<br>Phrasal verbs<br><br>Spelling: words ending in *y* (WB)<br>Similes (WB) | The passive<br>Complex sentences<br>Question forms<br><br>Comparison and contrast (WB)<br>Genitives and apostrophes (WB) | Help with speaking: long turn<br>Help with word-building:<br>  cloze tasks | **Paper 1**: Lexical cloze task<br>**Paper 2**: Preparing a report<br>**Paper 3**: Comprehension questions<br>          Summary skills<br>**Paper 4**: Three-option multiple-choice questions<br>          Selecting an answer<br>          Four-option multiple-choice questions<br>**Paper 5**: Talking together about a visual prompt<br>          Expressing likes and dislikes |
| **UNIT FOUR** *A Fine Romance* 63 | | | | |
| Relationships<br>Personal<br>  qualities | Abstract nouns<br>Idiomatic expressions<br>Phrasal verbs<br>Proverbs<br><br>Spelling: common errors (WB)<br>Word building (WB) | Linking words and phrases<br>Inversions<br><br><br><br>Uses of *get* (WB)<br>Inverted commas (WB) | Help with multiple-choice<br>  questions<br>Help with Use of English:<br>  transformations | **Paper 1**: Lexical cloze task<br>          Multiple-choice questions<br>**Paper 2**: Essays<br>**Paper 3**: Comprehension questions<br>          Cloze passage<br>          Summary skills<br>**Paper 4**: Three-option multiple-choice questions<br>          Four-option multiple-choice questions<br>          Sentence completion task<br>**Paper 5**: Talking together about a visual prompt |
| **UNIT FIVE** *All Right on the Night* 84 | | | | |
| The performing<br>  arts<br>Entertainment | Prepositions<br>Dictionary skills<br>Word stress<br><br>Spelling and<br>  pronunciation (WB) | Linking expressions<br>Reported speech<br><br><br>Clauses with *whatever*,<br>  *however*, etc. (WB)<br>Reported speech (WB) | Help with Use of English:<br>  summary writing<br>Help with listening:<br>  three-way matching tasks | **Paper 1**: Lexical cloze task<br>          Gapped text task<br>          Reading for main points and<br>            specific information<br>**Paper 2**: Magazine articles<br>          Reviews<br>**Paper 3**: Summary skills<br>          Comprehension questions<br>**Paper 4**: Four-option multiple-choice questions<br>          Sentence completion task<br>**Paper 5**: Expressing likes and dislikes<br>          Long turn |

|  | Vocabulary | Grammar Focus | Help Sections | Exam Focus |
|---|---|---|---|---|
| **UNIT SIX** *Tip of my Tongue* 106 | | | | |
| Memory<br>Information<br>technology | Collocation<br>Prefixes<br>Record keeping<br>Phrasal verbs with 'up'<br><br>Word stress (WB)<br>Prefixes and suffixes (WB)<br>Word building (WB) | Conditionals<br><br><br><br>Gerund and infinitive (WB)<br>Relative pronouns (WB)<br>Commas and clauses (WB) | | **Paper 1**: Reading for specific information<br>Lexical cloze task<br>Gapped text task<br>**Paper 2**: Narratives<br>**Paper 3**: Word-building cloze task<br>Summary skills<br>Transformations<br>Cloze passage<br>**Paper 4**: Three-option multiple-choice questions<br>Listening for specific information<br>Note taking task<br>Sentence completion task<br>**Paper 5**: Talking about personal abilities<br>Talking together about a visual prompt |
| **UNIT SEVEN** *A Matter of Taste* 127 | | | | |
| Taste<br>Art and design<br>Culture | Adjectives<br>Synonyms<br>Compound words<br>Prefixes<br><br>Spelling: *cede/ceed/sede* (WB) | Inversions<br>Exemplification<br>Expressing concession<br><br><br>Gerund and infinitive (WB)<br>Wishes and regrets (WB) | Help with speaking:<br>Part Two | **Paper 1**: Multiple-choice questions<br>Lexical cloze task<br>**Paper 2**: Letters<br>Giving opinions<br>**Paper 3**: Summary skills<br>Comprehension questions<br>Cloze passage<br>Word-building cloze task<br>**Paper 4**: Matching task<br>Sentence completion task<br>**Paper 5**: Developing a topic |
| **UNIT EIGHT** *Go your own Way* 149 | | | | |
| Advertising<br>Hierarchies<br>Deception | Advertising<br>Definitions<br>Language of deception<br>Idioms<br>Phrasal verbs<br><br>Proverbs (WB)<br>Spelling (WB) | Parts of speech<br><br><br><br><br><br>Reporting verbs (WB) | Help with writing:<br>reports and proposals | **Paper 1**: Lexical cloze task<br>Gapped text task<br>**Paper 2**: Proposals<br>Newspaper articles<br>**Paper 3**: Word-building cloze task<br>Comprehension questions<br>Cloze passage<br>**Paper 4**: Matching task<br>Three-option multiple-choice questions<br>Sentence completion task<br>**Paper 5**: Long turn<br>Expressing opinions |
| **UNIT NINE** *Nose to the Grindstone* 170 | | | | |
| World of work<br>Recruitment/<br>job applications | Definitions<br>Proverbs<br>Idiomatic expressions<br>Business terms<br>Word stress<br><br>Spelling: common errors (WB)<br>Word building (WB) | Reference skills<br>Nouns formed from phrasal<br>verbs<br><br><br><br>*So/Nor/Neither* (WB)<br>Predicative *so/not* (WB) | Help with the Writing Paper | **Paper 1**: Lexical cloze task<br>Multiple-choice questions<br>Gapped text task<br>**Paper 2**: Formal letters<br>**Paper 3**: Cloze passage<br>Comprehension questions<br>Summary skills<br>Word-building cloze task<br>**Paper 4**: Three-option multiple-choice questions<br>Four-option multiple-choice questions<br>Listening for specific information<br>Sentence completion task<br>**Paper 5**: Talking together about a visual prompt<br>Giving opinions |
| **UNIT TEN** *The Road Ahead* 193 | | | | |
| Travel<br>Tourism | Phrasal verbs<br>Definitions<br><br>Group nouns (WB)<br>Topic-specific lexis (WB)<br>Spelling: checking your work (WB) | Noun phrases | Help with the Speaking Test | **Paper 1**: Gapped text task<br>Lexical cloze task<br>Multiple-choice questions<br>**Paper 2**: Proposals<br>Describing a place<br>**Paper 3**: Summary skills<br>Cloze passage<br>**Paper 4**: Three-option multiple-choice questions<br>Four-option multiple-choice questions<br>Matching task<br>**Paper 5**: Talking together about a visual prompt |

# Introduction

This book is designed to help you prepare for all aspects of the Proficiency examination. Each unit in the book includes a wide variety of tasks and exercises, all designed to help you to develop your vocabulary and practise the reading, writing, listening and speaking skills you need to pass the examination.

There are Help sections throughout the book which explain the main task types in the examination and give advice about how to approach each task. There is also further practice of the Use of English exercises in the Exam Practice section at the end of each unit.

The separate Workbook provides further exercises in the areas of grammar, vocabulary and writing skills, as well as giving the opportunity for more practice of the exam-style tasks and exercises.

Below is a description of the revised Proficiency examination.

## The Certificate of Proficiency in English

The Proficiency examination is the highest level examination in English as a Foreign Language offered by the University of Cambridge.

The examination has five papers. Each represents 20% of the total marks. They can be summarized as follows:

### Paper 1   Reading Comprehension (1 hour 30 minutes)

This paper is divided into four parts. The first part tests your knowledge of vocabulary, collocation, phrasal verbs and other aspects of usage through multiple-choice gap-fill questions based on three short texts.

The second part tests comprehension of gist, content, tone and register in passages of written English. There are four short texts on a related theme, each with two multiple-choice questions. The fourth part has similar questions on one longer text.

The third part is a gapped text where some of the paragraphs have been removed. This task tests your knowledge of coherence and cohesion in written texts.

### Paper 2   Writing (2 hours)

In this paper you have to produce two pieces of writing of between 300 and 350 words each. The first is a compulsory task based on written input material. In the second you have to do one writing task from a choice of four. You may be asked to write letters, reviews, reports, proposals, articles or essays.

Examiners who mark each piece of writing give credit for good organization, task fulfilment, and the quality and range of language used. Examples of marked writing tasks can be found on pages 216–218.

### Paper 3   Use of English (1 hour 30 minutes)

This paper tests your knowledge and control of the English language. There are five parts:

- Cloze passage (Help section on page 17)
- Word-building cloze (Help section on page 54)
- Gapped sentences (Help section on page 25)
- Key word transformations (Help section on page 79)

The fifth part contains two short passages on the same topic, each followed by two comprehension questions.

A final task in the fifth part is to write a summary, based on points taken from both texts. There is a Help with Summary Writing section on page 91.

### Paper 4   Listening (40 minutes approximately)

This paper tests your understanding of seven recorded listening texts. You hear each text twice. There are four parts to the test:

- Part One has four short texts with two multiple-choice questions on each text. These test your gist understanding of the text.
- Part Two has one long informational text with nine sentence completion items. These test detailed understanding of the text.
- Part Three has one long text with five multiple-choice questions. These test attitude and opinions expressed in the text.
- Part Four has one long conversational text with a three-way matching task. This tests understanding of opinions and whether the speakers agree or disagree.

There are Help with Listening sections on pages 28 and 98.

### Paper 5   Speaking (19 minutes approximately)

This paper tests your ability to discuss and comment on issues and express opinions. There are three main parts to the test. You take the test together with a partner, with whom you work in Part Two.

- Part One. You each talk about yourselves in response to the examiner's questions.
- Part Two. You talk about a set of visual prompts with your partner.
- Part Three. You each speak for two minutes on a topic, and then take part in a broader discussion led by the examiner on issues related to your talks.

The examiners are looking for vocabulary, interactive communication, discourse management, pronunciation as well as control and range of grammar. There are Help with Speaking sections on pages 49, 130 and 209.

UNIT 1

# Sign of the Times

### SPEAKING 1
***Expressing opinions***

1   Discuss the following with your partner.

Your favourite food:
- why you like it
- when you like to eat it
- how it should be prepared

The importance of these things in food:

| | | |
|---|---|---|
| taste | colour | texture |
| smell | temperature | presentation |

2   Some visitors from overseas are coming to visit your area for a day and want to find out about the local cuisine. What would you recommend they eat? Talk about:

| | |
|---|---|
| restaurants | breakfast |
| snacks | bars |
| lunch | drinks |
| dinner | home cooking |

3   What do these terms mean?
   a   convenience food
   b   fast food
   c   organic food
   d   genetically-modified food

4   What do you think of these types of food?

# UNIT 1 Sign of the Times

## USE OF ENGLISH 1
### Comprehension

■ 1 Look at this headline. What do you think the article is going to be about?

■ 2 Read both parts quickly to find out what happened in each of these years or decades.

| 1880s | 1904 | 1921 | 1950s | 1960s | 1970s | 1980s | 1990s |

■ 3 Read the article again and answer questions **1–13** with a word or short phrase.

# Crisis in a Sesame Bun

### Part 1: The Hamburger – origins and early history

DESPITE THE BAD publicity surrounding 'Mad Cow Disease' in the 1990s, the hamburger remains an icon for the twentieth century. In its provenance, preparation, purchase and very place of consumption it tells in microcosm the history of the century. In each decade its character and its image subtly reflected the shifting fashions and preoccupations of the era.

10 Its origins are cloaked in an uncertainty that only assists its status as a characterless object to which each generation may add whatever relish it chooses. Its connections with the German city of Hamburg are unclear. Although every culinary civilization has had some form of ground meat patty, most food historians do accept a link with the eponymous Baltic port.

Thus the hamburger enters history as the
20 plain but honest food of poor but ambitious immigrants to the United States. Indeed, according to one food expert, it had its origins in the fare of a German-owned shipping line, on whose vessels in the 1880s Hamburg beef was minced and then mixed with breadcrumbs, eggs and onions and served with bread.

But it was at the World Fair in St Louis in 1904 that it first became a symbol of mass-produced cuisine. It was there that the bun
30 was first introduced and the result was wildly popular. Soon after, in 1921, the first hamburger chain was established. But generally the burger remained a wholesome home-made dish. Older Americans still cherish childhood memories of Mom grinding good fresh steak and, after adding onion and seasoning, taking the result straight out to the charcoal grill in the garden, but like all things American, when exported it has been
40 debased and perverted.

The hamburger first entered British consciousness as part of the post-Second World War spending spree, when beef became a symbol of the new prosperity. When, in the late 1950s, the frozen beefburger was introduced (renamed to avoid unnecessary questions about why it did not taste of ham), the thin little cake of bland rubbery meat was a glamour product. It was
50 somehow foreign and, of course, frozen, which was then the height of new technology.

1 Explain in your own words what is meant by the phrase 'the hamburger remains an icon for the twentieth century'. (lines 2–4)

2 In your own words, explain why the writer regards the hamburger as an essentially 'characterless' object.

3 What is referred to by the phrase 'the eponymous Baltic port'? (lines 17–18)

4 What is the 'result' referred to in line 30?

5 In what way has the hamburger been 'debased and perverted'? (line 40)

6  What is a 'spending spree'? (line 43)

7  Explain in your own words why the hamburger was renamed 'beefburger' in Britain in the 1950s.

8  What is meant in this context by the phrase 'a glamour product'? (line 49)

### Part 2: The Hamburger in the Modern Age

The symbolic importance of the burger cannot be underestimated. Under its beefburger guise, it was the first of the new range of 'convenience' foods which were about to make the world a better place and begin the liberation of women from the drudgery of home-cooking and housework. The older generation did not approve, which made it all the better. In the Sixties the hamburger was a symbol of the techno age – perfectly circular and streamlined. It was as uniform and relentlessly predictable as only the latest technology could make it.

True, there were those who rebelled against it, but to most the hamburger was a reflection of the national love affair with Americana. It was a phenomenon which was made flesh in Seventies London with the trendy burgers of the Great American Disaster and the Hard Rock Café, and in many other cities round the world.

In the Eighties another subtle shift occurred. People became aware that America was no longer another place but a culture which had spread throughout the world. And the hamburger became globalized, too, in the form of McDonald's.

With its US home market, like the fat in its burgers, heavily saturated, McDonald's looked abroad. By the end of the Eighties it had grown to such a size that every day 28 million global citizens ate there and the Big Mac became omnipresent.

McDonald's stormed the world, but its successes also drew upon it in the Nineties the criticisms which were levelled at that era. Food experts began to see the world's changing culinary tastes as a symbol of what is wrong with the new consumerism. 'The hamburger is a metaphor for our times – cheap, convenient and an indication that we have given up any real interest in what we eat,' said the leading food writer Frances Bissell, lamenting the trends of our increasingly obese society towards snacking on the hoof or before the TV instead of eating proper meals.

Then along came 'Mad Cow Disease' and even though the average person was told they had more chance of winning the National Lottery than contracting 'Mad Person Disease', with it came the dreadful realization that the cheap, convenient, easy way out might, in the end, turn out to be none of these things.

Adapted from an article by Paul Vallely in *The Independent*.

9  Why is the word 'convenience' in line 55 in quotation marks?

10  What do you understand about the writer's view of Britain from the phrase 'the national love affair with Americana'? (lines 67–68)

11  Why did McDonald's decide to open branches outside the USA?

12  What is meant by the phrase 'snacking on the hoof'? (lines 96–97)
    Why is this phrase particularly appropriate to the article?

13  Why does the author compare 'Mad Person Disease' with winning the National Lottery?

UNIT 1 *Sign of the Times*

## VOCABULARY 1
### Definitions

■ 1   Choose the best definition (**A**, **B** or **C**) for each of these words as it is used in the context of the article.

1   provenance (line 4)
    **A**   range of ingredients    **B**   place of origin    **C**   number of varieties

2   preoccupations (line 9)
    **A**   special developments    **B**   recurrent problems    **C**   particular interests

3   fare (line 23)
    **A**   food provided    **B**   price of the ticket    **C**   type of journey

4   wholesome (line 33)
    **A**   traditional    **B**   ordinary    **C**   healthy

5   cherish (line 35)
    **A**   value    **B**   confess to    **C**   mention

6   bland (line 48)
    **A**   soft textured    **B**   lacking in taste    **C**   pale coloured

7   drudgery (line 58)
    **A**   loneliness    **B**   long hours    **C**   dull work

8   omnipresent (line 84)
    **A**   well-regarded    **B**   reasonably priced    **C**   found everywhere

9   lamenting (line 95)
    **A**   criticizing    **B**   regretting    **C**   describing

10  obese (line 96)
    **A**   overstressed    **B**   overworked    **C**   overweight

## WRITING 1
### Summary skills

■ 1   Look at this phrase from the first part of the article.

*it tells in microcosm the history of the century*

What do you understand by the term 'microcosm'?

■ 2   Look at the first part of the article only. In your own words, explain how the hamburger changed to suit the fashions of different periods in the first half of the twentieth century. Write no more than 70 words.

Use the questions below to help you structure your summary.

1   What do we know about the hamburger at the beginning of the century?
2   What important thing started in the 1920s?
3   What made hamburgers popular in Britain in the 1950s?

How will you link the ideas together? Look at the words and phrases in the box. Can you use any of these in your summary?

| first | later | originally | when |
|---|---|---|---|
| before | at first | after that | since |

## GRAMMAR 1
### Review of past tenses

**1**

1 Look at the article on pages 2 and 3 again. For each paragraph, look through quickly and decide what tense most of the main verbs are in (e.g. simple present, past simple, present perfect, etc.). Why is each tense appropriate to each paragraph?

2 Find some examples of the present perfect and past perfect tenses in the article. Underline them.

Why has this tense been used in each case?

**2** Put the verbs in brackets into the correct tense (present simple, present perfect, simple past, or past perfect).

The name hamburger (**1**) _____ (date) back to German immigrants travelling to the USA in the 1880s. It's only since 1902, however, that hamburgers (**2**) _____ (serve) in a bun. Before the 1920s, when the first chain of hamburger restaurants (**3**) _____ (open), most hamburgers (**4**) _____ (cook) at home.

The fashion for hamburgers in Britain (**5**) _____ (start) in the 1950s, and by the 1970s hamburger restaurants (**6**) _____ (become) some of the most fashionable in London. In the 1980s, McDonald's (**7**) _____ (decide) to expand their operations outside the USA and by the 1990s they (**8**) _____ (open) restaurants in most countries in the world.

Since 1980, people (**9**) _____ (begin) to question the assumption that fast food, and hamburgers in particular, (**10**) _____ (represent) progress.

📖 N.B. The Workbook has further work on past tenses.

## PHRASAL VERBS 1
### With 'out'

**1** Look at this extract from the article and underline the phrasal verb. What does this phrasal verb mean in this context?

*…with it came the dreadful realization that the cheap, convenient, easy way out might, in the end, turn out to be none of these things.*

**2** Complete each gap with a suitable verb to make more phrasal verbs with *out*.

1 Guests leaving the hotel are asked to _____ out of the hotel before 11 o'clock in the morning.

2 The investigation into the causes of the accident will be _____ out by a team of experts.

3 A foot injury has forced Fred to _____ out of Saturday's race.

4 The address is so badly printed that I can't _____ out the street name.

5 She went to the dentist's to have a tooth _____ out.

6 I decided to _____ out some of the ingredients from the recipe, as I wasn't sure they would taste nice in a cake.

📖 N.B. The Workbook has further examples of phrasal verbs with *out*.

UNIT 1 *Sign of the Times*

## SPEAKING 2
### Talking together about a visual prompt

**1** Look at the picture below. Talk about the picture with a partner using words and phrases you have learnt from the article about hamburgers. Talk about:
- the people; what they are doing and why; how they are feeling
- how you feel about the picture
- the images presented in the picture

**2** Now look at all the pictures. You have been asked to help design a poster on the theme 'icons of the twentieth century' which will symbolize twentieth century life. The poster will feature three pictures; one of a hamburger plus two others.

1 Look at these images and talk about how suitable each would be for the poster. Discuss your choices in relation to the following areas:
- the century as a whole
- people all round the world
- the future

Think about the positive and negative aspects of your choices.

2 Agree on the three images you want to put on the poster with the hamburger and then write a short report explaining your decision. (100 words)

Sign of the Times  UNIT 1

UNIT 1 *Sign of the Times*

## LISTENING 1
### Part One
### Matching

■ 1  Before you listen discuss these questions with your partner.

1  What is the attitude towards cigarette smoking in your country? Is this attitude changing?

2  Where is it possible to buy cigarettes:
   - in your country?
   - in any other countries you know about?

3  Do you think the sale of cigarettes should be restricted? Talk about:
   - age of buyers
   - places where they are sold
   - price controls
   - level of tax imposed on them

■ 2  You will hear part of a radio discussion about supermarkets selling cut-price cigarettes. For questions **1–9**, decide whether the opinions are expressed by only one of the speakers, or whether the speakers agree.
Write **J** for Joanne, **N** for Nigel or **B** for Both, where they agree.

1  There is little doubt about the harmful effects of smoking.   ☐ 1
2  Supermarkets are setting a bad example to the young.   ☐ 2
3  Supermarkets have a hypocritical attitude.   ☐ 3
4  The price of cigarettes affects how easy people find it to give up smoking.   ☐ 4
5  More people will start smoking if cigarettes are cheap.   ☐ 5
6  Supermarkets are using cheap cigarettes to attract new customers.   ☐ 6
7  Poor people often spend a lot of their money on cigarettes.   ☐ 7
8  Supermarkets should consider giving up the sale of all cigarettes.   ☐ 8
9  Supermarkets seem to regard smoking as an equivalent risk to eating unhealthy foods.   ☐ 9

### Part Two
### Sentence completion

■ 1  Look at these phrases from the listening text. Some words or short phrases have been removed. Look quickly to see if you can remember or guess the missing words or phrases.

This is one of the (**1**) _____ biggest preventable causes of death.

That (**2**) _____ is inconsistent with promoting a cheap cigarette.

They (**3**) _____ have a leaflet warning of the dangers of smoking.

It's the (**4**) _____ biggest factor that encourages smokers to increase their intake.

They are (**5**) _____ big chains that they can (**6**) _____ afford to sell their cigarettes (**7**) _____ more cheaply.

If supermarkets are (**8**) _____ interested in health, they should be reviewing the (**9**) _____ question of whether they sell tobacco products (**10**) _____ .

There's (**11**) _____ as a safe level of cigarette smoking.

Now listen again to check for the missing words.

## VOCABULARY 2
### Prefixes

■ 1  Look at these phrases from the listening text. What type of words have been underlined?

*This has <u>enraged</u> health campaigners.*
*It <u>encourages</u> smokers to increase their intake.*
*It's the factor that will <u>enable</u> adolescents to take up smoking.*

■ 2  Complete each sentence using the correct form of a word from the box and the prefix *en*.

| circle | close | danger | sure | roll | visage |
|--------|-------|--------|------|------|--------|
| force  | lighten | rich | list | joy | large |

1  To get your copy of the report, please write _____ a stamped, addressed envelope.

2  Laws aimed at preventing young people from taking up smoking are very difficult to _____ .

3  The old town is now _____ by a ring of modern suburbs.

4  The supermarket is being _____ and will soon have a super new bakery and delicatessen.

5  I'm going to _____ on a course to learn word-processing skills.

6  I'd like supermarkets to _____ that young people are not tempted to buy cigarettes there.

7  I can't _____ a meal in a restaurant where people are allowed to smoke.

8  I wonder if I could _____ your support in an anti-smoking campaign.

9  The plain meat sauce can be _____ with herbs and spices if you prefer.

10  People who smoke actually _____ the lives of themselves and others.

11  Do you _____ any problems in convincing the supermarkets to change their policies?

12  I don't seem to have understood so far, I wonder if you could _____ me?

## SPEAKING 3
### Expressing opinions

■ 1  Do you think that smoking should be banned in certain places?

Talk to your partner about:

- public transport
- places of entertainment
- schools and colleges
- eating places
- other public places

UNIT 1 *Sign of the Times*

## HELP WITH WRITING: ARTICLES

There are two parts to Paper 2 of the examination. You must produce two separate pieces of writing.

In Part One there is one question which you must answer. It is based on a short text. In Part Two, there is a choice of three general questions, or you may write about a set text, if you have studied one of them.

In both parts of the paper, each question includes information about:
- the context – who you are and why you are writing
- the text type – whether you are writing an article, a review, a proposal, a report or an essay
- the target reader – who is most likely to read your piece of writing

Help sections in this book will help you to prepare for each text type, and for both Part One and Part Two questions. The following section will focus on articles.

■ 1  Where do you usually read articles?
What style are they usually written in?

■ 2  Look at the following Part One Writing task. Can you identify:

- the context?    • the target reader?

The following comments were made during a public discussion on smoking which was broadcast on local radio. You attended the discussion and have decided to write an article for your local newspaper, responding to the points raised and giving your opinion.

*I believe you should live life to the full, and smoking can be enjoyable and exciting. It makes you feel cool and rebelious... I guess it's all part of growing up.*

*Quite apart from the obvious dangers to your health, smoking is just anti-social. I think it should be banned in all public places.*

*If you look at a non-smoker at a crowded party, he or she doesn't know what to do. Smoking can really help you feel confident socially.*

■ 3  Look at plans A and B. Is either of them suitable? If not, why not?

■ 4  Now look at plans C and D. Which one is best? Now expand on these notes.

■ 5  Think about the introduction and end to your article. How can you catch the attention of your target readers? How do you want your readers to feel once they have read your article? How should it end?

**A**
Introduction
What I think about smoking
Why attitudes need to change
What the Government should do
Conclusion

**B**
Introduction
The discussion –
    when, where, what, why?
Summarize what was said
Analysis of comments
Conclusion

**C**
Introduction
Is smoking part of growing up?
Can it improve your social life?
Is it damaging to your health?
Should it be banned in public?
Conclusion

**D**
Introduction
Does smoking damage your health?
Can it improve your social life?
Should it be banned in all public places?
Is it part of growing up?

Look at the following phrases. Do they come from the beginning or the end of an article?

a   There can be few people who can honestly claim never to have touched a cigarette.
b   Smoking is becoming more popular with young people despite the danger to health.
c   If you smoke regularly near to a baby you could give them a fatal disease.
d   It seems to me that some young people spend more money on smoking than they do on clothes.
e   The blonde-haired school girl strolled down the street chatting with her friends; she looked about 14. She paused to light a cigarette, then…
f   On the whole it seems that young people are ignoring all the information available to them about the effects of smoking.
g   We will never reduce the number of smokers unless we also reduce the advertising.
h   Is it right to try and control people's lifestyles?
i   Smoking kills! That's common knowledge.

**6**   Look at the words and phrases in the box. Most of them are used in written English when making lists of points or adding information when building up an argument. Which would you use to:
● make a contrast?       ● draw a conclusion?

| to begin with | moreover | however | furthermore | what's more |
| likewise | secondly | therefore | in addition | yet |

**7**   Now write paragraphs using the information from above. Try to use some of the linking words from the box where appropriate.

📖 N.B. The Workbook has further work on linking words.

## ✎ WRITING CHECKLIST

Before you begin any piece of writing there are six KEY things to think about. Following this Writing Checklist will help you to cover all the points that are considered when your writing is marked.

- Why am I writing?
- Who am I writing to?
- What is the best style to write in?
- What points should I include?
- How should the piece of writing be organized?
- How will the target reader feel after reading it?

1   Look at this Part Two Writing task.

*The student magazine in your school or college is planning a special 'Healthy Lifestyle' issue, and has asked for contributions from present or former students. You decide to write an article advising students on how to live a healthier life. Your article should give advice on smoking, food and eating within the college, the sports facilities available and the importance of using them.*

Write your article in **300–350** words.

Notice that the same text type, an article, may appear in both parts of Paper 2.
In which part of the Writing Paper is there input material which you must use?
In which part of the Writing Paper can you be a little more imaginative and inventive?

2   With a partner, go through the Writing Checklist and discuss the questions.

3   Now compare your ideas with another pair. Together prepare a plan for your article.

4   How are you going to begin and end your article?

5   Now write your article, remembering to check everything carefully when you have finished.

UNIT 1 *Sign of the Times*

## READING 1
*Multiple choice*

■ 1 Before you read the article discuss these questions with your partner.

1 Why are people frightened of going to the dentist?
2 Talk about a good or bad experience you, or someone you know, has had at the dentist.
3 What is a phobia? What sort of things do people have phobias about? How common do you think dental phobia is?
4 What advice would you give someone who is afraid of going to the dentist?

■ 2 Read the article about dental phobia.

# AFRAID TO OPEN WIDE

**RECENT RESEARCH** carried out by dentists and psychiatrists has shown that fear of the dentist is listed fifth among commonly held fears in many countries. Although figures are not available, some degree of dental phobia is estimated to affect about 30% of all adults, with many unable even to entertain the idea of dental work being done under anaesthetic.

As with most forms of phobic behaviour, the origins of dental fear tends to be found in childhood or adolescence. A traumatic dental experience is generally central, possibly with a critical or inconsiderate dentist, or maybe backed up by unfavourable experiences related by others, especially family members. Such experiences can influence adult behaviour despite any amount of educational and media coverage to the contrary.

The consequences of dental phobia can be traumatic in themselves. Over many years, a condition which is treatable can deteriorate into one which is not. Phobic patients are highly likely to suffer from dental disease and end up slowly losing their teeth or in emergency services.

When Clare Lodge was eleven, she visited a dentist who decided to do about twelve fillings in one session. 'I had to have a lot of injections, was enormously frightened and in pain for days and days afterwards,' she recalls. 'I was a dental phobic for years after that. Although I was still young enough to be forced to go, I refused to have injections because they had become associated with pain. When I was older I stopped going to the dentist for good.'

'I was very lucky – I didn't have many problems with my teeth; but recently I realized I had broken a tooth and really needed a filling.'

Ms Lodge, a training consultant, eventually got help – from a new dental service called Feelgood Dentistry which provides psychotherapy for dental phobics. 'I have to say I was sceptical at first,' she says, 'the therapist made me play back the scene when I was eleven in my mind – but as though I was sitting in the cinema and watching it on the screen. He told me to imagine the picture getting smaller and smaller, and in black and white. Then he asked me to play the film backwards – so that the last thing that happened was the injection coming out of my mouth'.

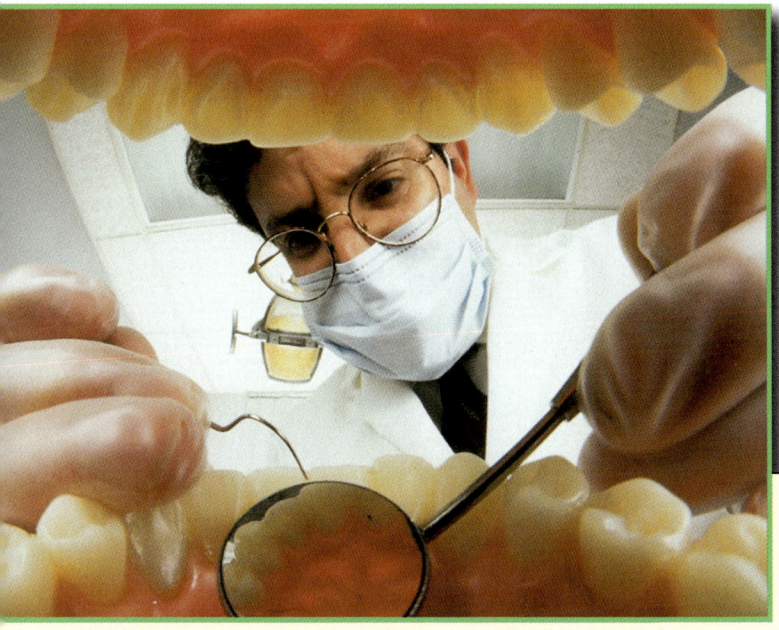

Feelgood Dentistry is a group of professionals with a particular interest in helping dental phobics by providing them with psychotherapy services. They have discovered a 'talking cure', an effective and friendly form of treatment, which often produces dramatic results. Graduated, controlled exposure of patients to the feared
60 stimulus is the guiding principle behind treatment. Like Clare Lodge, the patient first has a session, in a room near the surgery, with a psychotherapist who will work with them to help them leave their fear in the past. They will then have a consultation with the dentist. Psychotherapy is more effective if patients go immediately into the surgery, even if only for a consultation, rather than waiting several weeks.

The group also hopes to demystify the dentist and his equipment. All dentists do not cause pain. Clare Lodge
70 had not been to the dentist's in eighteen years when she went to Feelgood Dentistry. 'It put everything into perspective,' she says. 'The therapist made me appreciate that what I'd gone through as a youngster was not a huge drama; simply an insignificant moment in my life. On that occasion when I was a child, that particular dentist caused me pain. This does not mean to say that my childhood experience will be repeated.'

'When I finally underwent dental treatment, the original nightmare situation was back in history. I felt on top of
80 the situation. It wasn't completely pain-free, but it was manageable. Until that point, the idea of ever seeing another dentist had been a major ordeal, one that I felt I could never put myself through again.'

Adapted from an article by Sandra Alexander in *The Independent*.

### 3 Now answer the questions 1–5. Choose the answer (A, B, C or D) which you think fits best.

1 When the writer refers to 'educational and media coverage' he is making the point that

   A he disagrees with its message.
   B it has had a lot of influence on the public.
   C it has proposed an unrealistic theory.
   D there hasn't been enough of it.

2 In the years immediately following her dental trauma, Clare Lodge

   A refused to go back to the dentist at all.
   B only went to the dentist when she was in pain.
   C was fortunate enough not to need dental treatment.
   D had no choice but to continue going to the dentist.

3 When Clare first went to Feelgood Dentistry she felt

   A embarrassed that it was necessary.
   B defensive about her problem.
   C doubtful about their methods.
   D reluctant to talk about her problem.

4 How does the Feelgood Dentistry group help phobics?

   A The dentists are trained as psychotherapists.
   B The dental treatment takes place gradually, over time.
   C A psychotherapist is present during the dental treatment.
   D Patients overcome their fears before having dental treatment.

5 Which word or phrase reflects Clare's feelings about her therapy?

   A demystify (line 68)
   B put everything into perspective (lines 71–72)
   C an insignificant moment (line 74)
   D caused me pain (line 76)

UNIT 1 *Sign of the Times*

**4** Look at these pairs of words and decide what difference in meaning, if any, there is between them.

| | | | | |
|---|---|---|---|---|
| 1 | **a** anaesthetic<br>**b** painkiller | 7 | **a** associated<br>**b** connected | |
| 2 | **a** adolescence<br>**b** childhood | 8 | **a** sceptical<br>**b** cynical | |
| 3 | **a** traumatic<br>**b** upsetting | 9 | **a** psychotherapist<br>**b** psychiatrist | |
| 4 | **a** inconsiderate<br>**b** tactless | 10 | **a** demystify<br>**b** clarify | |
| 5 | **a** consequences<br>**b** results | 11 | **a** injections<br>**b** inoculations | |
| 6 | **a** deteriorate<br>**b** improve | 12 | **a** treatable<br>**b** curable | |

## PRONUNCIATION 1
*Word stress*

**1** Look at the words in the box. Underline the stressed syllable in each one.

> anaesthetic    adolescence    traumatic    inconsiderate
> consequences   deteriorate    injections   associated
> sceptical      psychotherapy  psychiatrist demystify

**2** Listen to check and compare your pronunciation of these words with that in the recording. If you find these words difficult to pronounce, practise saying them with your partner.

## VOCABULARY 3
*Prepositions*

**1** Complete each sentence with a suitable preposition. Then look back at the article on pages 12 and 13 to check.

1 Research has been carried _____ by psychiatrists.
2 Dental work is often done _____ local anaesthetic.
3 The consequences _____ dental phobia can be traumatic.
4 A treatable condition can deteriorate _____ one which is not.
5 Clare was _____ pain for days after her treatment.
6 Phobic patients are likely to suffer _____ dental disease.
7 Feelgood Dentistry has a particular interest _____ helping phobics.
8 Feelgood Dentistry provides phobics _____ a cure.
9 Patients have a consultation _____ a dentist.
10 Clare says the treatment put everything _____ perspective.

Sign of the Times **UNIT 1**

## GRAMMAR 2
### Causatives

■ 1  Look at these phrases:

*She went to the dentist to have a tooth filled.*
*Her teeth are not straight, so she'll have to have a brace fitted.*

What grammatical form is common to them? When do we use this form?

■ 2  Look at the words connected with the dentist. How many of them can be used with this form? Write some example sentences.

| | | | | |
|---|---|---|---|---|
| drill | fill | brace | take out/extract | decay |
| chair | X-ray | bib | crown | plate |
| check-up | injection | polish | hygiene | |

📖 N.B. The Workbook has further work on causatives.


## SPEAKING 4
### Describing an event

■ 1  Read the words of someone describing the first stages of the process of visiting the dentist.

Who is *you* in this passage?
How many different present tenses can you find?
Are the verb forms active or passive?
Underline three linking phrases which sequence the narrative.

■ 2  Now describe the experience of going to the dentist, doctor or optician for a check-up, from when you arrive to when you leave. Use this speaker's words as a model to start you off.

Think about:

- what you do on arrival/the waiting room
- when you are called/the room as you walk in
- where you sit/what you can see from there
- the person present/what he or she says/does
- what you have to do
- how you feel before/during/afterwards

Don't forget to vary your present tenses, use both active and passive verb forms, and use some sequencing phrases beginning with *after*, *before* and *when*.

> 'You go into the waiting room and you can read magazines which are provided for people who are waiting. Before you get called in you're often asked to go and register or fill in some forms at the reception desk. And when you've done that, the dentist puts her head round the door and calls you in and you're feeling very nervous at this point. And you go in and lie down on the dentist's chair, and you're asked to open your mouth. This can get really painful, just holding your mouth open for a long time. And when that's over, the dentist tells you if you need to come back to have some treatment or whether your teeth are OK.'

UNIT 1 *Sign of the Times*

## WRITING 2
### *Descriptive writing*

The article 'Afraid to open wide' on pages 12 and 13 describes how people can overcome dental phobia.

**1** Discuss with a partner:
- In which situations are you particularly nervous?
- Which situations make you feel very happy and relaxed?
- What physical reactions do you have in these sorts of stituations?

**2** In descriptive writing you need colourful words and phrases to create atmosphere and to stimulate the imagination of the reader.

1 Look again at the article on pages 12 and 13 and find the following phrases which describe a feeling of nervousness and tension. Discuss the meaning of the phrases, and how they are used in the article.

   **a** A traumatic dental experience (line 22)
   **b** enormously frightened (line 35)
   **c** a huge drama (line 74)
   **d** an insignificant moment (line 74)
   **e** a nightmare situation (line 79)
   **f** a major ordeal (line 82)

2 Look at the following phrases and decide which of them can be used in a frightening situation, and which can be used in a pleasant situation. Write **F** for frightening and **P** for pleasant.

| | |
|---|---|
| I was scared out of my wits. | My hair stood on end. |
| I was on cloud nine. | I was having the time of my life. |
| I felt very content. | It sent shivers down my spine. |
| I was petrified. | I was over the moon. |
| I had butterflies in my stomach. | I was shaking like a leaf. |
| I couldn't believe my luck. | It went like a dream. |

Which of the phrases express the strongest feelings?
In what context might you use some of these expressions?

**3** You have decided to take part in a creative writing competition organized by an English language magazine which is read by people studying English in your country. The judges are looking for both interesting content and good use of language.

Choose **one** of the two topics below and write an essay of **300–350** words.

1 Describe an event which you were not looking forward to. Say why you felt apprehensive about it and what happened in the end.

2 Describe a very special day in your life. Say how you prepared for it, how you felt beforehand and how things went on the day.

✎ Remember to use the Writing Checklist on page 11.

*Sign of the Times* **UNIT 1**

# HELP WITH CLOZE PASSAGES

Each of the exercises in this section is designed to develop skills that will help you to do the various cloze tests in the examination. There are cloze tests in both Paper 1 (multiple-choice vocabulary) and Paper 3 (grammar cloze and word-building cloze). Later Help sections will give specific advice on each of these.

**■ 1** You are going to look at a number of short texts connected with the growing and production of tea.

First discuss the topic of tea with your partner. Talk about:
- where tea is grown
- the plant itself
- different types of tea
- where tea is popular
- how to make a cup of tea

**■ 2** Now look at this paragraph about the history of tea drinking.

1 Read the paragraph through first to understand the whole context, but ignore the gaps.

2 Now think about the missing words. For each space, decide if the missing word is:
- a noun
- a verb
- an adjective
- a preposition
- another type of word

Don't write the word yet, just identify the <u>type</u> of word that is missing.

### *The Legend of Tea Drinking*

The legends surrounding the origins of tea drinking are almost as (**1**) _____ as the different types, or blends, of tea available today, and they (**2**) _____ from region to region. Indian and Japanese tales (**3**) _____ a devout Buddhist priest called Bodhidharma, (**4**) _____ was attempting a seven-year, sleepless contemplation of Buddha when he began to (**5**) _____ drowsy. In the Indian version, he plucked a (**6**) _____ leaves from the tree under which he sat and, (**7**) _____ chewing them, found that the sleepiness (**8**) _____ him. The Japanese story is slightly different; the priest cutting (**9**) _____ his drooping eyelids in frustration and throwing them (**10**) _____ the ground. Where his eyelids landed, two tea bushes sprang (**11**) _____ , and their leaves had the property (**12**) _____ fending off sleep.

3 Look at the words in the box. Divide them into nouns, verbs, prepositions, adjectives and other words.

| describe | feel | few | to | left | on |
|----------|------|-----|-----|------|-----|
| of | off | plentiful | up | vary | who |

4 Put one of the words from the box into each of the blanks in the text.

# UNIT 1 Sign of the Times

**3** In this continuation of the text, all the prepositions have been omitted.

1. First read the paragraph to get an idea of the context.
2. Now draw a line to show the places where you think there should be prepositions, but don't worry about which prepositions to use. The first one has been done for you as an example.

The Chinese legend, however, is the most popular and certainly the most believable. / The year 2737 BC, the Emperor Shen Nung was boiling some water the tree called Camellia Sinensis when some leaves fell the pot. He found that the result was a pleasant new beverage which was a great improvement boiled water. Modern tea comes the same species which the emperor discovered. The Chinese discovered that it could produce a wide range flavours and characteristics. This is achieved growing the plants different soils and climates and different altitudes rather like vines. Indeed many tea varieties are often compared fine wines.

3. Look at the prepositions in the box. Which will fit into each of the blanks you have indicated?

| at | in | into | from | under | to | on | through | of | in |

**4** In the next piece of text, ten words are in the wrong form, e.g. a verb form instead of a noun, or an adverb instead of an adjective, etc.

1. First read the paragraph to get an idea of the context.
2. Then read the paragraph again carefully and underline the words which seem to be wrong.
3. Finally, write in the correct forms of the words. The first one has been done for you as an example.

In time, the Chinese <u>perfection</u> three quite distinct types of tea by variation the processing technique; these were green tea which is unfermented, red tea which is partially fermented and black tea which is full fermented. Black tea, which was tradition produced solely in China, spread to India in 1839 and is now cultivated and processes all over the world. Tea can be growth in almost any region with a warm tropical or sub-tropical climate and plenty of rainfall. Left uncultivated, the tea plant – which is reality a tree – would reach a high of around nine metres. It is kept well pruned, however, to make it easy to pick. After about three to five years, depends on the altitude, the plant is ready for pick, when the top bud of the bush and the adjacent two leaves are plucked off.

_perfected_
_____
_____
_____
_____
_____
_____
_____
_____
_____

*Sign of the Times* **UNIT 1**

■5  In the next text, choose the best alternative (**A**, **B**, or **C**) to complete each of the numbered blanks.

People often ask how to (**1**) _____ about making the perfect cup of tea. Making a good cup of tea is not difficult, (**2**) _____ there are a number of golden rules which (**3**) _____ is as well to follow. Firstly, only use fresh, high-quality tea which should be kept in an airtight container, (**4**) _____ from any strong smelling items. Always use fresh cold water (**5**) _____ hot or reheated water contains less oxygen and gives a flat, stale taste. Warm your teapot (**6**) _____ rinsing it in hot water. This ensures the water stays (**7**) _____ boiling point when it touches the tea. It is important to use the right amount of tea. You should put one teaspoonful of tea (**8**) _____ person into the pot, (**9**) _____ an extra spoonful 'for the pot', as it is called. Finally, do (**10**) _____ sure your teapot is clean, but never put it in a dishwasher or use detergents on it, rinsing it in cold water is usually sufficient.

| | | | | | |
|---|---|---|---|---|---|
| 1 | **A** start | **B** go | **C** get |
| 2 | **A** also | **B** or | **C** but |
| 3 | **A** it | **B** there | **C** people |
| 4 | **A** away | **B** afar | **C** alone |
| 5 | **A** not | **B** as | **C** while |
| 6 | **A** or | **B** by | **C** and |
| 7 | **A** on | **B** to | **C** at |
| 8 | **A** per | **B** for | **C** each |
| 9 | **A** added | **B** adding | **C** addition |
| 10 | **A** makes | **B** making | **C** make |

■6  Now fill each of the numbered blanks in this last part of the text with **one** suitable word as you would in the examination.

Remember:
- Read through the passage first to get an idea of the context.
- Think about the form of the words which are missing.
- Check that the word you choose fits into the grammar of the sentence.
- Check that the word you choose fits into the sense of the passage.

Don't forget that when making a pot of tea, brewing time is critical. Pour in the boiling water and (**1**) _____ the tea brew for three to five minutes, (**2**) _____ on the size of the tea-leaf being used. If the strength is not to (**3**) _____ liking, adjust the amount of tea used, (**4**) _____ than the brewing time.

Another thing which is important (**5**) _____ to stir the tea before (**6**) _____ it out. Some people turn the pot three times one way and three times the other, which (**7**) _____ the same job. Tea will taste unpleasantly stewed (**8**) _____ left in the pot for more than ten minutes. It is also better (**9**) _____ to use a tea cosy or other form of teapot cover, as this will simply speed (**10**) _____ the stewing process.

Now look back at your answers. Which of them has made:
- a verb and preposition which always go together (a collocation)?
- a grammatical phrase used in comparisons?
- an idiomatic phrase?
- a phrasal verb?

UNIT 1 *Sign of the Times*

## EXAMPLE PRACTICE 1

**1** For questions **1–6**, read the text below and decide which answer (**A**, **B**, **C** or **D**) best fits each gap.

### *Vegetarians and Others*

Unfortunately, the word 'vegetarian' still presents to many minds a quite inaccurate picture of the diet and beliefs of people who (**1**) _____ animals (and, in the case of vegans and certain religious sects, all animal products) from their eating habits. Many, it has to be admitted, do become quite obsessed with what, when and how they eat, and extreme food faddists, (**2**) _____ vegetarian or not, have often given more moderate categories of vegetarian an undeserved (**3**) _____ . This unfortunate tendency has long been one of the social hazards of (**4**) _____ to unorthodox ideas of any kind.

The activities of health and food addicts, often reported in the media and proving to be increasingly focused on such issues as genetically-modified species and the production of organic foodstuffs, should, however, not be (**5**) _____ with the ethic, nor necessarily with the practice, of true vegetarianism. It is fair to say that in the wide world of food reform, there are certainly many vegetarians to be found, but many of the so-called food reformers are no nearer to genuine vegetarianism than a Masai tribesman or any other (**6**) _____ supporter of the meat-with-or-without-two-veg school of thought.

| | | | | | | | |
|---|---|---|---|---|---|---|---|
| **1** | **A** | exclude | **B** | prohibit | **C** | forbid | **D** | outlaw |
| **2** | **A** | although | **B** | whether | **C** | unless | **D** | whereas |
| **3** | **A** | distinction | **B** | estimation | **C** | consideration | **D** | reputation |
| **4** | **A** | subscribing | **B** | enlisting | **C** | enrolling | **D** | subjecting |
| **5** | **A** | blamed | **B** | confused | **C** | mistaken | **D** | jumbled |
| **6** | **A** | sharp | **B** | slight | **C** | keen | **D** | crisp |

**2** For questions **1–15**, read the text and think of the word which best fits each space. Use only **one** word in each space. There is an example at the beginning (**0**).

## *Deep-fried Mars Bar*

I did not, (**0**) __*at*__ first, believe in the deep-fried Mars Bar, considering it to be an urban myth, or something made (**1**) _____ by journalists. Then I visited Scotland and saw it with my (**2**) _____ eyes. Indeed, as if that weren't (**3**) _____ , I even tasted it.

Available at fish and chip shops, it is probably the most cardiologically lethal concoction yet devised, even in a nation as hooked (**4**) _____ its cholesterol as Scotland. 'It doesn't (**5**) _____ if it's healthy or not, if you enjoy it,' explained Lynne Dodd, echoing the general stoicism (**6**) _____ she cheerfully fried a Mars Bar for me at Gino's Fish Bar, in Queen Street, Dunoon near Glasgow.

Snickers may also be deep fried she confided, (**7**) _____ not Kit Kats which have a tendency (**8**) _____ explode into the fat, imparting (**9**) _____ chocolate flavour to subsequent batches of chips.

At Gino's, which has, (**10**) _____ times, dispensed as many as fifty fried Mars Bars in a day, the recipe has a ghastly simplicity.

Heat the fat to more than four hundred degrees. Smother the Mars Bar (**11**) _____ a batter of yellow flour, water and seasonings, of the (**12**) _____ used for frying fish. Immerse in the boiling fat for three to four minutes. Serve (**13**) _____ chips.

I confess that I found a very small taste of the confection palatable, with a flavour reminiscent (**14**) _____ a profiterole. A little does, however, (**15**) _____ a long way. Indeed, I think that one such bar would be quite sufficient to satisfy the curiosity of quite a large number of investigators.

**3** Read the text again and answer the following short-answer questions.

1 What is implied by the phrase 'cardiologically lethal concoction'? (paragraph 2)
2 Which phrase in paragraph 4 best reveals the writer's own feelings about the deep-fried Mars Bars?
3 In your own words, explain the point that the writer is making in the last sentence.

UNIT 2

# Call of the Wild

**SPEAKING 1**
*Talking together about a visual prompt*

1. Look at the pictures. With a partner, compare and contrast the relationship between people and animals shown in each one.

2. To what extent do humans exploit animals? Is this right? avoidable? inevitable?

   Talk about:

   | | |
   |---|---|
   | pets | working animals |
   | circuses | films/TV/advertising |
   | zoos | hunting |
   | factory farming | testing chemicals on animals |

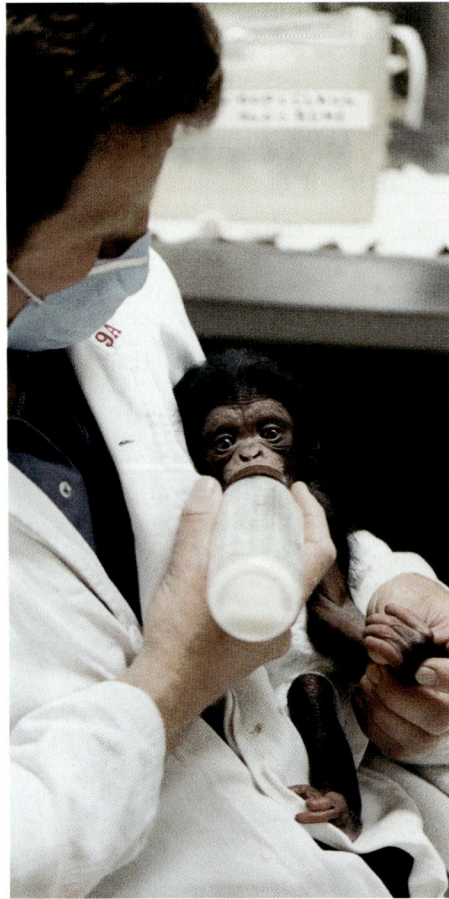

Call of the Wild  UNIT 2

## SPEAKING 2
### Expressing opinions

1 Look at this advertisement which was placed in a national newspaper. Who do you think placed the advertisement?

> **A PUPPY IS FOR LIFE NOT JUST FOR YOUR BIRTHDAY**

2 What message is it giving?

3 Is the message relevant to exotic pets?

4 What problems do people face when they buy unsuitable pets? What are the solutions to these problems?

## LISTENING 1
### Four-option multiple choice

1 You will hear a radio interview with a woman who has made a film about the problems associated with the keeping of baby orang-utans as pets. For questions 1–7, choose the answer (**A**, **B**, **C** or **D**) which fits best according to what you hear.

1 What was Sarah's original aim in making the film?

   **A** to inform people about orang-utans
   **B** to investigate one particular relationship
   **C** to help the foundation raise money
   **D** to expose the illegal trade in animals

2 How did Sarah feel when she first met Dai Dai?

   **A** disgusted
   **B** amazed
   **C** frightened
   **D** delighted

3 What impressed Sarah most about Dai Dai?

   **A** the clothes she wore
   **B** how much she understood
   **C** how obedient she was
   **D** her musical talent

4 Why did Mrs Chang decide not to keep Dai Dai?

   **A** She was concerned about the future.
   **B** She was in financial difficulties.
   **C** She didn't have the necessary commitment.
   **D** She was losing control of the animal.

5 What is the main aim of the centre Dai Dai went to in Borneo?

   **A** to protect the animals from tourists
   **B** to make sure the animals are healthy
   **C** to make the animals less dependent on humans
   **D** to show the animals what to eat in the wild

6 What does the episode at the end of the film show?

   **A** how close Mrs Chang and Dai Dai were
   **B** how Dai Dai wasn't ready for release
   **C** how little Mrs Chang understood Dai Dai
   **D** how like humans orang-utans are

7 How can we best summarize Sarah's attitude towards Mrs Chang?

   **A** Mrs Chang's behaviour was appalling.
   **B** Mrs Chang's concern was touching.
   **C** Mrs Chang's opinions were unimportant.
   **D** Mrs Chang's feelings were unnatural.

2 How does the story of Dai Dai and Mrs Chang make you feel?

Talk about:
- How can situations like this be avoided?
- Do you know of any similar stories?
- What problems do you think Dai Dai will face in the wild?
- What will Mrs Chang's life be like now?

23

UNIT 2 *Call of the Wild*

## GRAMMAR 1
### Cause and result

**1** Read the introduction to the radio interview. Complete the text with a word from the box; some words can be used more than once. Then listen to check.

| with | there | which | where | this | such | that |

Some years ago, (**1**) _____ was a popular childen's TV soap opera in the Far East (**2**) _____ starred a pet orang-utan. (**3**) _____ led to a demand for (**4**) _____ animals (**5**) _____ resulted in enormous smuggling from the island of Borneo to other Pacific rim countries (**6**) _____ the babies were bought as luxury pets. (**7**) _____ fashion has now resulted in a large number of orang-utans (**8**) _____ are proving too much for their owners to cope (**9**) _____ .

**2** Now answer these questions.

1 When do we use *which*, and when do we use *this*?
2 When should *that* be used instead of *this*?
3 Why did the speaker use *such* and not *these*?
4 What is the difference between *led to* and *resulted in*? Why did the speaker use both these forms?

**3** Read these sentences about tarantulas. Link each sentence using suitable pronouns and the forms *resulted in* and *led to* to make a paragraph.

An episode of a popular British soap opera showed two girls buying a pet tarantula.

Demand for tarantulas in Britain increased.

Tarantula sales at the Pet City shop quadrupled.

Most of the spiders were bought by teenage girls and young mothers.

Many people have been bitten by tarantulas.

The bite is painful like a bee sting.

Many tarantulas have been killed or abandoned by owners who no longer want them.

📖 N.B. The Workbook has further work on expressing cause and result.

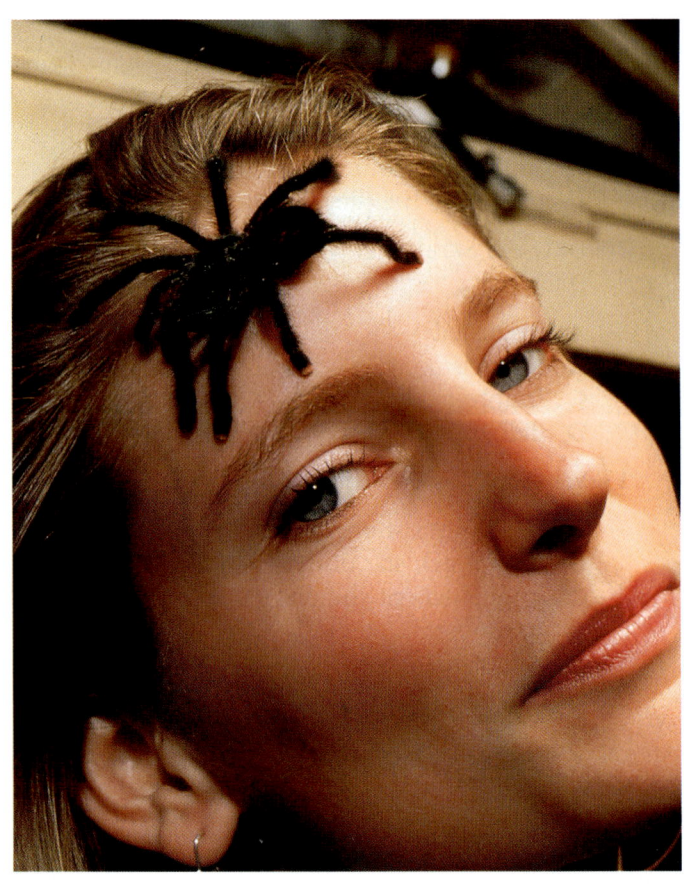

*Call of the Wild* **UNIT 2**

## HELP WITH GAPPED SENTENCES

**1** In the Use of English Paper, Part Three involves finding the one word which will fill a gap in three different sentences.

Look at this example:

Each of the words in the box fits into one of the gaps in sentences **a**, **b** and **c**. However, only one of them fits in all three sentences. Which is it? Why?

| worried | involved | concerned | aware |

**a** Nowadays, many scientists are _____ about the increase in pollution levels and the effects of global warming.

**b** All those _____ in the project had to produce a detailed report of their activities.

**c** This is a deplorable situation and, as far as we are _____ , it is entirely of your own making.

## REMEMBER

- There are no words to choose from; you must supply the missing word.
- The same word, in the same form, must fit in all three gaps.
- The word will have a slightly different meaning in each of the sentences.
- Some words will form part of phrasal verbs, common expressions or collocations. Look at this example:

    **a** Tony finally <u>gave</u> up smoking last year.
    *(key word is part of phrasal verb)*
    **b** The audience <u>gave</u> the speaker a big round of applause.
    *(key word is part of a common collocation)*
    **c** Tanya <u>gave</u> a lot of money to charity last year.
    *(key word is part of a common expression)*

- Sometimes the word will be influenced by the grammar of the surrounding sentence. Look at this example:

    **a** Please, <u>help</u> yourself to more vegetables, don't wait to be asked.
    *(key word is followed by a reflexive pronoun)*
    **b** Jane couldn't <u>help</u> laughing when she saw Graham's appalling haircut.
    *(key word is part of a longer verbal phrase)*
    **c** Patti is getting a friend to <u>help</u> her with her maths homework.
    *(key word is followed by a dependent preposition)*

### How to approach these questions

- Read all three sentences first.
- Decide which type of word is needed (e.g. verb, noun, adjective, etc.).
- Decide which form of the word is needed (e.g. plural/singular, present/past, etc.).
- Look for clues before and after the gap in each sentence.
- When you think you've found the word, check that it fits both the meaning and the grammar of all three sentences.

# UNIT 2 Call of the Wild

**2** Now try the following Part Three examples.

1. Studying on this degree course calls for a good deal of _____ as well as a genuine interest in the subject.

   A single _____ of this self-tanning product may not, in all cases, guarantee lasting results.

   If you send in your letter of _____ after the closing date, it is unlikely to be considered.

2. Our rooms are at the back of the hotel and _____ a magnificent view of the botanical gardens behind.

   Sue really wanted to help Trevor, but was up to her eyes in work and just couldn't _____ the time.

   I really can't _____ to let an opportunity like this slip through my fingers.

3. Keep a _____ eye on the baby, she tends to pull things off the table.

   For my 18th birthday last year, all my _____ relations clubbed together and bought me a new computer.

   It's going to be a very _____ contest, as the two competitors are very evenly matched.

4. Paul is convinced that some treasure was once _____ under the apple tree in his garden.

   Professor Damian strode off down the corridor, deep in thought, his hands _____ in his pockets.

   Because she wanted to forget her various misfortunes in life, Mariel _____ herself in her work.

5. When you're on a diet, however bland the menu may seem, you must resist the temptation to _____ your fish and vegetables in oil or butter.

   The constant chattering of the children tends to _____ out the noise of the factory next door.

   It's by no means unusual even for wild animals to _____ in the river, because the current is very strong.

6. Denise _____ a hand wearily over her forehead as she contemplated all the work there was still left to do.

   Shane's comments _____ unnoticed because everyone was distracted by the sounds coming from outside.

   Through lack of foresight, the organization seems to have _____ up a golden opportunity.

7. My therapist is helping me to _____ with my phobia about insects.

   The next person to _____ the cards was Wendy, and as she did so, a tense silence fell on the players.

   These shops _____ mainly in exotic pets, but you can also find the more unusual breeds of dog and cat on sale too.

Call of the Wild UNIT 2

## USE OF ENGLISH 1
### Cloze passage

■ 1  What is happening in each of these photos? What might the outcome be?

■ 2  Match these headlines to the photographs.

*Fishermen to the rescue of feathered friend in need*     *Mass strandings spark frantic rescue missions*

■ 3  Look at the words in the box. How many of them are prepositions?

| at | back | brought | in | long | no | over | one |
|----|------|---------|----|----|----|------|-----|
| or | result | their | to | up | when | which | with |

■ 4  Look at the text. Before trying to put in the missing words decide which gaps need prepositions. Then look back at the list in the box and decide which preposition fits each gap. The first one has been done for you as an example. Then complete the remaining gaps with the other words from the box.

### Strandings

All (**0**) _over_ the world, strandings of dolphins and whales are becoming more common and environmentalists claim that this may be Nature ringing the alarm bells, believing it is the sea itself (**1**) _____ is enduring a slow death (**2**) _____ about by pollution. Some dolphins found dying off America and in the Mediterranean were nearly all infected (**3**) _____ a virus, but heavy pollution had also suppressed their immune systems.

Individual strandings are mainly the (**4**) _____ of illness or injury. The animals cannot either navigate (**5**) _____ swim properly and accidentally come ashore. It is even possible that they may choose to strand themselves as a response (**6**) _____ their condition. In the southern hemisphere, mass strandings of these animals are common and everywhere (**7**) _____ plight sparks frantic rescue missions to refloat them by well-meaning humans. Such strandings happen (**8**) _____ the animals are in a large group and their leader becomes disoriented and swims ashore. They then all follow and, as (**9**) _____ as the leader remains stranded, (**10**) _____ amount of work by human rescuers will persuade the others to go (**11**) _____ to sea.

(**12**) _____ piece of good news is that when people succeed (**13**) _____ refloating whales, the survival rate can be encouraging. In New Zealand, where most stranded whales are fit and merely lost, (**14**) _____ to 90% survive. One signal, at least, that all may not be wrong (**15**) _____ sea.

27

UNIT 2 *Call of the Wild*

## HELP WITH LISTENING: SENTENCE COMPLETION TASKS

■ 1   In Part Two of the Listening Test, you have to do a sentence completion task.

### REMEMBER

- The task tests your ability to record information and stated opinions from the text.
- Read and listen to the instructions carefully. Think about the speakers and the context to help you feel ready.
- Read the questions and think about what the answers might be, both in terms of the meaning and what type of word or phrase is needed.
- The questions follow the order of information in the recording.
- A lot of the information from the listening text is included in the sentences on the page, both before and after the gap. Be careful not to repeat it.
- Most answers require you to write between one and three full words, or sometimes a number, for each answer. Don't try to write long answers.
- The answers that you need to write are all words you hear in the recording, but they are not in the same sentences as this is not a dictation.
- You do not have to change the form of the words you hear in order to complete the sentences, but you must check that the sentence you have created is grammatically correct and that the words you have written are spelt correctly.

■ 2   You will hear part of a radio programme about attempts to save stranded whales in Britain. For questions **1–10**, complete the sentences with a word or short phrase.

---

The Whale and Dolphin Protection Society aims to create a network of what it calls [_____ 1 _____] across the country.

Volunteers are trained using a full-length inflatable whale which is [_____ 2 _____] to make it heavy.

Rescuers put a [_____ 3 _____] under the whale so it can be moved out to sea.

To ensure their survival, stranded whales shouldn't be allowed to [_____ 4 _____].

Without help, stranded whales always die because, even at sea, they are unable to move [_____ 5 _____].

Teresa says that during the rescue, whales don't appear to be [_____ 6 _____].

Over 2000 whales in New Zealand have been saved by what's called the [_____ 7 _____].

Most whales which come ashore in Britain are [_____ 8 _____].

One problem is that many live strandings occur in [_____ 9 _____] places.

Teresa is surprised at the [_____ 10 _____] of volunteers training today.

---

■ 3   Look at these student answers to question 9. Decide whether each of them is a good answer or not and why.

*places which are remote*   *no people*   *turn up in remote*
*really remote*              *remote*      *where there aren't people*

## VOCABULARY 1
### Idiomatic phrases

■ 1   Do you know the name of this bird? Why is it famous?

■ 2   Look at this sentence.

*I'm afraid the project has no future; it's as dead as a dodo.*

■ 3   Now complete each idiomatic phrase with a word from the box.

| bee | bull | cat | chicken | dog |
|---|---|---|---|---|
| fish | fly | lamb | pig | snake |

1  It's time to be brave and take the _____ by the horns.

2  Terry went meekly into the exam room, like a _____ to the slaughter.

3  Misfortune was to _____ Charles for the rest of his life.

4  From this point the road begins to _____ down hill to the coast.

5  I've eaten too much, I've made a real _____ of myself.

6  Philip's such a gentle man, he wouldn't hurt a _____ .

7  Grandfather looked like a _____ out of water at the disco.

8  John's got the big match tomorrow, but I'm sure he's going to _____ out at the last minute and stay at home.

9  Carol arrived at the party and made a _____ line for the sandwiches as she hadn't eaten for hours.

10  Lisa walked in tentatively, like a _____ on a hot tin roof.

📖 N.B. The Workbook has further work on animal vocabulary.

## SPEAKING 3
### Discussing pros and cons

■ 1   What can be done to help animals that are in danger of extinction?

Which of these ideas would you favour? What are the advantages and drawbacks of each idea?

- ban hunting
- create nature reserves
- go back to natural farming methods
- stop the expansion of cultivation
- breed animals in zoos
- set up captive breeding programmes and then release animals into the wild

■ 2   Talk to your partner about:

- What good can animal welfare organizations do?
- How can people help them? Financially? Practically?
- What different types of organization are there?
- Why do some people not support them?
- Would you be willing to help an animal welfare organization?

UNIT 2 *Call of the Wild*

## READING 1
## Multiple choice

**1** Before you read the article discuss these questions with your partner.
- Which animals are threatened with extinction? Why?
- How important is it to preserve the natural habitats of rare animals?
- Is it worth trying to save all the different species of wild animals on the planet?
- What is the purpose of zoos? Do you approve of them?

**2** You are going to read an article about conserving endangered species. Read quickly to find:
- who Gerald Durrell was.
- what he was famous for.
- the countries he operated in.

# A RARE ANIMAL

The late Gerald Durrell was one of the leading names in wildlife conservation. As the zoologist who proved that zoos could save wildlife, the author of 37 books translated into 31 languages, a presenter of 14 television series with 150 million viewers worldwide, and a man with a wonderful sense of humour, Durrell probably raised the world's collective conservation consciousness more than all other naturalists put together.

John Hartley was personal assistant and friend to Durrell for more than 30 years at Jersey Zoo, established by Durrell in 1959. Hartley works at the Wildlife Preservation Trust (WPT), which was created at the zoo four years later. 'Much of the conservation effort in zoos today is a result of Gerald Durrell developing ideas, and then proving that they work,' he says. Through a renowned training programme, the WPT has passed on Durrell's legendary expertise in breeding captive animals to more than 800 trainees from over 75 different countries. 'The programme is aimed at people who, at some time in their lives, are going to be involved with breeding programmes in developing countries, though not necessarily affiliated with zoos,' explains Hartley. 'Until we started this, there would not have been a lot of experience in the countries where most of our trainees come from, and that's not a criticism – it's a fact.'

Indeed, the very first person on the programme, Yousoof Mungroo, is now director of the recently created first national park of Mauritius, an island which was once home to many unique species. When Durrell visited the island in 1976, he discovered, to his surprise and dismay, that a number of birds, notably the pink pigeon and the Mauritius kestrel, were about to go the same way as the most famous of former Mauritian inhabitants, the dodo, now extinct. In response, Durrell rapidly established a comprehensive programme for breeding and releasing these endangered species, while simultaneously trying to argue for the importance of biodiversity on the island.

Incredibly, the battle to save these species is now being won. Durrell, Hartley and Mungroo brought up and then released so many kestrels that their numbers have risen from just 4 to over 150. The pink pigeon's numbers are not so spectacular, but research into the pigeon is part of the WPT's ongoing work and the long-term strategy is to guarantee its independent existence.

Durrell repeated his techniques for many other species from around the world, including the reptiles of Round Island and the golden lion tamarins of Brazil. Many are kept at the zoo in Jersey, but many are also kept in their country of origin, and often in their immediate habitat. Some people have questioned whether the ability to keep animals *in situ* means that zoos are still necessary, but Hartley still repeats Durrell's assertion that they are.

'The difference is that our zoo was established with the intention of creating conservation programmes for endangered species, at a time when nobody else was doing that. Now, thank goodness, more zoos have followed that lead,' he says. 'By having these species here in Jersey, we are able to show them to people who can write cheques and help conserve them. We funded the whole of the restoration of Round Island, for instance, by having a few of its reptiles in Jersey which caught the eye of one wealthy philanthropist.'

Hartley accepts, however, that despite the excellent example which Durrell's zoo has set, there is still a long way to go. 'There are too many animal collections stretching limited resources too thinly. But I believe that it is important that endangered species are kept in captivity so that people can see them properly. This is part of the conservation effort, because it stirs the imagination in the people who give us funds.'

Stirring imaginations, and stimulating worldwide interest in wildlife through his books, was Durrell's life blood. 'I know, from handling the correspondence from millions of people out there who we have never even seen or met, but who are involved in conservation, professionally or voluntarily, that they are doing it as a result of Gerald's books,' says Hartley with glee.

Of course, Durrell has not been without his critics: like many conservationists, he was accused of favouring animals over people. The reality, however, is that he recognized the enormous, unquantifiable value that animals bring to people's lives, and devoted his own life to preserving that.

**3** Now read the article again more carefully and answer the questions **1–5**. Choose the answer (**A**, **B**, **C** or **D**) which you think fits best according to the text.

1 According to the first paragraph of the article, Gerald Durrell's most important achievement lay in

A raising the profile of zoos throughout the world.
B making people aware of conservation issues.
C providing wild animals with a safe environment.
D promoting the notion that animals can be fun.

2 According to John Hartley, the current focus of the WPT's work is to

A pass on the skills needed to set up captive breeding projects.
B give support to those working in zoos in various countries.
C ensure that Gerald Durrell's pioneering work is not forgotten.
D draw on the experience of conservationists from different countries.

3 The writer expresses pleasant surprise about

A the long-term effect of Durrell's early work.
B the commitment and determination of the WPT.
C Durrell's ability to locate animals in danger of extinction.
D the capacity of certain species for surviving in different locations.

4 What does John Hartley say about bringing endangered species back to Jersey Zoo?

A It works better than trying to conserve them in their natural surroundings.
B It has attracted criticism from some members of the public.
C It is a financially efficient way of ensuring their survival.
D It has proved successful only with certain species.

5 Which phrase from the text best reflects the problem facing the present generation of conservationists?

A limited resources (line 83)
B kept in captivity (line 85)
C favouring animals over people (line 103)
D unquantifiable value (line 105)

## UNIT 2 Call of the Wild

**4** Now read the text again and answer these questions.

1 In your own words, explain what the phrase 'the world's collective conservation consciousness' (lines 8–9) means.

2 Explain what the writer means by the expression 'go the same way as'. (line 39)

3 Which two expressions in paragraph 4 give us the idea that the WPT will continue to be heavily involved in conservation projects on the island?

4 Which three expressions in paragraph 5 are used to describe alternatives to keeping animals in zoos like the one in Jersey?

5 Which phrase in paragraph 7 echoes the idea introduced with the phrase 'people who can write cheques'? (lines 73–74)

6 In your own words, explain the expression 'Durrell's life blood'. (line 92)

7 What does the expression 'with glee' (lines 98–99) tell us about John Hartley's feelings about Durrell's achievements?


## GRAMMAR 2
### Relative pronouns

**1** Look at these two phrases from the article. What is the function of *who* in these phrases? What other words can be used in this position?

*As the zoologist who proved that zoos could save wildlife, …*
*The programme is aimed at people who, at some time in their lives, are going to be involved with breeding programmes.*

**2** Complete each sentence about Gerald Durrell and his work with a suitable relative pronoun.

1 Durrell made television programmes _____ had 150 million viewers worldwide.

2 Jersey was the place _____ Durrell set up his first zoo.

3 The Wildlife Preservation Trust is an organization _____ Durrell set up.

4 Gerald Durrell, _____ conservation techniques were very successful, also wrote a number of best-selling books.

5 Reptiles from Round Island, _____ were kept at Jersey Zoo, caught the eye of a wealthy philanthropist.

6 Mauritius was the island on _____ Durrell did much of his early work.

7 Durrell was grateful to his financial backers, _____ support enabled him to continue with his work.

8 Gerald Durrell will be remembered as the man without _____ many species would have become extinct.

📖 N.B. The Workbook has further work on relative pronouns.

## PHRASAL VERBS 1

**1** Look at this extract from the article and underline the phrasal verb.

*Durrell, Hartley and Mungroo brought up and then released so many kestrels that their numbers have risen from just 4 to over 150.*

**2** Write one word in each gap to complete the phrasal verb in the context.

1 The Mauritus kestrel has been _____ back from the verge of extinction.
2 Jersey Zoo helps other conservationists to keep up _____ the latest techniques.
3 The WPT was _____ up a few years after Jersey Zoo.
4 Many conservation projects are in danger of running _____ of funds.
5 Durrell wasn't afraid to _____ up to the challenge of saving rare species.
6 Without Durrell's intervention, rare species of bird may have died _____ .
7 Durrell can be credited with _____ about a change in attitudes towards zoos.
8 Jersey Zoo is able to count _____ the support of some wealthy backers.
9 Through his books, Durrell got the conservation message _____ to a wider public.
10 Visiting Jersey Zoo _____ out to be more interesting than I'd expected.

## READING 2
### Lexical cloze

**1** Read this extract from a travel article. For questions **1–6**, decide which answer (**A**, **B**, **C** or **D**) best fits each gap.

I've never had a great deal of sympathy with the idea of keeping animals in cages. To my (**1**) _____ , it has always seemed rather a cruel thing to do. But a recent visit to Jersey Zoo has (**2**) _____ me over to the idea that captive breeding can be an important step in the conservation of species that are in (**3**) _____ of extinction.

At Jersey Zoo, rare animals such as the Mexican thick-billed parrot and the Majorcan midwife toad, are kept in conditions that, as far as possible, (**4**) _____ those of their natural environment. This is important, because if the animals breed successfully, their (**5**) _____ can be returned to their country of origin and released into the wild with a (**6**) _____ chance of survival.

| | | | | | | | |
|---|---|---|---|---|---|---|---|
| 1 | A | opinion | B | mind | C | sense | D | view |
| 2 | A | led | B | brought | C | won | D | caught |
| 3 | A | menace | B | threat | C | risk | D | danger |
| 4 | A | remake | B | replicate | C | recover | D | remember |
| 5 | A | offspring | B | outcome | C | upshot | D | downfall |
| 6 | A | greater | B | surer | C | tougher | D | broader |

**2** What do you think about Gerald Durrell's approach to conservation? In what other ways can endangered species be saved?

UNIT 2 *Call of the Wild*

## WRITING 1
### Formal letters

■ 1 Look at these quotes made by representatives of various animal welfare organizations in a magazine article. Which of the representatives would agree with each of the statements **1–7** below? Some of the statements reflect the views of two organizations.

1 Most of our work involves research. ☐

2 It is not our normal policy to use our funds for saving injured animals. ☐☐

3 Our organization's aim is to save animals' lives at all costs. ☐

4 Our organization's main concern is the countryside in general. ☐

5 Some well-intentioned people have the wrong attitude towards animals. ☐

6 We do not believe in keeping animals in cages. ☐☐

7 We try to understand how animals feel. ☐

**REPRESENTATIVE A**
We take in injured, harmed, unwanted, run over, shot, mentally damaged animals of all kinds. If a bird's lost a wing, we don't count it as a reason why it should die. The only difference between this sanctuary and others is, if you bring us a heap of bones which is bird, by the time you've got back into your car, we have decided how we're going to make it into a bird again, and we won't have wrung its neck before you get home.

**REPRESENTATIVE B**
If somebody finds, say, a rabbit that's been run over and has a broken leg, the last thing one should do is take it to a vet and waste money on trying to pin it together and then put it in a cage. The kindest thing to do is knock it on the head. Now that would horrify the average town dweller, but what we're trying to do is preserve genuine rural habitats. I'm afraid the trouble is, and it may seem unkind to say it in this way, but certain people are merely over-sentimental about animals, and it really tells you more about the people concerned than it does about the well-being of wildlife.

**REPRESENTATIVE C**
As far as we're concerned the important thing is quality of life. If we feel an animal can be repaired relatively quickly, and returned to the wild, then we'll help it. What we hate is keeping animals in captivity, and if we think that's going to be the case, we'd rather put it to sleep. If an animal hasn't got its freedom, its whole reason for being has completely gone and it's unlikely to be happy or lead a proper life. People are very good at projecting their emotions onto animals and looking at them and deciding whether they're happy or not. An animal may look happy if you throw some food in to its cage, but if that animal's natural instinct is to hunt for it, this will not feel right for the animal. Living in captivity is really stressful for animals. It has to be.

**REPRESENTATIVE D**
It was only during the oil spill off the coast that we really began to get involved in animal rescue. And we were using about 160 litres of water per bird to get them cleaned up so that they could be released again. We actually did some very rough sums and came up with a figure of about £35 per bird to wash it, and, of course, this whole operation was quite outside our normal sphere of activity. But, as a wildlife organization we couldn't just sit there and watch the birds suffer what would be a lingering death. So we hope that people will help us to pay for clearing up that mess, by lending financial support to our regular study programmes, which suffered as a result.

Call of the Wild **UNIT 2**

**2** Which of the organizations do you think has the best ideas? Choose the one which appeals to you most.

Read the paragraph you have chosen again, this time in more detail.

**3** If you were thinking of offering to help out at the organization on a voluntary basis, what else would you like to know about it? Make a list, for example:

*How old are the other volunteers? How many hours a week do you ask volunteers to work?*

**4** Plan a letter of enquiry to your chosen organization, requesting further information and offering to help as a volunteer. Think about what you want to know, and what they may want to know about you.

**5** When you have finished, explain to your partner which organization interested you and why. Then talk through your plan with your partner and ask your partner for other ideas about the content of your essay.

**6** Look at the following letter, which was written to one of the animal welfare organizations. For questions **1–10**, complete the gaps with one of the words or phrases from the box.

> To begin with
> I would be available
> regarding
> Before going any further
> in response to
> I would welcome the opportunity
> currently
> In addition
> I would appreciate it
> I was wondering whether

I am writing **(1)** _____ an article about your work which I read in a recent issue of the Boxton Times, and I am extremely interested in the work you do with animals. I am a 25-year-old student **(2)** _____ following a course in Environmental Studies at university. As I will have some spare time during the summer holidays, **(3)** _____ you would be in need of any assistance in your animal sanctuary during this period.

I feel I may be of use to you for a number of reasons. Firstly, I am a keen animal lover and, although I have not actually worked with wild animals, as a teenager I helped out at a stables every weekend, where I gained considerable experience of working with horses. Subsequently, I got a part-time job in a veterinary surgery, where I worked with a wide range of domestic pets. Finally, the preservation of our natural environment is an integral part of my course, and I would like to give my support to any organization that has a genuine concern for the protection of wild animals.

**(4)** _____ , I would be grateful if you could answer a few queries about your organization. **(5)** _____ , could you tell me your exact location and whether I could reach you by public transport from the city centre? As I may need to consider staying near to the sanctuary, **(6)** _____ if you could give me any information you may have **(7)** _____ accommodation in the immediate vicinity. **(8)** _____ I would like to know what hours I would be expected to work, and if you generally have other volunteers of my age working with you.

I do hope that my letter is of interest to you since **(9)** _____ to become involved in your work. **(10)** _____ to come for an interview at your convenience.

**UNIT 2** *Call of the Wild*

■ **7** Read the completed letter on page 35 again and decide what the main topic of each paragraph is.

■ **8** Think about the letter of enquiry you have planned and discussed with your partner.

1 Will the letter be formal? Semi-formal? Informal?

2 The beginning and ending of a letter are very important and must be appropriate for the style of the letter. Look at the possible openings (**A–C**) and endings (**1–4**) on this page.

What is the style of each opening and closing?

In which type of letter would you use these phrases?

3 Choose the opening and closing that would be best for your letter of enquiry.

■ **9** Using the letter on page 35 as a model, plan the following letter of enquiry.

*You have read a newspaper article about an international children's charity which does a lot of work with orphaned children. The charity has recently opened a Children's Aid Centre in your area and you would like to do some voluntary work there. Write a letter to the charity, expressing your interest and asking for more information about its work and how you may help.*

✏ Remember to use the Writing Checklist on page 11.

Now write your **letter** in **300–350** words.

📖 N.B. The Workbook has further work on formal and informal expressions.

**A**
To whom it may concern:
I write with reference to …

**B**
Dear Sir/Madam,
I am writing to express my interest in …

**C**
Dear animal lovers,
I read the bit about you in …

**1**
An early reply would be appreciated,
Yours faithfully

**2**
I look forward to hearing from you,
Yours faithfully

**3**
Write back soon,
Best wishes

**4**
I remain,
Very truly yours

## HELP WITH READING: GAPPED TEXT TASKS

Part Three of the Reading Paper is a 'gapped text'. In this task, paragraphs have been removed from the text and placed after it in random order. You have to decide which of the paragraphs fits into each gap in the text. There is one extra paragraph which does not fit in any of the gaps.

■ 1  First read the short introduction to the text on page 38 carefully. It will help you understand the main idea of the text. Then 'speed read' the remaining paragraphs of the main text to get an idea of the content and structure of the whole article.

■ 2  Now look again at the first paragraph in the main text. Then read through the options **A–H** on page 39 until you find one which follows on from it in terms of meaning and ideas.

Does the second paragraph in the main text follow on from the option you have chosen?

If it doesn't flow into the following paragraph in the main text, then you have probably chosen the wrong option. If so, find another option and repeat the process until you indentify the one missing paragraph which does link with the text both before and after the gap.

### Looking for links

The first paragraph in the main text (page 38) concerns the domestication of the horse, ending with the fact that the horse was pre-adapted for a domestic role. The beginning of option **C** picks up on this idea, mentioning things we take for granted as useful in horses, such as speed, size and intelligence.

Option **C** ends with 'the evolutionary changes it has undergone in response to a changing diet'. This idea links with paragraph 2 of the main text, where we read about horses switching from eating leaves to eating grass.

Option **C** is therefore the correct answer for gap 1.

Now look at gap 2 in the same way.

### Rejecting a link

Some options look like they may fit into a gap, until a detailed reading of the content shows them to be wrong. For example, at first sight, option **G** seems to link with the text on either side of gap 3.

However, the changes to the horse described in **G** (larger head, eyes distanced from the mouth, larger brain) do not actually relate to the idea of being larger and more energy efficient, which is found in the third paragraph of the main text.

This rules out option **G** in gap 3.

Now continue in the same way for the remaining gaps.

When you have finished, explain to a partner the links you have seen on either side of each gap. If you think your partner is wrong, explain why you reject his or her links.

# The Horse

*There are many theories as to how and why horses and humans have developed such a special relationship over the ages. Here we present one scientific explanation.*

Of the more than 4,000 species of mammals that have inhabited the earth over the past 10,000 years, the horse is one of only a dozen or so which have been successfully domesticated. Domestication is not simply a matter of human intention. If it were, it is possible that we would now be sitting at home with a hyena curled at our feet. The ancient Egyptians apparently tried, but they were unsuccessful because the hyena was not 'pre-adapted' for a domestic role. The horse was.

| 1 |

As the Ice Age advanced and forests died away to be replaced by windswept savannah, many herbivores were forced to switch from leaves to grass as their main source of food. The little leaf-browsing predecessor of our modern horse – the ur-horse – began to change and adapt to a new ecological niche on the plains.

| 2 |

On the plains, competition for sustenance was stiff. Horses adapted, learning to thrive on the poorest quality grasses, forage on which cattle would have starved. Horses needed to eat huge amounts to extract enough nutrition, so they began to increase in size. In a mammal, the amount of energy expended is proportional to the amount of heat lost through the exposed surface area. It is more energy efficient to be large.

| 3 |

As a result, horses became more of a force. They also developed new social systems to suit life on the plains. In the food-rich forests, ur-horses were solitary and territorial. Distances between individuals meant that stallions mated with one, or just a few females. But those horses which were driven onto the open plains, where food was patchier, adopted a new roaming lifestyle. They began to band into groups for mutual protection and for breeding purposes.

| 4 |

This process was a brilliant evolutionary strategy for horses. It was they who first discovered our mutual compatibility and without it, it is unlikely that they would have survived. Horses began to hang around human settlements, finding they had more to gain than to lose. Even if some became food for the humans, more grew sleek on the crops robbed from the fields. Then, with the close of the Pleistocene era and a gradual warming of the global climate, forests began to creep back over the land. Grassland animals, like mammoths, slowly vanished. By 10,000 years ago, it seems likely that in North America, at least, horses had disappeared.

| 5 |

If the horse used humans to supply food and protection, humans found that the innately social behaviour of the horse could be drawn upon to forge a useful relationship. Their bonding instinct was invaluable. Even nowadays some trainers, for instance, will deal with a particularly aggressive or recalcitrant animal by denying it companionship. The socially deprived horse quickly comes to accept and bond with its trainer.

| 6 |

Less in doubt is the fact that, like most social animals (including humans), horses also developed hierarchical structures within the herd. Degrees of dominance are established at first by a fight, perhaps, but later, once rank has been established, by symbolic threats. Thus, although a group of horses may squeal, lunge and lash out, actual violence is rare. The horse developed a keen ability to read and interpret social signs, to react to the threat – to the lowered head and stretched neck, for example, which is the preliminary to a bite.

| 7 |

The much-discussed ability of the horse to 'mind-read' stems from the same ability to interpret signs. If a horse starts to canter a few moments before its rider tells it to, or becomes alert as its rider thinks about an upcoming jump, it is probably because it is picking up on unconscious cues from the rider, such as the sudden tensing of muscles or tightening of the rein.

**A** This instinct gives horses the capacity to recognize and remember other individuals by sight, smell and sound. This may explain why some riding horses refuse to co-operate with an unfamiliar rider or why certain horses can be managed only by one particular person.

**B** Breeding colonies developed because a male could no longer claim mates simply by guarding a tract of land. And strong bonding instincts developed. It is these bonding instincts which people were to draw upon in the domesticization of the horse.

**C** Much of what we take for granted as useful in the modern horse – speed, size and intelligence, for example – can be explained through the evolutionary changes it has undergone in response to a changing diet.

**D** Although horses do have a relatively large brain, most of it is employed simply in keeping their feet in the right place. Carnivores, needing to anticipate the complex actions of elusive prey, are good at solving problems. The herbivorous horse has no need of this particular mental trick and is no more adept at solving problems than a guinea pig. But this doesn't mean we can dismiss the horse, which has other important innate skills.

**E** When this happens, speed naturally increases too, as does lifespan. It is a remarkable fact that almost all mammals live an average of 1.5 billion heartbeats. Since small animals have faster metabolisms their lifespans are correspondingly shorter.

**F** This is what underlies the perhaps surprisingly peaceful subordination of the horse to the human. Merely to carry a whip in one's hand is often enough to make a horse behave.

**G** The head grew longer, with the eye positioned at some distance from the mouth, so that on exposed spaces it could keep a wary watch for predators while it grazed. A larger brain began to develop, probably because, as a grazer, it needed greater tactile sensitivity in its lips to choose its food.

**H** This explodes the romantic myth that certain feral horses on that side of the Atlantic are survivors of some ancient prehistoric line. The horses that populate the world today may all be descendants of animals domesticated some 6,000 years ago on the windblown plains of the Ukraine.

## VOCABULARY 2
### Collocation

The gapped text contains a number of useful adjective–noun word partnerships or 'collocations'.

■ **1** For the two sets of words in box 1, match each adjective from column A with a noun from column B to find the most strongly-linked combinations of words. Look back at the text to check your answers.

■ **2** Now look at other nouns in box 2 which often partner the adjectives *social* and *mutual*. In each case, circle the noun which does not go with the adjective. Then, for each combination, write a brief sentence to show how it is used.

*Example*: She has a busy *social life* and is a popular girl.

**1**

| A Adjectives | B Nouns |
|---|---|
| social | instinct |
| open | strategy |
| evolutionary | systems |
| mutual | behaviour |
| social | plains |
| bonding | compatibility |

| A Adjectives | B Nouns |
|---|---|
| hierarchical | changes |
| breeding | myth |
| evolutionary | structures |
| innate | colonies |
| romantic | skills |

**2**

| SOCIAL | history reforms sciences mood customs life worker drinker |
|---|---|
| MUTUAL | friend respect affection dislike consent companion relationship |

UNIT 2 *Call of the Wild*

## EXAM PRACTICE 2

**1** For questions **1–15**, read the text below and think of the word which best fits each space. Use only **one** word in each space. There is an example at the beginning (**0**).

### *Suspect is Blue Large and Hairy*

A Peruvian blue-backed tarantula spider (**0**) <u>which</u> escaped inside an English magistrate's court last November and had long been presumed dead, has (**1**) _____ something of a comeback (**2**) _____ the height of a fraud trial.

A 'large hairy spider' scuttled along a skirting board just (**3**) _____ the defendant, a 47-year-old arachnophobe, was listening to the evidence against him. Barney Cosgrave, the solicitor (**4**) _____ client was taken home after the hearing suffering (**5**) _____ shock, said, 'We're all thinking of coming in with rubber bands or cycle clips on (**6**) _____ trousers next week'. *line 8*

(**7**) _____ eight-legged intruder was initially thought to be a harmless raft spider, Britain's largest, but not venomous, species, (**8**) _____ events took a more exciting turn (**9**) _____ the magistrate's clerk reported the incident. (**10**) _____ then did anyone make the connection with a young man who had brought his pet tarantula into the courthouse in a plastic box, last November, quite legitimately, and later reported that both spider and box had (**11**) _____ missing.

One of the Natural History Museum's leading spider specialists was consulted and it was learnt that this is by (**12**) _____ means a placid spider and people would be well-advised not to handle it. (**13**) _____ its venom is mild for most people, it is very (**14**) _____ more aggressive than the Mexican red-kneed tarantula, the one some people allow to crawl over their hands.

The court was sprayed over the weekend (**15**) _____ a penetrating chemical, but a search of the building's nooks and crannies yesterday failed to reveal a corpse.

**2** Read the text again and answer the following short-answer questions.

1 In your own words, explain the significance of the 'rubber bands or cycle clips' mentioned in line 8.

2 Which phrase from the text establishes that the spider was originally in the court for a good reason?

3 Which expression from the text suggests that the building would be a good place for a spider to hide?

**3** For questions **1–5**, think of **one** word only which can be used appropriately in all three sentences.

1. The calculator is small enough to _____ into the inside pocket of my jacket.

   After the forced entry, we decided to buy a new lock and employed a locksmith to come and _____ it.

   I often have trouble finding shirts which _____ me comfortably around the neck.

2. So many things had happened that afternoon that Paul felt the need to go for a long walk to _____ his head.

   I think they are going to _____ that land and build a new housing estate on it.

   Imagine my disappointment, after waiting so long for payment, when the bank refused to _____ the cheque.

3. Let's go and have something to eat because the train's not _____ for another 50 minutes.

   Vanessa gave the problem _____ consideration, but then decided to do nothing about it.

   Terry hadn't taken any paid leave for some years and several weeks' holiday were _____ to him.

4. The trouble with a lot of modern fabrics is that the colours _____ after just a few washes.

   When she gets very tired, my grandmother's voice tends to _____ into a whisper.

   Once he'd settled into his new life in Australia, Gordon's painful memories began to _____ away.

5. The weather tomorrow will be mostly _____ with temperatures about average for the time of year.

   I think it's only _____ to say that the team didn't play as well as on other occasions.

   Our relatives live a _____ distance away from us, so we don't get to see them very often.

UNIT 3

# A Word in your Ear

**SPEAKING 1**
*Talking together about a visual prompt*

1   Talk to your partner. Look at these pictures which are all concerned in some way with language.

   Choose one of the pictures and say what is happening and find out what your partner thinks about it. Use the words and phrases in the box to help you.

It looks as if/though…

(s)he looks + adjective

(s)he seems/appears to be + adjective

(s)he seems/appears to be + verb + *-ing*

I get the impression that (s)he is…

Maybe/perhaps (s)he is…

(s)he could/may/might be…

(s)he must/can't be…

It looks like + (a) noun

*A Word in your Ear* UNIT 3

**2** Now look at all the pictures. An international charity is publishing a book entitled *The World's Languages in the 21st Century* and needs to choose a photograph to use on the cover. Talk together about the issues raised by each of the pictures and decide which one would make the best cover.

**3** Talk to your partner about:
- the advantages of knowing a foreign language
- the problems people have in learning a foreign language
- good and bad ways of learning a foreign language

43

UNIT 3  *A Word in your Ear*

## LISTENING 1
*Three-option multiple choice*

■ 1  You will hear four extracts in which different people are talking about language learning. There are two questions for each extract. For questions **1–8**, choose the answer (**A**, **B** or **C**) which fits best according to what you hear.

**Extract One**

1  What is the speaker complaining about?

   A  people's attitude to language learning
   B  people's inability to learn languages
   C  people's laziness as language learners

2  He mentions tennis as an example of an activity which

   A  can be learnt relatively easily.
   B  some people have a particular gift for.
   C  requires more effort than language learning.

**Extract Two**

3  What does the speaker think of what she calls 'teach-yourself' language manuals?

   A  They are as good as a teacher.
   B  They may be better than people think.
   C  They are no substitute for attending a course.

4  Why does she recommend using more than one book?

   A  to prevent boredom
   B  to sample different teaching methods
   C  to compare the explanations given

**Extract Three**

5  What is the speaker talking about?

   A  motivating yourself to learn a language
   B  developing techniques for learning a language
   C  prioritizing the language skills you focus on

6  What does he recommend?

   A  reading texts in translation
   B  reading about a variety of topics
   C  choosing your own reading texts

**Extract Four**

7  What approach to language learning is the speaker suggesting?

   A  a systematic approach
   B  a practical approach
   C  a traditional approach

8  How did she view the learning of vocabulary as a teenager at school?

   A  as largely pointless
   B  as a necessary exercise
   C  as a good grounding

■ 2  Do you agree with what the four speakers say about language learning?
Which one do you feel is making the most valid point?
Talk about your own experiences as a language learner. Which language learning activities do you find particularly useful/difficult/enjoyable?

# READING 1
## Lexical cloze

**1** Discuss these questions with your partner.

1 The British are said to be very poor at learning languages. Why do you think this is?

2 How important is it to try and learn the language if you are:
- visiting a country on holiday?
- working with people from another country?

**2** For questions **1–6**, read the text about British attitudes to language learning and decide which answer (**A**, **B**, **C** or **D**) best fits each gap.

### Decline and Fall

Recent figures have again shown a decrease in the number of students taking language degrees at British universities. Students are now more likely to study subjects like media studies or sports science than they are to (**1**) _____ for a course specializing in foreign languages. The number of students (**2**) _____ up places on language degree courses was down by almost 10% last year and language courses now rank amongst the ten least popular choices alongside music and mechanical engineering.

A serious (**3**) _____ of bilingual secretaries has already been identified in the British workforce and this is a (**4**) _____ of concern for the Government as international trade continues to be of increasing importance. The Government has been a keen supporter of programmes like Socrates and Erasmus, which have (**5**) _____ more than 12,000 people to study in another European country for a year, and (**6**) _____ improve their language skills, without paying tuition fees. Interest in languages, however, does not seem to have increased as a result.

| | | | | | | | |
|---|---|---|---|---|---|---|---|
| 1 | **A** select | **B** choose | **C** pick | **D** opt |
| 2 | **A** keeping | **B** taking | **C** setting | **D** giving |
| 3 | **A** drawback | **B** shortfall | **C** downturn | **D** undergrowth |
| 4 | **A** creation | **B** cause | **C** reason | **D** result |
| 5 | **A** enabled | **B** entitled | **C** enriched | **D** enlightened |
| 6 | **A** despite | **B** whereas | **C** thereby | **D** albeit |

**3** Why do you think British students are attracted to subjects like media studies and sports science?
How can more students be encouraged to study languages?

UNIT 3 *A Word in your Ear*

## USE OF ENGLISH 1
*Summary skills*

1. Read both parts of the article and then answer the questions **1–13** with a word or short phrase.

# Mind your language

*The theme of this year's London Secretary Show is 'communication across language and cultural barriers'. Our reporter, Ken Philips, interviews two seminar leaders from the show, and gets a sneak preview on the need for secretaries to communicate internationally.*

**Part One**

Business is becoming more international and secretaries will increasingly need international communication skills. English is often the only means of communication, but as two seminars at the forthcoming London Secretary Show will attempt to point out, there are many advantages for British secretaries in not simply falling back on the convenience of saying **it** in English.

In the UK, ironically, despite the fact that the country is becoming more popular as a location for international business, the reputation of the local workforce for linguistic expertise is plummeting. Vicky Collins of *Herald Language Enterprises* will focus on **this** in the first part of her seminar, and prove that communication across language and cultural barriers is easier than most British secretaries imagine. 'I am not advocating instant fluency in five foreign languages for every secretary, but as any traveller will testify, a little knowledge in a foreign language is a matter of basic politeness, which gets any transaction, business or otherwise, off to a good start. It is really quite easy to learn a language superficially. Secretaries should surely be able to offer at least basic hospitality, such as asking a visitor to sit down, in **their** own first language.'

Collins has written and published a series of guides on the business use of a number of languages. Her seminar at The London Secretary Show will move on to cover global communications as a whole, especially the issue of sensibility to other cultures. Collins explains: 'The business cultures of some countries offer more potential pitfalls than others. The wrong message can be conveyed as easily by body language as by the spoken word.' Collins warns British business people against the common British and American custom of beginning a meeting with a joke or light-hearted remark, for example. **This** could well create an unfavourable impression among clients used to a more formal business culture where work and play are kept apart.

---

1. In your own words, explain what is meant by 'falling back on the convenience'. (lines 15–16)

2. In your own words, explain what is ironic about the situation described in the UK.

3. Which word in paragraph 2 of Part One is used to indicate a rapid change?

4. In your own words, explain what is meant by the term 'body language'. (lines 47–48)

5. What point does the example of the joke or light-hearted remark in paragraph 3 of Part One serve to illustrate?

**Part Two**

Teresa Watts of the language consultants *Meridian* will be conducting a seminar on coping on the telephone in French, German and Spanish. She says there is no knowing when **such skills** might become necessary. 'Even if a secretary currently never has to deal with clients who do not speak English, it may be necessary in the future. And a secretary is often the first point of contact between the company and the outside world. It is quite possible that, as such, secretaries may well find themselves liaising between the English-speaking world and a non-English speaking company.'

It is widely recognized that the telephone is an intimidating instrument on which to conduct a conversation in a foreign language. 'Indeed, some people are not entirely happy with **it** in their mother tongue. But its very immediacy makes it a useful tool for developing language skills,' Watts says. *Meridian* offers courses in language tuition conducted entirely over the phone. Watts does not believe that someone has to be fluent in order to communicate in a foreign language by telephone, or even have any serious grounding in the language at all.

*Meridian* specializes in training in languages for specific purposes. **Its** clients include staff at ports and airports who have to issue simple instructions or directions in more than one language. Staff are trained to cope with the limited phrases they need by acting out scenarios.

Watts believes the **same methods** can be applied to secretaries. 'It is not generally assumed that secretaries will be able to pass the time of day with clients in another language, but the language being spoken should be identified, and some sign should be given to the caller that they will be passed on to someone who can deal with the call. A simple "Hang on" in the given language will convey that the call is not a dialogue of the deaf,' she says. **Such an approach** also requires no knowledge of irregular verbs or complicated tenses. Even a handful of **such phrases** can increase confidence and make the experience of handling a foreign language call 'exhilarating rather than intimidating'.

---

6 Which phrase in paragraph 1 of Part Two points to the importance of the secretary's role in the company?

7 In your own words, explain why a telephone might be 'an intimidating instrument'. (line 73)

8 In your own words, explain why *Meridian* considers courses conducted over the telephone so effective.

9 Which word in paragraph 2 of Part Two is used to mean 'a basic knowledge'?

10 Explain what you understand by the term 'acting out scenarios'. (line 92)

11 In your own words, explain the phrase 'to pass the time of day'. (lines 95–96)

12 What is implied by the phrase 'dialogue of the deaf'? (line 103)

13 Which word in paragraph 4 describes a feeling of positive enjoyment?

**2** In a paragraph of not more than 75 words, summarize **in your own words as far as possible**, the approach that secretaries should adopt towards learning languages, according to Vicky Collins and Teresa Watts.

**3** Do you agree that language courses should have a cultural aspect to them? What would this involve for your language?

UNIT 3  *A Word in your Ear*

## GRAMMAR 1
### The passive

1. Look at this sentence from the article.

   *It is not generally assumed that secretaries will be able to pass the time of day with clients in another language, but the language being spoken should be identified, and some sign should be given to the caller that they will be passed on to someone who can deal with the call.*

2. Underline the verbs in the sentence which are in the passive.

3. Rewrite the sentence so that all the verbs are in the active voice.

4. Compare the two sentences. Why did the writer choose the passive for this sentence?

5. Look back at the article. Find two other examples of the passive and decide why it has been used in each case.

   N.B. The Workbook has further work on the passive.

## VOCABULARY 1
### Collocation and referencing

1. Can you remember how the following collocations with 'language' were used in the text?

   language barriers    body language
   foreign language     language skills
   first language       language tuition

   Now explain the following collocations to your partner. Either give an example or say how they are used. You can start anywhere on the wheel.

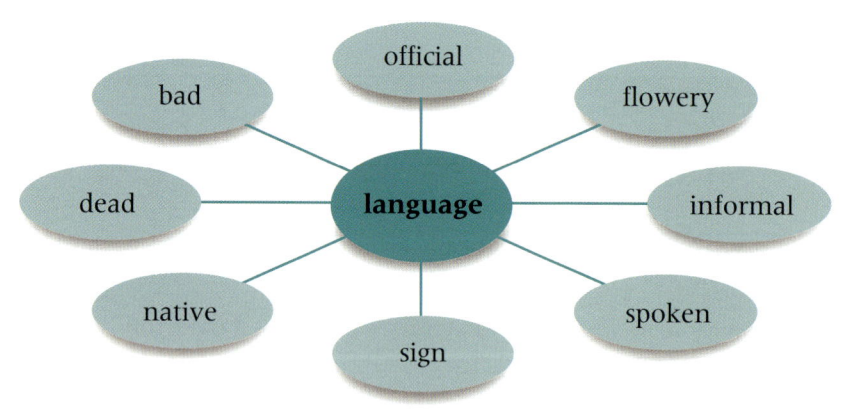

   *[Wheel diagram with 'language' in center connected to: official, flowery, informal, spoken, sign, native, dead, bad]*

2. Look back at these words and phrases which are in **bold** in both parts of the text. In each case say what each word or phrase is referring to.

   **Part One**
   1. it (line 16)
   2. this (line 23)
   3. their (line 36)
   4. This (line 52)

   **Part Two**
   5. such skills (line 61)
   6. it (line 76)
   7. Its (line 87)
   8. same methods (line 93)
   9. Such an approach (line 104)
   10. such phrases (line 107)

## HELP WITH SPEAKING: LONG TURN

**1** Part Three of Paper 5, the Speaking Test, is divided into a number of phases. In the first phase, you and your partner both have the chance to speak for about two minutes on different, but related topics. This phase of Part Three is called your 'long turn' and the following section will help you prepare for it. A Help section later in the book will help you prepare for the other parts of the Speaking Test.

## REMEMBER

- You have to talk for about two minutes.
- You cannot choose the topic.
- There is no time to prepare.
- The topic of your talk is written on a prompt card.
- There are ideas to help you on the prompt card.
- You cannot give a prepared speech, as you don't know what topic you will be given, but you can prepare yourself in other ways.

### How to approach the long turn

1 Remember your audience.

   - Your partner and the examiners are listening to what you say.
   - Try to make your talk interesting for them.
   - Explain what you want to say clearly, and keep looking at them to make sure they are following you.

2 There's plenty of time!

   - Don't go too fast. Give yourself time to think and allow yourself natural pauses.
   - To avoid running out of things to say, you need to develop each point you make before moving on to the next one.
   - Give examples of everything you say. This also adds interest for the listener.
   - Don't just say what *you* think about a topic, but say what other people think. Say why they think that way and why you don't agree with them.
   - Don't just talk about yourself. Say how the issue affects different types of people, in different places.
   - Don't just talk about now. Say what has happened in the past, how views have changed, and what you think will happen in the future.

3 Structure what you say.

   - Use the ideas on the prompt card to help you organize your ideas.
   - You could treat the ideas on the card as headings for the parts of your talk.
   - You do not have to use the ideas on the prompt card, but they are there to help you.
   - If you like, you can also introduce your own ideas, as long as they are relevant to the topic.
   - Try not to repeat yourself.
   - Learn useful phrases and expressions. These give you time to think, and also act as signposts which help listeners follow your arguments. Look at the useful phrases in the box on page 50.

UNIT 3  *A Word in your Ear*

| | |
|---|---|
| **Giving an example:** <br> for example <br> for instance <br> an/one example of this is <br> if we take the example of X <br> X serves as a good example of this | **Sequencing words:** <br> firstly <br> secondly <br> next/then <br> finally <br> lastly <br> last but not least |
| **Introducing a new idea:** <br> the first thing (I'd like) to mention <br> to begin with <br> another point to consider is <br> which leads me on to another point <br> and, of course, we shouldn't forget | **Bringing an idea to its conclusion:** <br> to sum up <br> in the final analysis <br> on balance <br> taking all the arguments into consideration <br> in conclusion |

■ 2  Before attempting a long turn, discuss the following questions with your partner.

1  What would be the advantages of having a world language which everyone could speak?

2  What problems would there be in choosing which language to use?

3  What problems would be involved in getting everyone to learn the language?

■ 3  Decide who is Student A and who is Student B.

Now look at the following prompt card. Student A should talk for two minutes on this topic.

> Would the world be a better place if everyone was forced to speak the same language?
>
> ◆ ease of communication
> ◆ educational implications
> ◆ which language?

Now look at this prompt card. Student B should talk for two minutes on this topic.

> Is English the best language for international communications?
>
> ◆ present role of English
> ◆ linguistic drawbacks of English
> ◆ cultural objections to English

■ 4  Now talk together on the same general theme for about four minutes. Here are some further questions to discuss.

1  Should everybody in the world be taught to speak English from an early age?

2  Should the grammar, spelling and pronunciation of English be simplified to make it easier for people to learn?

3  Should we protect our own languages against English by not allowing advertisers and the media to use English words?

## VOCABULARY 2
### Similes

■ 1  When people or things are likened to other things this is called a simile.

*Example:*
He's as deaf as a post.
The room was as cold as ice.

Match the beginnings of the simile in **A** with its conclusion in **B**.

| A | B |
|---|---|
| 1  as light as | nails |
| 2  as different | life |
| 3  as large as | a feather |
| 4  as hard as | a pancake |
| 5  as quick as | chalk and cheese |
| 6  as flat as | a cucumber |
| 7  as fresh as | a bone |
| 8  as good as | a daisy |
| 9  as cool as | a flash |
| 10 as dry as | gold |

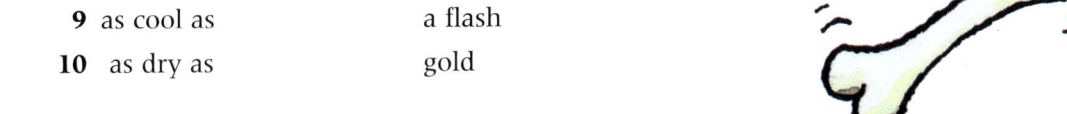

■ 2  Which of these similes would you use to talk about:

- people?
- places?
- objects?

📖 N.B. The Workbook has further work on similes.

## 🎧 LISTENING 2
### Selecting an answer

■ 1  Discuss these questions with your partner.

1  Do you often read books in translation?

2  Are most major works of fiction from other languages translated into your language?

3  Which important writers from your country are translated into other languages?

4  Have you ever read a book in both your own language and in English?

5  What did you think of the translation?

UNIT 3  *A Word in your Ear*

■ 2  You will hear two parts of a radio discussion on the subject of books which are international bestsellers. Listen to Part One. For questions **1–2**, choose the answer (**A**, **B** or **C**) which fits best according to what you hear.

1   Elizabeth says that her job involves

   **A**  choosing a small number of books to be translated into English.
   **B**  recommending which English books should be translated.
   **C**  selling to publishers books that she has translated.

2   Elizabeth says that in order to be successful in her work she has to

   **A**  find books which have a complex plot.
   **B**  anticipate which books might sell in large numbers.
   **C**  rely on her own judgement and not on other people's.

■ 3  Listen to Part Two and for each of the questions **1–7**, mark each box **A** or **D** to show whether the two guests agree or disagree.

1   The need to explain things clearly for the benefit of foreign readers.   ☐ 1

2   The acceptability of English humour to foreign readers.   ☐ 2

3   The extent to which writers should consider their readers as they write.   ☐ 3

4   The attitude of American publishers.   ☐ 4

5   The lesson to be learnt from literary classics.   ☐ 5

6   The attitude of British and American readers to books in translation.   ☐ 6

7   The growth in popularity of translated novels in the UK.   ☐ 7

■ 4  Imagine you have been asked to check a translation from your language into English. The translation has been done by a young inexperienced translator.

- What type of vocabulary mistakes would you expect to find in the translation?
- What type of grammar mistakes would you expect to find in the translation?
- What other type of mistakes do speakers of your language commonly make when translating into English?

■ 5  How can you make sure that you do not make these mistakes in your own writing?

## PHRASAL VERBS 1

**1** Look at each of these phrases or sentences from the listening text. Each one contains a phrasal verb. Underline the phrasal verb in each example and then choose the best definition **A**, **B** or **C**.

1 Mervyn's latest novel has really taken off internationally.
   A been successful
   B been released
   C been removed

2 A new international market for books is opening up.
   A being offered
   B becoming accessible
   C gaining acceptability

3 The very same books are taken up by almost all my publishers.
   A adopted
   B translated
   C recommended

4 A lot of authors toss in local references which are meaningless to people in other countries.
   A include intentionally
   B include disrespectfully
   C include casually

5 American publishers will pick you up on the smallest point.
   A reject you
   B question you
   C criticize you

6 A good translator will sort out those little problems for readers in other languages.
   A rearrange
   B clarify
   C omit

## SPEAKING 2
### Expressing likes and dislikes

1 Talk to your partner about a book you have bought, read or used recently which you found particularly enjoyable, useful or interesting.

2 Look at the types of book in the box and say which three you buy, read or use most regularly and why.

| | | |
|---|---|---|
| cookery books | (auto)biography | thrillers/crime novels |
| modern literature | science fiction | educational books |
| manuals | romantic novels | travel books |
| puzzle books | classic literature | reference books |

3 What type of person do you think buys which type of book?

4 Which type of book do you think is the most popular in your country?

UNIT 3  *A Word in your Ear*

## HELP WITH WORD-BUILDING: CLOZE TASKS

■ **1** In Part Two of the Use of English Paper, you have to complete a word-building cloze.

### REMEMBER

- Only one word fits in each space.
- The word must be formed from the base word printed on the right of the text.
- Most words will be longer than the base word and are formed by:
  adding a suffix, e.g. *announce* ➔ *announce<u>ment</u>*
  adding a prefix, e.g. *successful* ➔ *<u>un</u>successful*
  changing the form of a word, e.g. *seek* ➔ *sought*
  adding a word to form a new compound word, e.g. *bag* ➔ *<u>hand</u>bag*

  Often more than one change will be necessary, e.g. *true* ➔ *<u>untruthfully</u>*

- The word must make sense in the sentence, not just in the line with a gap, and also must match the sense of the text as a whole. So it is important to:
  — read the whole text through before you begin
  — think about the meaning of the sentence containing a gap
  — think about whether the words you form need to be singular or plural, positive or negative

- The key words must be spelt correctly. Sometimes spelling changes occur as a result of adding prefixes and suffixes. Be careful of:
  double consonants, e.g. *admit* ➔ *admi<u>tt</u>edly*
  letters which are dropped, e.g. *ignore* ➔ *ignorance*
  sounds which change, e.g. *solve* ➔ *solution*

  📖 N.B. The Workbook has Help with Spelling sections designed to help you with this task.

■ **2** Look at the completed word-building task on page 55 and find one example of each of the following amongst the keys.

    **a** a compound word   _____

    **b** a word involving a spelling change   _____

    **c** adding two suffixes   _____

    **d** adding both a prefix and a suffix   _____

    **e** a negative prefix   _____

    **f** a word that must be plural in the context   _____

    **g** a noun formed from a verb   _____

    **h** a verb formed from a noun   _____

    **i** an adjective formed by adding a suffix   _____

    **j** a noun formed from another noun   _____

## Think before you Send

The issue of how to use e-mail effectively and (1) *professionally* — **PROFESSION**
in the work environment, without appearing too (2) *informal* — **FORMAL**
is something of a (3) *minefield*. According to one leading staff — **MINE**
(4) *recruitment* agency, the key is to think before you send. Be — **RECRUIT**
(5) *friendly*, but not too familiar, and keep your messages short. — **FRIEND**
Avoid (6) *abbreviations* unless you're sure the person you're writing — **BRIEF**
to will understand them, and always put a (7) *heading* in the — **HEAD**
subject box so that the recipient knows how to (8) *prioritize* what — **PRIORITY**
they receive. Finally, do remember to add the (9) *attachments* you — **ATTACH**
promised, but take great care when sending and forwarding them.
It's easy to send things to the wrong person, sometimes with
(10) *disastrous* consequences. — **DISASTER**

**3** Now try this task. The first one has been done for you as an example.

## Secrets of the Office Password

Millions of office workers switch on their computers each
morning and (0) <u>immediately</u> reveal quite a lot about their — **IMMEDIATE**
personalities. In many (1) _____ , it is necessary for an — **ORGANIZE**
(2) _____ to key in a personalized password before he — **EMPLOY**
or she can gain access to the company's computer (3) _____ . — **NET**
The choice of password is, however, generally left up to the
individual, and this is the area which has provided teams
of (4) _____ with such a good opportunity for research. — **PSYCHOLOGY**

According to a recent study, four distinct categories of password can
be identified, corresponding to four personality types. Most people,
rather (5) _____ , go for their own name, or that of a close — **PREDICT**
family member or beloved pet. Other, slightly more (6) _____ — **IMAGINE**
people choose their favourite football team, cartoon character or film
star. But around 11% actually choose a word that they feel in some
way is a (7) _____ of their character. Passwords like 'superstar', — **REFLECT**
'genius' or 'sexy' turned out to be surprisingly common amongst
this somewhat (8) _____ group, and it's difficult to believe that — **MODEST**
all were intended to be jokes. The smallest of the four categories,
however, was made up of the truly (9) _____ conscious. These — **SECURE**
were people who had taken the exercise seriously and had chosen a
password that was completely (10) _____ with any aspect of their — **CONNECT**
work and lives. Company secrets, it seems, will always be safe with them.

UNIT 3  *A Word in your Ear*

## USE OF ENGLISH 2
### Comprehension

■ 1  Look at the headline of the article on page 57. What do you think the article will say about book buying in Britain?

■ 2  Read the article quickly to find out what the following numbers refer to:

95,000   899   35   55
55,000   12   793   47   22

■ 3  Now read again more carefully and answer these questions.
1  Why has the writer used the expression 'chapters ahead'? (lines 2–3)
2  In your own words explain the term 'for pleasure'. (line 7)
3  What does 'the same' in line 14 refer to?
4  What does the word 'markedly' in line 15 mean?
5  What does 'the figure' in lines 17–18 refer to?
6  What are 'culinary titles'? (line 25)
7  What does the phrasal verb 'bore out' in line 31 mean?
8  Explain in your own words why 'trophy books' may be 'more purchased than read'. (lines 36/38–39)
9  What does 'they' in line 50 refer to?
10  What do you understand by the adverb 'steadily'? (line 56)
11  Explain in your own words the term 'consumer spending'. (line 61)
12  Which word is used in the article for the conclusions drawn from the information collected in the survey?

## GRAMMAR 2
### Complex sentences: Comparison and contrast

■ 1  Look at the first sentence in the second paragraph of the article.
1  How many pieces of information does the sentence give?
2  Which word provides the link between the two main parts of the sentence?
3  How is the punctuation of the sentence important?
4  Why has the writer chosen this type of sentence to present the information?

■ 2  Look at the next two sentences in the article. Which words provide the link between the two main parts of these sentences? Are they making the same type of link?

📖 N.B. The Workbook has further work on this type of sentence.

# The Joy of Reading Leaves Men on the Shelf

When it comes to reading habits, women are chapters ahead of men, a survey reveals today. The study of what Britons read – and when – found that 35% of men had not read a book for pleasure for five years or more, compared to only one in five women.

The survey, conducted by Book Marketing Ltd, also reveals that while 47% of women claimed to have finished a book in the previous fortnight, only 30% of men could say the same. Reading habits differ markedly with age; whereas only 18% of those aged 15 to 24 had read a book in the week before they were questioned, the figure for people aged between 25 and 34 was 21%, and 41% for those over 55.

Cookery books, with many titles linked to a television series, are the most popular type of book bought, although romantic fiction and puzzle books have the biggest volume of sales.

For example, culinary titles were bought by 21% of those who purchased a book compared to 18% who bought a crime story or thriller, 12% who bought a romantic novel and 7% who bought a work of 20th-century fiction. A quick look around London book stores yesterday bore out some of the findings, with a range of cookery books, romantic works and thrillers on the best-seller racks. Also selling well were novels that had won literary prizes and what one bookseller called 'trophy' books, titles which look good on the bookshelf, but which tend to be more purchased than read.

The finding that women are greater readers than men was supported by a quick survey of book buyers by this newspaper. 'I think it's because women are continually trying to change and improve themselves, and are more flexible and open to new experiences,' Liz Kay, a curator at the Tate Gallery, said. Tamsin Summerson, 22, said she was aware of the difference among her friends. 'If you ask a man what book they've just read, they're likely to have forgotten or they will change the subject. On the other hand, with a woman, you're likely to get into a lengthy discussion about it.'

But whichever sex you are, it is getting harder to be well-read. The number of books published in Britain has risen steadily in recent years, from just under 55,000 in 1987 to just over 95,000 today. Book prices have also risen from an average of £7.93 for a novel in 1991 compared with £8.99 today. Consumer spending on books has jumped from £755 million in 1985 to £1673 million.

Adapted from an article by Marianne MacDonald and Michael Streeter in *The Independent*.

UNIT 3  *A Word in your Ear*

## SPEAKING 3
### Constructing a questionnaire

1. The article talks about two surveys. How are the two surveys different? Why do you think the newspaper decided to carry out the second survey?

2. Look at the article.
   What questions did the Book Marketing Survey ask people? Make a list.
   What order do you think the questions were asked in? Why?

3. What questions did the newspaper survey ask people?

4. Do you think a survey of people in your country/school would find the same results as the two surveys in the article? Why (not)?

5. Design a questionnaire about the type of recorded music people buy. Your questionnaire should be quite short so that you can ask lots of people (i.e. about 8–12 questions) and should provide you with enough information to write a report. Your report should include:
   - information about the people interviewed
   - how much they spend on recorded music and what they buy
   - some subjective opinions

## WRITING 1
### Preparing a report

1. A local businessman, who is proposing to open a music shop in your area, has asked you to give him a report based on the results of your questionnaire on recorded music. What would be the best style and layout for such a report?

2. Read the two reports on page 59, written in response to this request.
   Are they written in an appropriate style?
   Which one will be more useful to the businessman? Why?

3. Look at the phrases and words that are underlined in report A; they are quite informal. Match them with phrases and words of a similar meaning in report B.

4. A report should be a well-organized piece of writing where the information is clearly set out in response to the question. It is often helpful to include headings and sub-headings, to help the reader find the information he or she needs.

   1. The headings are missing from report B. Think of some possible headings.

   2. What tenses would you expect to use in a report?
      Why is the passive often used?
      In a report, should you: **a** make suggestions? **b** express personal opinions?

5. Now look at the following exam question and plan your report. Then write your **report** in **300–350** words.

   *A youth club in your neighbourhood faces closure unless it can raise enough money to carry out major repairs to its premises. You are organizing a music concert, which will take place in three weeks time, to raise money for the youth club. Write a progress report to be presented at the club's next committee meeting. Explain what arrangements have been made for the concert and what remains to be done.*

   ✎ Remember to use the Writing Checklist on page 11.

   📖 N.B. The Workbook has further work on report writing.

*A Word in your Ear* **UNIT 3**

**A**

Dear Mr. Bradley,

Here are the results of the survey I did in May, about the type of music people like to buy. I spoke to about fifty people in the street and they all had different ideas, but the younger people seemed to spend a lot more money on buying music than the older people.

Most of the people in their twenties said they liked Pop music and they obviously knew a lot about the different artists. Although they didn't have a lot of money, they said they bought about four CDs a month. The people who bought the most music were the over 30s, and it was usually the men who were more interested in music. They liked all different sorts of music but they said it had to be good quality. These men I've just mentioned often bought CDs by post because it's easier that way.

Hardly anyone over fifty bought any music, because they said they preferred going to concerts or listening to the radio.

I hope this information is helpful to you and I wish you every success in your business.

Yours sincerely

Leo Andrews

**B**

To:        Mr. Bradley
From:      Anna Morris
Subject:   Purchase of recorded music

**1** _____

This report outlines the findings of a survey carried out during the period 10th–25th May to assess the type of recorded music bought by people in the area. Data was obtained from 50 men and women aged between 16 and 65, who responded to a questionnaire in a face-to-face interview in the shopping centre.

**2** _____

80% of respondents in the under-30 age group reported a preference for pop music, and demonstrated a keen awareness of the contemporary music scene. Amongst those questioned in the over-30 age group, however, only 10% are recorded as liking pop music, whereas 30% expressed a preference for classical music or opera. The remaining 60% of respondents in this age group listened to a wide range of musical styles, including jazz and folk.

**3** _____

In the under-30 age group, respondents reported buying an average of four CDs per month. Those under 20, often on a limited budget, favouring discount stores, whilst those over 30 were more likely to buy via mail-order for convenience. In the age group 30 to 50, men spent a considerably larger part of their income on recorded music than women did, whereas those over 50 bought very little recorded music at all, preferring to attend concerts or listen to the radio.

**4** _____

The results of the survey clearly suggest that people under 50 are the major purchasers of recorded music in this area, with pop music the most popular choice. Whilst the younger end of the market appears to be the most price sensitive, competition from mail-order companies is most likely to affect the market for classical music, jazz, etc. amongst consumers over 30. The strongest demand for recorded music appears to come from male consumers aged 20 to 50, who are most likely to buy good-quality pop music.

UNIT 3  A Word in your Ear

## LISTENING 3

*Four-option multiple choice*

**1** What are the qualities of a good novel? Talk about:

> plot   characterization   descriptions   tension   humour   style of writing

**2** You will hear an interview with a novelist who has written a book called *The Secrets of Best-seller Writing*. For questions **1–6**, choose the answer (**A, B, C** or **D**) which fits best according to what you hear.

1 Why did she refuse initially to write the book?

   **A** She was busy writing something else.
   **B** She found this sort of book irritating.
   **C** Other books on the subject were rubbish.
   **D** Other writers would probably want to write it.

2 She feels that books advising writers are often misleading with regard to

   **A** the nature of the readership.
   **B** the quality of the product.
   **C** the importance of reviews.
   **D** the attitude of the book business.

3 How did she feel about the number of people attending her talk at the book fair?

   **A** disappointed
   **B** surprised
   **C** gratified
   **D** nervous

4 John Grisham serves as an example of how

   **A** you can't teach people to write.
   **B** you can't predict who will be successful.
   **C** one successful writer benefited from advice.
   **D** some people dream of writing a best-seller.

5 What must all writers have before they can begin to write a best-seller?

   **A** an outline of the plot
   **B** a narrative instinct
   **C** some clear literary ideals
   **D** a true story as a base

6 Why does she feel that, as a novelist, she never gets 'writer's block'?

   **A** She has great self-discipline.
   **B** She has a fixed daily routine.
   **C** She's always found writing easy.
   **D** She trained in another field.

# EXAM PRACTICE 3

**1** For questions **1–8**, complete the second sentence so that it has a similar meaning to the first sentence, using the word given. **Do not change the word given**. You must use between **three** and **eight** words, including the word given. Here is an example.

*Example:* A lot of people attended the meeting.
**turnout**
*Answer:* There *was a very good turnout for* the meeting.

1 Why do you think your first novel was so successful?
   **account**
   How _____ of your first novel?

2 It's not Jane's intention to forgive Peter for embarrassing her.
   **no**
   Jane _____ Peter for embarrassing her.

3 What are the chances of the book becoming a best-seller?
   **likely**
   How _____ will become a best-seller?

4 As soon as it was published in translation, the book became a best-seller.
   **sooner**
   No _____ than it became a best-seller.

5 They discussed the acceptability of English humour to foreign readers.
   **how**
   They discussed _____ to foreign readers.

6 Samantha always wanted to be a writer when she grew up.
   **ambition**
   It _____ up to be a writer.

7 People often make the mistake of thinking that Fatima is a native speaker of English.
   **mistaken**
   Fatima _____ a native speaker of English.

8 Only part of the story he told has historical evidence to support it.
   **partially**
   The story _____ historical evidence.

UNIT 3  *A Word in your Ear*

**2**  For questions **1–5**, think of **one** word only which can be used appropriately in all three sentences.

1  The company found itself unable to cope with all the correspondence it received in other languages, and so decided to _____ more bilingual staff.

A good public speaker has to be skilled enough to _____ the attention of the audience.

Try to _____ him in conversation, while I slip into the office and look through the papers on his desk.

2  From what I _____ , he did not have much opportunity to study languages when he was young.

If you would all like to go and _____ up the picnic things, I'll bring the car round and open the boot.

Before there was television, people would all _____ round the piano in the evenings and sing.

3  From what I can see, Fiona will have to take her son in _____ before he becomes too ill-disciplined.

Just leave the job to Phil – he's an old _____ at repairing torn book jackets.

This company is the best I know, they always have a team of translators on _____ to help with enquiries from overseas customers.

4  There has been a steady _____ in the number of translated books published recently.

Because of their increased workload, the secretaries at the company put in for a _____ .

The house is situated on a slight _____ in an otherwise flat landscape.

5  The idea of working overseas for a year to learn a language has really _____ off in recent years.

Sometimes, I suspect that Colin has not _____ his writing career seriously enough.

I was particularly _____ by the beautifully well-kept flowerbeds along the seafront.

UNIT 4

# A Fine Romance

### SPEAKING 1
**Talking together about a visual prompt**

1. Look at the photographs and talk to your partner about:

   1. the relationships between the people and how the people are feeling:
      - about themselves
      - about others
      - about what they are doing

   2. what they are thinking about

   3. what type of person you think each one is:
      - what qualities they have
      - what failings they have

2. A magazine is organizing a photographic competition on the theme of 'togetherness', with the emphasis on couples. Talk to your partner and decide:
   - how well each of the photos matches the theme
   - which should come first, second and third in the competition and why

UNIT 4  *A Fine Romance*

**3** Which of these characteristics would you like your ideal partner in life to have? Choose the five most important. Say why you have chosen them.

| | | | | |
|---|---|---|---|---|
| modesty | loyalty | honesty | generosity | reliability |
| style | intelligence | bravery | judgement | patience |
| charm | sense of humour | faithfulness | sociability | talent |
| caution | resourcefulness | taste | common sense | beauty |

**4** Think about your ideal/perfect partner in life. Talk about what is important to you and why.

Physical appearance:
Height, weight, colouring, age, health and fitness, etc.

Status:
Money, social position, occupation, family background, education, etc.

Character:
Qualities and failings that matter.

Which would affect your choice most?

**5** Is your perfect partner similar to you or different to you? Is this significant?

Do men and women have different ideas of what makes a good partner?

**6** With your partner, look at this advertisement for an introductions agency. Talk about:

- what the agency is
- how it works
- what sort of people use them
- whether you think they are successful

### HAPPY HEARTS INTRODUCTION AGENCY

♥

*Find your perfect partner in life*

♥

*Our database holds details of 2000 single people*

♥

*All areas, all ages, all interests catered for*

♥

***Confidentiality guaranteed***

## READING 1
*Lexical cloze*

**1** For questions **1–12**, read the three passages connected with dating agencies and decide which answer (**A**, **B**, **C** or **D**) best fits each gap.

**A**
The Happy Hearts Introduction Agency is designed for individuals seeking a genuine one-to-one relationship. Clients are (1) _____ that entries will not be accepted on to our database if they state a race, creed, colour or nationality in the person (2) _____ and that all entries must be within the law. The Agency (3) _____ the right, therefore, to exercise its own discretion in refusing any entries which may (4) _____ offence or be in any way unlawful.

**B**
Hi. Tall, slim and exceptionally attractive. I'm a struggling musician who travels a great deal and has many friends. By nature, I'm caring and affectionate with a good (5) _____ of humour. Being very sociable, I have a (6) _____ to throw impromptu parties. My ideal partner is someone who is tolerant enough to (7) _____ with my unpredictable lifestyle, but brave enough to (8) _____ up to me sometimes. It's someone who will be there when I need them, but who will also leave me the space when I need to be by myself.

**C**
Once you've selected your ideal partner from our shortlist, naturally you'll be keen to get in touch with them. You can write a letter or e-mail to your chosen person through us, using the database code number on the printout. It couldn't be easier, and there's no need to give your personal (9) _____ if you don't want to. Sooner or later, if you (10) _____ it off, you may want to actually meet your new friend. Remember this is (11) _____ to you to decide; there's no pressure. But when you go to meet the person for the first time, we suggest you:
– tell a friend of your plans
– always meet in a public place
– don't give your address or phone number (12) _____ you're sure you want to continue with the relationship.

| | | | | |
|---|---|---|---|---|
| 1 | **A** refrained | **B** reminded | **C** recalled | **D** regulated |
| 2 | **A** striven | **B** pursued | **C** sought | **D** hunted |
| 3 | **A** requires | **B** remains | **C** reserves | **D** restores |
| 4 | **A** hold | **B** make | **C** take | **D** give |
| 5 | **A** sense | **B** style | **C** taste | **D** tone |
| 6 | **A** tendency | **B** habit | **C** failing | **D** weakness |
| 7 | **A** pick up | **B** work out | **C** put up | **D** try out |
| 8 | **A** keep | **B** stand | **C** stick | **D** look |
| 9 | **A** materials | **B** items | **C** points | **D** details |
| 10 | **A** strike | **B** hit | **C** set | **D** carry |
| 11 | **A** round | **B** back | **C** up | **D** over |
| 12 | **A** apart from | **B** unless | **C** in case | **D** otherwise |

UNIT 4  *A Fine Romance*

**2** Now for each text, talk about:
- who you think wrote it
- who it is talking to
- the style it is written in
- what you think about what it is saying

**3** Write either:

**a** Your own (real or imaginary) entry for the agency's database.
**b** Your reply to the person who wrote passage B.

Remember that you have to describe yourself in a flattering light and give a good idea of the qualities you are looking for in a perfect partner.

## LISTENING 1
### Three-option multiple choice

**1** You will hear two extracts in which different people are talking. For questions **1–4**, choose the answer (**A**, **B** or **C**) which fits best according to what you hear.

**Extract One**

You turn on the radio and hear this extract from a programme.

**1** What sort of programme is it?
  **A** a soap opera
  **B** a news report
  **C** a documentary

**2** What is described in this extract?
  **A** unrequited love
  **B** a romantic interlude
  **C** a touching reconciliation

**Extract Two**

You hear a man who has been married twice, talking about his weddings.

**3** During his first wedding ceremony, he disliked
  **A** the way he had to dress.
  **B** being the centre of attention.
  **C** receiving so many gifts.

**4** He enjoyed his second wedding more because
  **A** it was more relaxed.
  **B** it cost less money.
  **C** it took less time.

**2** Look at these words and phrases from Extract Two. Listen again, and then match each of the expressions in the box with its definition **a–g**.

> the outfits    a low-key affair    stay out of the limelight
> the hassle    over and done with    laid back    suited me down to the ground

  **a** not be the centre of attention
  **b** a lot of trouble
  **c** relaxed attitude
  **d** the clothes
  **e** ideal arrangement
  **f** not an extravagant occasion
  **g** finished with relief

*A Fine Romance* UNIT 4

## HELP WITH MULTIPLE-CHOICE QUESTIONS

**1** There are multiple-choice questions in both the Reading and Listening Papers of the Proficiency examination. In the Reading Paper, there are multiple-choice cloze questions in Part One (like those in exercise 1 on page 65) and multiple-choice comprehension questions in Parts Two and Four (like those on page 69). In all these tasks, you must choose the correct answer from the four alternatives.

In the Listening Paper, there are multiple-choice questions in Parts One and Three. In Part One, there are only three options, whilst in Part Three, there are four options. You should, however, approach the questions in the same way.

There are two types of multiple-choice comprehension question. Either a question is followed by alternative answers, only one of which is correct (e.g. questions 1 and 2 in the listening task on page 66) or there is an incomplete sentence with alternative possible endings, only one of which matches what is said in the text (e.g. questions 3 and 4 in the listening task on page 66).

## REMEMBER

- The order of questions follows the order of the text.
- Each question is based on one piece of text.
- You are being tested on whether you understand what the writer or speaker is saying. Don't be influenced by your own ideas about the subject; read or listen carefully to see what the writer or speaker says.

### How to approach multiple-choice <u>reading</u> questions

This section focuses on the multiple-choice questions found in Parts Two and Four of the Reading Paper of the examination. When attempting these types of reading task it is important to consider the following guidelines:

- Read the whole text first without pausing to think about difficult words.
- Look at the questions or incomplete sentences and find the relevant piece of text.
- Read the text again carefully and try to answer the question in your own mind before you look at the options **A–D**.
- Underline the important information in the text.
- Find the option which best matches your own answer.
- Read again to check that the other options are definitely wrong.

**2** Now try the following multiple-choice reading task about a woman with a difficult decision to make concerning her relationship with her boyfriend.

## UNIT 4 A Fine Romance

### READING 2
*Multiple choice*

■ 1  Read this extract from a novel carefully and for questions **1–6**, choose the answer (**A**, **B**, **C** or **D**) which you think fits best according to the text.

## Brief Conceit

*Laura had something important to say – if only she could make herself understood to Howard above the noise in the restaurant.*

It's our favourite restaurant, small and intimate, but it has its drawbacks: the service is pleasant but lazily inefficient, by necessity there's very little space between tables, and because the place is perpetually on the edge of bankruptcy, they serve just four small squares of ravioli and call it a main course. But everyone puts up with these things, and somehow you feel compensated
10   by the complimentary amaretti biscuits and tiny glasses of lemon liqueur that arrive with your bill.

Today I was meeting Howard there for lunch. I pushed open the green door, wondering if this would be my last visit. Marco, the head waiter, strode forward from the throng to greet me, his chubby face beaming. 'Signorina Laura! Howard has telephoned. He is running late,' he tutted, 'and asks you to order for him.' I chose a table with a good view of the door.

The air was filled with prattle and the clatter of knives and forks. I ordered mussels for Howard and squid for myself. As I kept watch, two tall women in slick jackets and high heels approached the table next to me. 'Can we be quick? We have a meeting at
20   two,' the woman with red hair said to Marco. They shrugged off their coats and slid into their seats. They were ordering their food, voices raised above the clamour, when Howard walked in like a tall, gawky bird in his flapping raincoat.

'Laura,' he shouted, leaning down to kiss me. 'Sorry I'm late.' Marco bore away the coat while Howard checked the specials on the menu to make sure I hadn't missed anything. Suddenly he looked up and smiled. 'You always choose the right thing for me,' he said. I was used to his abbreviated flashes of affection, but still not immune.

Our food arrived and as we ate, Marco glided in and out to fill and refill our glasses. Howard efficiently extracted his mussels but the squid was like rubber in my mouth and I couldn't swallow. 'Listen, Howard,' I began. 'Look at the colour of these shells; they're
30   like your eyes,' he said, in imitation of a romantic novel. The red-haired businesswoman glanced at Howard's discarded mussel shells at her elbow and started to talk over him.

'I've known you all this time, Maribel, and you've never told me why your parents gave you such an odd name,' she said to her friend. 'Don't you know that story, Francesca?' said Maribel. 'It's because my father was an explorer.'

I tried to ignore their conversation. 'Howard,' I tried again. I thought of my boss's words that morning, when he'd offered me a new job in the firm's Tokyo office. 'A wonderful opportunity that may never come up again,' he had said. 'You don't have any ties to hold you here in England, do you?' My future lay now in the hands of the man sitting opposite me.

40   'I can't hear,' Howard bellowed over Maribel's voice. 'One year my father was on an expedition to the North Pole, and was marooned by ice floes in Greenland,' Maribel was saying. The businesswomen took large gulps of wine. 'What's wrong with your squid?' said Howard, leaning forward to spear one with his fork. I thought I had his attention now. 'Howard, we've been going out together for a long time now, and I need to know if…' Howard waved the bread basket in the air until he caught Marco's eye. I swallowed a big mouthful of wine myself. 'I need to know if we're ever going to get married.'

68

'I hadn't a clue he did anything like that,' said Francesca. Howard ate more of my squid. 'This is great,' he said. 'The thing is, Howard, I've had this job offer in Japan.' Marco arrived with the bread, and Howard began with concentration to mop up the juices from his dish of mussels. 'Don't you like the squid, Signorina?' asked Marco above the din, his face lugubrious. 'Shall I bring you something else?' 'I'm just not hungry, Marco,' I explained. He nodded.

'Anyway, he was trapped by the ice floes and survived the entire winter on a lump of sugar a day,' continued Maribel. I took a deep breath. 'I've decided, Howard, there's only one thing which will stop me from going to Tokyo, and you know what it is.' 'Really?' Francesca said, her spaghetti slipping from her fork. Maribel nodded. Howard was still chewing away on my squid, reaching across the table with his long arms. 'Squirt a bit of lemon on it for me, sweetheart,' he murmured.

'Finally,' said Maribel, 'just as he was down to the last sugar lump, he was rescued by a Spanish trawler called Maribel. So I'm named after an old trawler.' 'A coffee for Laura, and the bill please,' called Howard. We threw our plastic cards into the saucer and Howard turned to Maribel. 'I couldn't help overhearing what you said… the way these tables are arranged,' he gestured at the few inches between us. 'I was enthralled, and I'm sure anyone would be. I produce television documentaries. May I give you my card?' She took it and stood up. 'Of course, thank you. But we must be going.'

'You don't want this after all, Signorina?' asked Marco, belatedly arriving with my coffee. 'Not really,' I said, suddenly feeling decisive, my eyes on the back of Howard's light, fluffy head as we followed the women to the door. 'You'll have to tell me about your name another time, Maribel. I didn't hear a word you said,' I heard Francesca say. 'I was riveted by that woman sitting next to you.'

'Goodbye, sweetheart. You were quiet today,' Howard said, and kissed me. 'Goodbye,' I said, and turned to Marco, who looked a little taken aback when, relishing my refound freedom, I kissed him too.

1 What aspect of the restaurant's service does Laura interpret cynically?
A the attitude of the waiter
B the layout of the tables
C the size of the portions
D the provision of free extras

2 In her description of the two women who arrive in the restaurant, Laura implies that they are
A more familiar with the waiter than she is.
B unaccustomed to the level of service provided.
C more elegantly dressed than Howard.
D unused to the level of noise found there.

3 How does Laura feel when Howard compliments her?
A annoyed by his insincerity
B embarrassed by his show of affection
C susceptible to his charm
D impervious to his attempts at flattery

4 Why is Laura so keen to get Howard's full attention during the meal?
A She needs to clarify something with him.
B She wants to ask his permission about something.
C She needs to inform him of a decision she's made.
D She wants to remind him about something.

5 From his behaviour during the lunch, we understand that Howard
A is pre-occupied with his own thoughts.
B wants to concentrate on his meal.
C is unaware that something is troubling Laura.
D needs time to think about Laura's problems.

6 What irony is revealed at the end of the story?
A Howard intended to finish the relationship anyway.
B Howard was more interested in Maribel's story than Francesca was.
C At neither table was communication actually taking place.
D Only Marco was listening to both conversations.

UNIT 4  *A Fine Romance*

**2** Find words or phrases in the text which mean the following (paragraph numbers in brackets):

   a  free of charge (1)
   b  crowd (2)
   c  trivial chat (3)
   d  noisy confusion (3)
   e  awkward in his movements (3)
   f  thrown away (5)
   g  shouted (8)
   h  sad and gloomy (9)
   i  extremely interested (11)
   j  not coming on time (12)
   k  extremely interested (12)

**3** Discuss the following questions with a partner.

   1  What impression do you have of Howard and Laura? Are they well-suited as a couple? Do you think they would be happy together as husband and wife?

   2  Look at the title of the story. Which of the characters would you describe as conceited?

   3  What decision do you think Laura will make?

## WRITING 1
### Essays

**1** Look at this Writing task.

*In class, you have read this text about stability in relationships. Your tutor has asked you to write an essay, saying how far you agree with the opinion given.*

*Write your **essay** in 300–350 words in an appropriate style.*

> Where both love and friendship are concerned, the strongest and most lasting relationships are based on fundamental difference: of personality, opinion and interests. For in both partner and friend, we seek the qualities missing in ourselves. If we are shy, we seek someone outgoing; if we're disorganized, we're attracted to someone tidy and practical.

**2** When you are writing a discursive essay, you are not giving just a personal opinion. It is a relatively formal piece of writing in which an argument is considered from opposing points of view. Both sides of the argument should be presented in a fair, objective way.

The outline of a balanced essay could, for example, look like this:

**Paragraph 1:**       A summary or overview of the topic with some background but without giving your opinion.

**Paragraphs 2 and 3:** Arguments in support of the idea put forward in the question, with justification and examples.

**Paragraphs 4 and 5:** Arguments against the idea put forward in the question, with justification and examples.

**Final Paragraph:**   A balanced consideration of the whole argument. You may give your opinion here, either indirectly or directly, but in a detached, non-emotional way, e.g. 'It seems that…/On balance, I am of the opinion that…'

**3** To write effectively it is important that you state both sides of the argument. Before writing, discuss the essay question with a partner. Together, make a list of points for and against the argument. This will form the plan for your essay.

**4** Linking words and phrases make an essay easier for the reader to follow. Look at the groups of expressions **1–5**. Which heading (**a–e**) fits each group best, according to how the linking expressions are generally used?

- **a** Stating a truth
- **b** Concluding phrases
- **c** Introducing a contrasting point or opinion
- **d** Stating a partial truth
- **e** Adding/Listing points

**1**
First of all, secondly, thirdly,
A further advantage is…
Another major drawback is…
Furthermore,
Moreover,
What's more,

**2**
Many people would argue that…
On the other hand…
It is widely claimed that…
Nonetheless/Nevertheless…
Opponents of… claim that…
Some experts advocate… (+ ing/noun)
In spite of,
Despite,

**3**
in fact…
in practice…
realistically…
It is a fact that…

**4**
To a certain extent…
There is some truth in this but…
In some cases… however,
To a limited extent…

**5**
All things considered…
Taking everything into account…
On balance…
To conclude…
All in all…

**5** When you are putting forward an argument you need to use words that stress or emphasize what you are saying, for example:

| obviously | needless to say | naturally | without doubt | clearly |

You can also change the word order of your sentence following certain adverbial expressions to add emphasis to your argument, for example:

*So intense is the feeling of 'love at first sight' that couples rarely give a thought to the future.*

*Only after two years of marriage did they begin to feel that they were not compatible.*

N.B. The Workbook has further work on using inversion for emphasis.

**6** Now, using your plan, write your **essay** in **300–350** words. Try to incorporate several of the words and phrases from exercises 4 and 5.

Remember to use the Writing Checklist on page 11.

UNIT 4 *A Fine Romance*

## LISTENING 2
*Four-option multiple choice*

▪ 1   What sort of things cause arguments in a relationship? Talk about:

| friends | different interests | family | work | moods | money |

▪ 2   Are arguments in a relationship a good thing or a bad thing?

▪ 3   You will hear a speaker from the Marriage Guidance Organization talking about the type of problems it helps couples with. For questions **1–5**, choose the answer (**A**, **B**, **C** or **D**) which fits best according to what you hear.

1   What do we learn from the organization's statistics?

   **A**  Marital problems are on the increase generally.
   **B**  People often fall out when they're away from their usual routine.
   **C**  People are now more open about marital problems.
   **D**  There is a tendency for more couples to seek professional help.

2   What is the main difference between what are described as 'parallel' and 'interactional' couples?

   **A**  their normal lifestyle
   **B**  their attitude to problems
   **C**  their commitment to marriage
   **D**  their leisure activities

3   In the 'power couple', both partners tend to be

   **A**  influenced by their peer group.
   **B**  unaccustomed to making decisions.
   **C**  interested in quite different things.
   **D**  unwilling to compromise with each other.

4   According to the speaker, when on holiday 'traditional' couples should

   **A**  consider not going away together at all.
   **B**  agree to spend the majority of their time together.
   **C**  seek out the company of other similar people.
   **D**  accept the need for completely separate social lives.

5   In general, the speaker regards holiday periods as

   **A**  an opportunity to review the success of relationships.
   **B**  more enjoyable for the female half of couples.
   **C**  the cause of unnecessary stress for couples.
   **D**  good for the well-being of individuals.

▪ 4   Do you agree that arguments are more likely on holiday?
Tell your partner about arguments you have had or witnessed in similar situations.

## USE OF ENGLISH 1
### Cloze passage

**1** Fill each of the numbered blanks in the passage with **one** suitable word from the box. The first one has been done for you as an example.

| behind | case | under | in | of | or | to | with |
|--------|------|-------|----|----|----|----|------|
| us | when | which | matter | into | ~~because~~ | the | who |

### How do you Row?

Arguments are inevitable in a relationship. A row occurs (**0**) _because_ two individuals are not the same. No (**1**) _____ how close you are, there will be conflicts unless, that is, you are in (**2**) _____ first throes of love – which, you have to admit, is a temporary illness, during (**3**) _____ you subsume yourself to the relationship and don't care which film you see.

(**4**) _____ private we've all experienced it. It's the moment (**5**) _____ sheer frustration rises (**6**) _____ the surface, and dignity goes into free-fall. Most of (**7**) _____ have had the heated slanging match full (**8**) _____ bile and vitriol, name-calling and offensive personal criticism. Often it starts quite trivially: in the supermarket over which brand of toothpaste to buy, (**9**) _____ on a night out over which type of restaurant to eat in. A lover's tiff is painful enough (**10**) _____ closed doors, but when your row turns into a public spectacle, it's humiliating.

If you're someone (**11**) _____ doesn't row, there's probably something wrong. You may manage to steer your way around conflicts most of the time, but one day, when you're tired or (**12**) _____ stress, there will inevitably be a head-on collision, so be prepared! Here is our psychologist's guide to the roles we take when we row, together (**13**) _____ some tips in (**14**) _____ your partner falls (**15**) _____ one of the categories.

**2** Look back at the text. In your own words explain what these words and phrases mean.

1. slanging match
2. first throes
3. free-fall
4. lover's tiff
5. name-calling
6. bile and vitriol
7. sheer

**3** Have you ever had either a lover's tiff or a slanging match? How did you feel: before? during? afterwards?

UNIT 4  *A Fine Romance*

## READING 3
*Matching*

**1** Look at the words in the box. They each describe a type of role people adopt when they row. Read some more of the text and match each description to its title by writing one of the words from the box in each space.

> Bullies   Weepers   Dramatists   Sulkers
> Revengers   Screamers   Slow-burners

### Which type are you?

a _____ find that words don't work for them, so they resort to violence. Until children learn to talk, they express themselves physically by grabbing things – and these people haven't learnt that adults can't get away with that. Education gives access to power through words; uneducated people tend to be more violent.

b _____ make a mountain out of a molehill. They feel that they are not being taken seriously, so they have to exaggerate their emotion. They couldn't get their own way as children, so they became manipulative and scheming. They cry wolf to get what they want.

c _____ fear they will lose the argument if they let you be heard, possibly because they came from a large family where they had to make a lot of noise to be heard. They are insecure and may have a short fuse.

d _____ are depressive types, prone to rumination, who nurse their self-hatred. They feel misunderstood and turn their aggression against themselves. As children they probably thought their siblings had a better deal. 'It's not fair' is the typical refrain of this type, who feel powerless and have given up trying to get their point across.

e _____ go for the sympathy vote. They were abandoned a lot as children. Now as soon as they start to get angry, they feel sad too. In childhood this may have been a successful tactic in gaining sympathy, particularly if they were attractive – who can resist a tearfully cute baby. It worked then and they are still trying it now.

f _____ are envious. When they were three years old they weren't just quietly jealous of their brother's or sister's toy, they would go and destroy it. If someone else has anything they want – be it physical or emotional – they are liable to damage it. If they think something bad has happened to them, they can't let it go. If they think someone has something better than they have, they want to spoil the other person's prize.

g _____ are passive-aggressive. They don't express aggression when they feel it, or when provoked, but it builds up and then comes out as a disastrous explosion. It can take a lot to get them wound up – they are not provoked by what annoys most people – but they can be cold, and inflict pain without regard.

*A Fine Romance* **UNIT 4**

■ 2 Here are some tips that the psychologist gave to anyone whose partner fell into one of the categories. Which tip do you think matches which of the types?

> ### Psychologist's Tips
> - Try to take them out of themselves, get them to open up.
> - Hide your kitchen knives.
> - Be calm and firm. Don't be a victim.
> - Give them a Kleenex tissue and tell them to grow up.
> - Find a way to give vent to their creative side.
> - Tell them they'll succeed by reason, not volume.
> - Hide your most treasured possessions and feelings.

■ 3 Do you recognize any of the types of personality described? In yourself? In other people you know?

■ 4 Is it better to have rows with family and friends or is it better to try and avoid them? Are there good and bad times to start a row? Should you intervene to try and stop two other people rowing?

■ 5 Explain in your own words what these words and expressions from the text mean (paragraph references in brackets).

1. resort to (a)
2. cry wolf (b)
3. a short fuse (c)
4. siblings (d)
5. tactic (e)
6. liable to (f)
7. wound up (g)
8. take them out of themselves (Psychologist's Tips)
9. give vent (Psychologist's Tips)

## PHRASAL VERBS 1

■ 1 Look at these two phrases from the article. Underline the phrasal verbs in each one.

*These people haven't learnt that adults can't get away with that.*
*They've given up trying to get their point across.*

■ 2 Complete each sentence with a suitable preposition.

1. After that big argument, John and Barbara got on much better _____ each other.
2. The argument began when Julie said that Tom was always trying to get _____ of doing the washing-up.
3. I enjoy writing letters, but I'm so busy that I never get _____ to it.
4. Mrs Black was never sure what her children were getting _____ to when she wasn't watching them.
5. 'How are you getting _____ with your homework, David?' said his father.

UNIT 4  *A Fine Romance*

## SPEAKING 2
### Discussing proverbs

**1** Look at these proverbs and common expressions. With your partner decide:
- what each one means
- if a similar saying is used in your language

A  Leave no stone unturned
B  Honesty is the best policy
C  Don't beat about the bush
D  Pride comes before a fall
E  Once upon a time
F  Attack is the best form of defence
G  Don't hide your light under a bushel
H  Many a true word is said in jest
I  Keep your eye on the ball
J  Make a clean breast of it

**2** Look at this magazine feature about how to win an argument. Do you agree with the points made?

### HOW TO WIN AN ARGUMENT

**1** Prepare. Preparation is the key. Understand all the facets of your argument, and your opponent's.

**2** Empower yourself. Everyone is capable of making the winning argument. Self-belief is utterly convincing.

**3** Relate your argument in the form of an example. Traditionally, we are tellers of tales and listeners. Use this familiar format to express your ideas.

**4** Tell the truth. Establish your credibility from the start. With credibility comes trust.

**5** State objectives clearly. If you want something, ask for it. Don't let others misinterpret your requests.

**6** Avoid sarcasm, scorn and ridicule. Use humour cautiously. Give respect to your opponent. Nobody admires the scoffer, the cynic, the mocker. Humour, when properly used, can be devastating, but beware, badly used, it can backfire catastrophically!

**7** Logic is power. If you have logic on your side, ride it for all it's worth and don't allow yourself to be distracted by red herrings. It may not always be fun, but logic is powerful.

**8** Act to win. Don't go on the defensive. Take the initiative. Take control.

**9** Admit the weaknesses of your argument at the beginning. You can expose your weak points better than your opponent, who will always expose them in the darkest possible way.

**10** Understand your power and your argument. With proper understanding you give yourself permission to win. But remember, arrogance, insolence and stupidity are close relatives.

**3** Decide which of the sayings or proverbs **A–J** matches each piece of advice **1–10**.

## LISTENING 3
### Sentence completion

**1** Before you listen, discuss the following questions with your partner.

1 What do you understand by the phrase 'madly in love'?
2 Do you think it is possible to measure the intensity of love?
3 What sort of criteria would be useful for determining how deeply in love people might be?
4 What questions could you ask them, what tests could you run?

**2** You will hear part of a talk by a scientist on the subject of the power of love. For questions **1–11**, complete the sentences with a word or short phrase.

---

### The power of love

The speaker quotes poets who describe the power of love as [___**1**___].

When two people are 'madly in love', their [___**2**___] may become linked together.

In the first part of Grinberg's experiment, volunteer couples looked at each other, but didn't [___**3**___].

The Faraday Cage is designed so that [___**4**___] between people is impossible.

Grinberg's subjects wore [___**5**___] which measured their brain waves.

Similar brain patterns were recorded between partners who also exhibited the greatest level of [___**6**___].

The speaker doubts that the results can be explained in terms of [___**7**___] by scientists.

Another possible explanation, rejected by the speaker, is that the experiments were not [___**8**___].

One interpretation of Grinberg's findings is that the mind may be located [___**9**___].

One implication of Grinberg's work is that people may need to be more careful about their [___**10**___].

Dr Grinberg feels that it's important for people to have [___**11**___] in business, schools and the family.

UNIT 4  *A Fine Romance*

**3** Look at this excerpt from the listening. Complete the passage with a word from the box; some words can be used more than once. Then listen again to check.

| there | this | three | these | first | them |
| their | second | that | who | third | |

(0) __There__ are only (1) _____ explanations for the results of (2) _____ experiments. The (3) _____ is a deliberate hoax by the scientists. (4) _____ seems extremely unlikely knowing (5) _____ academic background. The (6) _____ is (7) _____ the volunteers were communicating by some conventional means, (8) _____ is (9) _____ the experiments were not properly conducted. (10) _____ also seems very unlikely as the experiments were very carefully set up by experienced scientists (11) _____ had repeated (12) _____ many times with many different subjects. The (13) _____ possibility is (14) _____ some brains can communicate in an as yet unknown way.

### WRITING 2
## *Summary skills*

Complete this summary of how the experiment was conducted, using your own words.

First of all, _____

_____

_____

After that, _____

_____

_____

Then, _____

_____

_____

In conclusion, _____

_____

_____

## HELP WITH USE OF ENGLISH: TRANSFORMATIONS

■ 1  In Part Four of the Use of English paper you have to transform sentences from one structure to another. You are given a complete sentence which is followed by a word in bold and an incomplete sentence with between two and eight words missing from its centre.

*Example 1:*

You should take no notice of your critics.

**attention**

No _____ critics.

The sentence needs to be completed like this:

*Answer:* No <u>attention should be paid to your</u> critics.

- The new sentence must have a similar meaning to the original one, but must use the word in bold in the form it is given.
- You must not change the word in any way and you must use it in the new sentence.
- You must write no more than eight words, including the word in bold, in the gap.

The new sentence may express the same idea using a different expression, as in example 1, or it may require you to make grammatical changes as in example 2 below. Other changes may also be necessary to complete the new sentence.

*Example 2:*

Only a small number of people buy the works of this composer.

**demand**

There <u>is very little demand for the works of</u> this composer.

What has changed in the sentence? Why?
What has remained the same? Why?
What has been omitted?
What has been added?

Are there any other correct ways to complete the two example transformations?

■ 2  For each of the following transformations, choose the correct answer, **A**, **B** or **C**. Say why the other answers are incorrect.

1  Not everybody likes jazz music.

   **taste**

   Jazz _____ , it seems.

   A  music is not to everybody's taste
   B  music has not been tasted by everybody
   C  music is not something which everybody has good taste in

# UNIT 4 *A Fine Romance*

**2** Sue is unlikely to get the part in the new film.

**prospect**

Sue _____ in the new film.

A has no prospect of getting the part
B 's prospects of getting a part in the new film are not great
C has little prospect of getting the part

**3** The company has promised to investigate any complaints.

**looked**

The company _____ into.

A has looked any complaints
B has promised that any complaints will be looked
C 's promise about complaints was looked

**4** Duplicate tickets will not be issued for any reason.

**account**

On _____ issued.

A no account will duplicate tickets be
B no account will be taken of duplicate tickets
C duplicate tickets, no account will be

**5** The researchers had encountered problems with their camera equipment.

**come**

The researchers _____ equipment.

A came into problems with their camera
B camera equipment had come across problems
C had come up against problems with their camera

# REMEMBER

- Try to identify the target structure/language of each transformation sentence.
- Check that the new sentence is similar in meaning to the original sentence.
- Make sure you have used the key word and have not changed it.
- Have you used between two and eight words in the gap?
- In the exam you will write your answers on a separate answer sheet; make sure you write only the missing words on this sheet.

**3** For questions **1–9**, complete the second sentence so that it has a similar meaning to the first sentence, using the word given. **Do not change the word given**. You must use between **three** and **eight** words including the word given.

1 Samantha often talks at tedious length about her own problems.

   **tendency**

   Samantha's _____ problems can be tedious.

2 In my opinion, this novel needs a stronger plot.

   **mind**

   To _____ to be stronger.

3 As well as making you laugh a lot, that film really makes you think.

   **provoking**

   The film is _____ very amusing.

4 This exhibition confirms that Lawley is indeed a leading artist.

   **borne**

   Lawley's reputation _____ this exhibition.

5 I was really taken aback when Sue turned up at the party.

   **by**

   Sue's _____ complete surprise.

6 As the day wore on, the weather definitely seemed to be improving.

   **signs**

   As the day wore on, there _____ in the weather.

7 Most people think that Francine's dog broke the valuable vase.

   **widely**

   Francine's dog _____ the valuable vase.

8 They have turned the disused schoolroom into a restaurant.

   **converted**

   The disused _____ use as a restaurant.

9 What amazed everyone was the exceptional way in which Fiona coped with the incident.

   **of**

   To the _____ well with the incident.

# UNIT 4 *A Fine Romance*

## EXAM PRACTICE 4

**1** For questions **1–10**, read the text below. Use the word given in **capitals** at the end of some of the lines to form a word that fits in the space in the same line. There is an example at the beginning (**0**).

### *Blissful Memories*

When I was growing up, every summer we would go to
Connemara, that (**0**) *majestic* wilderness in the west of Ireland, **MAJESTY**
for our annual holiday. I would sit in the back of the family car,
reading aloud place-names from the roadmap: Lackavrea,
Lugganimma, Bunnahown. The words sounded strange;
somehow (**1**) _____ , and I loved the music in my father's voice **MAGIC**
as he sang them back. Out of all these idyllic summers, one
still stands out with a luminous (**2**) _____ . The holiday had **CLEAR**
begun with the usual (**3**) _____ of arrangements and arguments **EXPLODE**
in the house. These were not just run-of-the-mill domestic
squabbles, either. My parents' (**4**) _____ had long been troubled, **MARRY**
and recently the rows seemed to have (**5**) _____ seriously. And **WORSE**
yet, after the first few days in Connemara, I noticed that something
strange had begun to happen. My parents seemed to be getting
along well. There was a new (**6**) _____ between them, a feeling **CALM**
of lightness and ease which was (**7**) _____ . One of them would **INFECT**
laugh when the other made a joke, a gentle and (**8**) _____ **VAGUE**
exasperated laugh. I recall a succession of long walks through gorgeous
scenery, of vivid colours and Atlantic air and, although (**9**) _____ **ADMIT**
the memory plays tricks, there wasn't even a hint of a (**10**) _____ . **AGREE**

**2** Read the text again and answer the following short-answer questions.

1. In your own words, explain what the writer means by the phrase 'idyllic summers'.
2. What phrase does the writer use to describe typical family arguments?
3. What does the writer suggest with the phrase 'although the memory plays tricks'?

**3** For questions **1–9**, complete the second sentence so that it has a similar meaning to the first sentence, using the word given. **Do not change the word given.** You must use between **three** and **eight** words including the word given.

1 One of the actors was too ill to appear that night.

   **prevented**

   That night, one actor _____ by illness.

2 What astounds me is that you paid the money before seeing the goods.

   **it**

   I find _____ the goods before you paid for them.

3 The price of computers has fallen significantly in the last five years.

   **fall**

   There has _____ computers in the past five years.

4 Sarah finds it easy to learn foreign languages.

   **comes**

   Sarah has no _____ languages.

5 She was appointed to the committee for two years only.

   **period**

   Her _____ of two years only.

6 Tony agreed to appear in the play on condition that he didn't have to sing.

   **long**

   Tony said, 'I _____ I don't have to sing.'

7 Over the years, unpainted woodwork tends to rot.

   **left**

   Over the years, if woodwork _____ for it to rot.

8 I'd prefer you not to smoke in the car, if you don't mind.

   **whilst**

   I'd rather _____ the car.

9 I'm sorry we're unable to invite Mark to the party.

   **possible**

   I wish it _____ Mark to the party.

UNIT 5

# All Right on the Night

**SPEAKING 1**
*Expressing likes and dislikes*

1. Look at the genres of film listed in the box. Can you think of a recent film that fits into each of the categories? What other genres of film are there?

   > thriller   science fiction   comedy   western
   > costume drama   horror   romance   cartoon

2. Which of these genres do you particularly like or dislike? Why?
   What are the conventions of the genre in each case?
   Why are these types of film popular? Who do they appeal to?
   What types of film are becoming more/less popular? Why is this?

3. Look at these three video covers. What do the films all have in common?

   At what age should young people be allowed to see films like these?

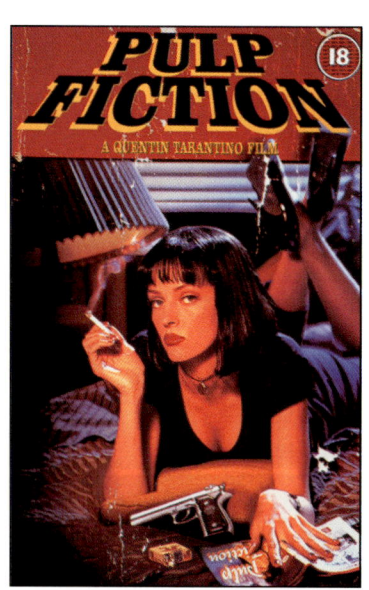

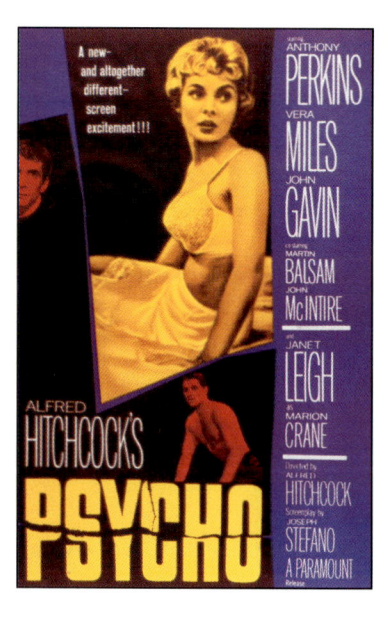

4. Talk to your partner. Do you agree with the following?

   - All modern Hollywood films look the same.
   - Explicit sex scenes in films are degrading to women.
   - Scenes of violence on film lead people to be more violent in real life.
   - Film censorship is an evil thing that seeks to stifle artistic expression.

*All Right on the Night* **UNIT 5**

## LISTENING 1
*Four-option multiple choice*

**1** You will hear a radio programme about violence in films. For questions **1–4**, choose the answer (**A**, **B**, **C** or **D**) which fits best according to what you hear.

1 What does Dr Drew feel about the research that's been carried out?

   A There's too much of it.
   B It hasn't been well conducted.
   C It has been unsuccessful.
   D It has been inconclusive.

2 Dr Drew thinks that advertising

   A leads people to behave unpredictably.
   B affects people differently to movies.
   C sets out to alter people's tastes.
   D makes use of views people already hold.

3 What does the interviewer feel about explicit violence on film?

   A She likes advanced warning of it.
   B It never fails to shock her.
   C She's become hardened to it.
   D It holds no interest for her.

4 According to Dr Drew, what is the main problem with violent films?

   A They fail to use good imagery.
   B They don't have interesting plots.
   C They leave little to the imagination.
   D They are in bad taste.

## PRONUNCIATION 1
*Word stress*

**1** Look at these words from the listening. Underline the stressed syllable in each word.

   *Example:* ac<u>claim</u>ed

   reaffirmed    distasteful    inconclusive    unsuccessful    unpredictably

   Now listen to check.

**2** Now draw lines on the words in exercise 1 to show the boundaries between:

   • root words    • prefixes    • suffixes

   *Example:* ac|claim|ed

   What general rules can you identify about the stress in words like these?

**3** Listen to these groups of words and underline the stressed syllable in each word.
   1 real   reality   realism   really   unreality
   2 photograph   photographic   photography   photographer
   3 family   familiar   unfamiliar   familiarity
   4 market   marketing   marketable   unmarketable
   5 person   personal   impersonal   personality   impersonation
   6 inform   informative   uninformative   information
   7 product   production   productive   unproductive
   8 manage   manager   management   mismanagement

UNIT 5 *All Right on the Night*

## READING 1
*Lexical cloze*

■ 1   For questions **1–12**, read the two texts below and decide which answer (**A**, **B**, **C** or **D**) best fits each gap.

### Film posters

Film posters used to be considered worthless ephemera once they'd (**1**) _____ their purpose – to get bums on seats. They took up too much space in warehouses and were destroyed by the thousand. No one (**2**) _____ it worthwhile to lay them down on acid-free paper to (**3**) _____ them from discolouring, still less to (**4**) _____ against pinholes and creases, in (**5**) _____ of the day when they might be worth large sums of money.

With the passage of time, however, more and more people came to regard film posters as works of art, and as the traditional art market is normally beyond ordinary people's (**6**) _____ , film posters represented images they could afford.

| | | | | |
|---|---|---|---|---|
| 1 | **A** served | **B** performed | **C** satisfied | **D** delivered |
| 2 | **A** appreciated | **B** considered | **C** imagined | **D** wondered |
| 3 | **A** avoid | **B** hide | **C** store | **D** prevent |
| 4 | **A** keep | **B** guard | **C** shield | **D** save |
| 5 | **A** prediction | **B** investment | **C** anticipation | **D** foresight |
| 6 | **A** stretch | **B** touch | **C** clutch | **D** reach |

### The Collectors

The market for film posters is partly (**7**) _____ by nostalgia, but today serious collectors regard posters as an investment and prices have risen as a result. David Hutchinson is a typical collector with what he is (**8**) _____ to call an addiction. 'I loved film posters as a child and I've been (**9**) _____ ever since', he says. People collect posters of well-known films, or ones they (**10**) _____ with some memory, like their first date. Sometimes, (**11**) _____ , a poster of an obscure 1920s film may have a fantastic image and that's what (**12**) _____ . Only posters with good graphics are of interest to serious collectors. Modern posters, using photographic rather than drawn images, are not so stylish and are reproduced on a very large scale. As a result, they are less collectable.

| | | | | |
|---|---|---|---|---|
| 7 | **A** driven | **B** pushed | **C** powered | **D** urged |
| 8 | **A** merry | **B** happy | **C** jolly | **D** funny |
| 9 | **A** hooked | **B** nailed | **C** stuck | **D** fixed |
| 10 | **A** accompany | **B** correlate | **C** associate | **D** affiliate |
| 11 | **A** regardless | **B** although | **C** moreover | **D** however |
| 12 | **A** counts | **B** reckons | **C** catches | **D** minds |

■ 2   In your own words, and using information from both passages, write a paragraph of no more than 75 words explaining why certain types of film posters have become highly collectable in recent years.

*All Right on the Night* UNIT 5

## LISTENING 2
*Sentence completion*

■ 1   Look at the picture of Marilyn Monroe.

Have you ever seen a Marilyn Monroe film?
What type of film do you associate with Marilyn Monroe?
What type of parts did she play?
Why is she such an important figure in film history?
What else do you know about her?

■ 2   You will hear a radio discussion about Marilyn Monroe.

For questions **1–9**, complete the sentences with a word or short phrase.

Sue says the play doesn't require her to do an [__1__] of Marilyn.

Sue says the play shows us that Marilyn was really a rather [__2__] person.

David's story shows us that Marilyn could control the extent to which people [__3__] her.

David points out that Marilyn couldn't really choose the type of [__4__] she was given.

In the 1950s, Marilyn was regarded as rather [__5__] by most middle-class audiences in the USA.

Now people realize how much the [__6__] created people's idea of Marilyn.

Sue admires Marilyn because she was a good [__7__] as well as being a good actress.

Sue tells us that Marilyn felt that the costumes for *The Seven Year Itch* were too [__8__].

Sue was surprised to learn that Marilyn [__9__] the famous dress herself.

■ 3   Discuss these questions with your partner.

How was the real Marilyn different from the image?
Do modern film stars have more control over their screen image?

87

# UNIT 5 All Right on the Night

## READING 2
*Gapped text*

**1** What is a child prodigy? Can you think of any famous examples? How would expect such a young person to behave?

### The Everyday Prodigy

*It is 10am, bright but bone-chillingly cold, in New York. There is packed snow on the sidewalks. I am grateful to be sitting, notebook at the ready, with Mike and Dave the photographers, in a well-heated limousine, parked outside the university library. Our driver is waiting to transport Midori, graduate student in psychology and one of the world's greatest violinists, to our photoshoot and interview in Brooklyn. She has been in the library, as she is most days, since 7am.*

**1**

'I'll take the underground railway,' she tells us on emerging, seemingly fresh as a daisy, a rucksack of psychology books in one hand, the other holding tight to her precious 1734 Guarnerius del Gesu, snug in its violin case. 'I get car sick, so it'll be impossible for me to read in the limo. If I meet you at the Clarke Street entrance, I can work on the train.'

**2**

She leaves me with no choice but to detach myself from the rest of the team and set off in hot pursuit. 'You see, for me,' she duly explains, 'being part of a community is as natural as breathing. When I was younger I was very lucky because my environment was properly balanced, and even though I had started to play in concerts, I was allowed to have the basic responsibilities of a child. I wasn't chauffeured to school or given permission to skip classes.'

**3**

In the middle of playing Leonard Bernstein's Serenade with Bernstein himself conducting the Philharmonic, she broke a string on her violin. Without missing a note and maintaining perfect composure, she borrowed the concert-master's fiddle, broke another string, borrowed another instrument and gave a performance which left critics and audience stunned by her brilliance.

**4**

This refreshing humility is further evident when we catch up with the rest of the team in Brooklyn. When it comes to star behaviour, Midori appears to register absolute zero on the Richter scale of artists' demands. Apart from her rigorously defined two-hours-only time slot for this interruption to her busy schedules, she asks for nothing. No make-up, hairstylist, hot coffee, or even a pair of warm boots. Midori, her mind on an essay she is eager to finish, has black slip-on shoes, totally unsuitable, let it be said, for slippery suburban kerbsides covered with snow.

**5**

Midori set up her non-profit-making body in 1992. It serves New York City's public schools by providing comprehensive music education for children who normally have little or no access to the arts. 'It's for every class, not necessarily just for children who want to play an instrument, and it's definitely not about me going into a school to give a performance. I do that sometimes, but I'm very much against the idea of having one random recital at a school and calling it "Music Education"', she says.

**6**

As we return to the university, I sense that these desires to repay a debt to society and shun a life of glorious stardom result from Midori having lived under the glare of publicity for so much of her life. This probably also goes a long way to explaining why Midori closely guards her privacy. She has a circle of good friends and her family, but if there is any love relationship in her life, it's nobody's business but hers.

**2** Read the article about a young musician on page 88. Six paragraphs have been removed from the text. Choose from the paragraphs **A–G** below the one which fits each gap (**1–6**). There is one extra paragraph which you do not need to use.

A  'I believe that, as a musician, I have a responsibility to give something back, and I see that responsibility not in terms of my individual musical ability but in wider terms – of being a human being, a full person', she explains.

B  As a result, Midori became the most celebrated prodigy in years, acclaimed for her technical genius and a maturity of expression beyond her years. 'I figured out early on that I actually liked getting older,' she tells me. 'Not just because I was always branded as "the youngest", but because as I grew I saw opportunities to learn more.'

C  Indeed, Midori is absolutely clear about what it takes to be a musician. 'To do it for the fame, money, status and celebrity might work, but it certainly won't last', she says.

D  Physically, Midori is slight and fragile, but she leaves us in no doubt that she has an iron will. Nothing is going to make her change her mind. We look on in disbelief, horrified that we are about to lose the focus of our attention.

E  When the shoot is over, even Midori's principles succumb temporarily to the lure of a warm back seat and a chance to wiggle her toes in the direction of a heater. Not that she uses the time to chin-wag with the chauffeur, preferring instead to ring her PA and discuss the reordering of letterheads and a dozen other details concerning her educational foundation, Midori and Friends.

F  This is no mean feat when one considers that yesterday she flew to and from a blizzard-bound Boston for a sold-out afternoon concert. Her recital programme might have sapped the strength of lesser mortals, consisting as it did of very demanding and diverse works by, among others, Bach, Poulenc and Beethoven.

G  Travelling on the underground is not typical of internationally acclaimed classical musicians, particularly that most treasured of rarities – a child prodigy who has remained at the top of the tree long into adulthood. Midori gave her first public concert aged six, made her debut with the New York Philharmonic orchestra five years later, then, at 14, hit the headlines of *The New York Times*.

**3** Did Midori conform to your idea of a prodigy?

Make a list of the words which seem to describe her character and attitudes.

# UNIT 5 *All Right on the Night*

## VOCABULARY 1
### Prepositions

**1** Look at these fixed phrases and expressions from the text. Complete each phrase with a suitable preposition. Then look back at the text on pages 88 and 89 to check. Numbers in brackets refer to the main text on page 88, and letters to the missing paragraphs on page 89.

1  I'm grateful to be sitting, *notebook _____ the ready*, with Mike and Dave… (paragraph 1)

2  Our driver is waiting to transport Midori, *graduate student _____ psychology*… (paragraph 1)

3  *She leaves me _____ no choice but to* detach myself from the rest of the team… (paragraph 3)

4  …and *set off _____ hot pursuit*. (paragraph 3)

5  *When it comes _____ star behaviour*, Midori appears to register absolute zero… (paragraph 5)

6  Midori, *her mind _____ an essay* she is eager to finish, … (paragraph 5)

7  …I'm very much _____ the idea of having one random recital at a school… (paragraph 6)

8  …these desires to repay a *debt _____ society* and shun a life of glorious stardom… (paragraph 7)

9  …having lived _____ *the glare of publicity* for so much of her life. (paragraph 7)

10  …acclaimed for her technical genius and a maturity of expression _____ her years. (paragraph B)

11  …diverse works by, _____ others, Bach, Poulenc and Beethoven. (paragraph F)


## SPEAKING 2
### Long turn

**1** Choose one of the two questions in the box and talk about it on your own for two minutes. Use the points below the question to help you.

> Why do celebrities in the film and music industries often seem to have unhappy private lives?
>
> - pressures of the job
> - lifestyle
> - the role of the media
>
> Why do some music and film stars become enduring celebrities whilst others fade into obscurity?
>
> - natural talent
> - good career management
> - ability to get media attention

# HELP WITH USE OF ENGLISH: SUMMARY WRITING

In Part Five of the Use of English Paper, there are two texts to read on the same theme. After each text, there are two short-answer comprehension questions about the text. The main task is a summary writing task. You must use information from both texts to write a summary that answers the question set in the given number of words.

## How to approach the tasks

**1** The short-answer questions

- Read through both texts before you begin to answer the questions.
- Answer the short-answer questions on each text first before looking at the summary task.
- Your answers to these questions do not need to be full sentences, but they must be clear to the examiner. The questions may, for example:
  - ask you to find and write down words or phrases from the text.
  - explain the meaning of a word, phrase or part of the text.
  - explain what words and phrases in the text refer to.
- Use your own words for these answers; don't copy from the text unless you are told to.
- Explain yourself clearly, but be careful not to write too much.
- There are some examples of short-answer questions on pages 92 and 93.

**2** The summary task

- Read the instructions carefully and underline the important words in the task.
- Read the texts again and locate the parts of the texts which are relevant to the summary before you begin to write.
- Write a list of the points you will include and choose the most logical order.
- Make sure that your points answer the question exactly. Do not include irrelevant information.
- Express the ideas clearly and simply. Be careful not to repeat yourself.
- Think about how to link your ideas. Use some of the linking expressions in the box below.
- Use your own words to express the ideas in the text. You may need to use some names and other words from the text, but don't copy whole phrases and sentences.
- You should include at least one content point from each text.
- You get marks for both content and language, so check your spelling and punctuation.
- Check that your answer is within the word limit given.

## Linking expressions

| Sequencing | Contrasting | Adding | Concluding |
|---|---|---|---|
| firstly | although | as well as | therefore |
| secondly | despite | another | for this reason |
| thirdly | while | by the same token | in conclusion |
| finally | whereas | in addition | to sum up |
| | on the other hand | added to that | |
| | at the same time | | |

UNIT 5 *All Right on the Night*

## REMEMBER

- In the exam you will write your short answers and the summary on a separate answer sheet.

**3** For questions **1–5**, read the following texts about genius. For questions **1–4**, answer with a word or short phrase. You do not need to write complete sentences. For question **5**, write a summary according to the instructions given.

### *Can you Make a Genius?*

When the artist Whistler was asked if he thought that genius was hereditary, he replied that he couldn't really say since he hadn't had any children. Science hasn't got very much further than this smart aleck response. Last week's television programme entitled 'Can you make a Genius?' revisited the familiar 'is it Nature or is it nurture?' debate, without burdening itself with any preliminary reflection on what constitutes genius, or whether making geniuses is even desirable.

It may be, in fact, that genius is not an absolute quality, but is the victim of changing fashions. One minute, a work of art may be hailed as a work of genius and the next reviled as worthless. For this reason, it seems that genius can only reliably be conferred on individuals in hindsight. And while the musical prodigies we heard on the programme had a timeless quality to their virtuosity, you couldn't really say the same for the man who could calculate 99 to the power of 11 in his head. Is not his showy brand of genius also vulnerable to changing times? Today we have pocket calculators that can work out 99 to the power of 11, whereas we still don't have a machine that can paint or sculpt as gloriously as Michelangelo. I mean, we are not impressed by someone who can handwash their clothes as efficiently as a washing machine, are we?

1 Which phrase tells us the writer's attitude towards Whistler?

_____

2 In your own words, explain what the writer thought was lacking in the television programme he describes.

_____

**All Right on the Night** UNIT 5

### Gene Genius

Of the sixty or so members of the Bach family who lived in the 17th and 18th centuries, more than fifty were professional musicians of one kind or another, and at least one was hailed as a genius. So does this mean that musical talent is in the genes? Or was it simply a habit, in those houses echoing to the sound of music, that each young Bach would acquire musical skill? And it's not just the Bachs. Many leading contemporary musicians come from, or may well go on to found, musical dynasties. But the problem with the genetic idea is that there is no solid evidence either to prove or disprove it. Detailed genetic studies have been beyond the scope of science, while the psychological research that has been done to date leaves plenty of room for furious argument.

Essentially, this is the old nature vs. nature debate, but with added layers of complexity since genius remains much easier to identify than it is to describe. We can safely attribute exceptional amounts of originality, imagination, skill, dedication and so on to the greatest artists, but unless we allow the likes of Shakespeare and Mozart something else as well, we miss a vital aspect of their achievement. But what exactly is this something else? Its essence is all bound up with its inexplicability – with our sense that genius is unpredicted and unpredictable, that it defies rational explanation.

*line 10*

Adapted from an article by Hugh Alersey-Williams in *The Independent*.

3  In your own words, explain what the writer means by the phrase 'beyond the scope of science'. (line 10)

   _____

4  Which phrase in the second paragraph is used instead of the word 'genius'?

   _____

5  In a paragraph of between **50 and 70** words, summarize **in your own words as far as possible**, the reasons given in the texts to explain why it's difficult to be sure what genius is.

   _____
   _____
   _____
   _____
   _____
   _____
   _____

# UNIT 5 All Right on the Night

## USE OF ENGLISH 1
### Comprehension

**1** Read this article and answer the short-answer questions which follow it.

# Opera's Wedding of the Century

**OF ALL SINGING marriages this must be the most spectacularly operatic ever. Love, tragedy and triumph abound in the story of Roberto Alagna and Angela Gheorghiu. Alagna was hailed the new Pavarotti after a couple of performances of 'La Boheme' and 'Romeo and Juliet'. Meanwhile Gheorghiu's 'Traviata' had catapulted her to overnight stardom at 29. It was certainly good for business when they announced their love for each other.**

Now married, both are musical sensations in their own right and I met them in a London recording studio singing love songs for a new disc. Whatever the cynic might have to say about media-hype and 'marketability', there can be no disputing the sheer uniqueness of this musical phenomenon.

Roberto Alagna is a small man who tends to remain relatively still while singing. But his stance, with feet spread squarely apart, arms out at his sides like a fighter entering a fray, back arched and head tilted slightly upwards, lends him a tremendously imposing presence. When the most strenuous and demanding high note falters and is to be consigned to digital limbo, or a song goes sadly awry for the fourth time, his face never fails to light up in amusement.

In contrast, Gheorghiu with fluid movement of arms and hands, conducts the passage of her voice as if coaxing it, manipulating it. She fidgets, looking like she's unable to find the most comfortable way to stand. When mistakes are made she might clasp herself in exasperation or feign banging her head against the music stand, but this is not serious vexation – more the humorous antics of an extrovert perfectionist striving to produce the results she knows she's capable of. They often end with her bursting into fits of giggles.

Throughout the session producer David Groves exhibits total composure and control, in spite of the frenetic rate of communication with the conductor and the arduous nature of eliciting the very best from the singers. Whatever imperfections he elucidates, there are always compliments accompanying them, and his patience seems limitless.

After an hour of tussling with a particularly tricky piece his message to the conductor is 'I think Roberto is a fraction behind Angela, but the phrasing is perfect.' Then, turning aside to those gathered around him and without a hint of irritation: 'It would be so wonderful if they could just end up in the same place at the same time!'

70 Then he is suddenly satisfied, announcing: 'Boheme, please, Boheme.' After the travails of the previous hour, the relief at the prospect of singing from this opera is palpable. It's the work that brought them together and 'O Soave Fanciulla' obviously touches on something special. The soloists share a plane apart, their pointing fingers, furrowed brows and bubbling laughter culminating in an embrace that bridges
80 the two-foot gulf between them. And unbelievably, there's not a camera in sight.

1 Which two words in the first paragraph tell us about the speed of Angela's rise to fame?

2 In your own words, explain why some people might be cynical about the new disc.

3 What does the phrase 'consigned to digital limbo' in lines 33–34 imply about the song which has just been recorded?

4 What do you understand by the word 'fidgets'? (line 41)

5 In your own words, compare briefly the reactions of Roberto and Angela to mistakes they make.

6 Which three words in paragraph five are used to emphasize the difficulties of David Groves' work?

7 Which phrase in paragraph five provides an example of David Groves' great patience?

8 What does 'palpable' as used in line 74 mean?

9 In your own words, explain what it is that the writer finds so surprising at the end of the piece.

2 Find words or phrases in the article that mean (paragraph numbers in brackets):

a publicity (2)
b way of standing (3)
c a fight (3)
d turns out badly (3)
e trying hard (4)
f hold tightly (4)
g pretend (4)
h gently encouraging (4)
i uncontrollable laughter (4)

UNIT 5 *All Right on the Night*

## GRAMMAR 1
*Reported speech*

1. Look at these two sentences from the article. Both are in direct speech.

    *'I think Roberto is a fraction behind Angela, but the phrasing is perfect.'* (said David)

    *'It would be so wonderful if they could just end up in the same place at the same time!'* (said David)

2. Rewrite the sentences in reported speech.

    David said _____

    David said _____

3. Which two general rules of reported speech do these examples illustrate?

4. What other types of changes are necessary in reported speech?

    📖 N.B. The Workbook has further work on reported speech.

## WRITING 1
*Magazine articles*

1. Work with a partner. You are both journalists working for two different magazines.

    **Student A:** You write for a young peoples' Pop music magazine called *Music Now*. You have interviewed Angela Gheorghiu. Read the notes about her below, which were made during the interview. Using the information in the article on pages 94 and 95 and your imagination, add some more notes about your impression of the opera singer, including her appearance and personality.

---

### ANGELA GHEORGHIU: The Inside Story

**Discovered:** Bucharest Music Academy 1990

**Big break:** Violetta in *La Traviata* receives such outstanding reviews that TV channels immediately clear their schedules for immediate transmission. The CD wins 'Disc of the Year'.

**What the critics say:** 'She is the most affecting Violetta for decades.' 'Will she be spoilt by instant success?' 'She's stable, focused, extremely choosy.' 'I just hope this early success doesn't go to her head and take out the spontaneity and emotion.'

**What she says about herself:** 'There was never any question of "Oh, what a promising voice!" I was born with this voice. Right from when I was a little girl, it was clear that I would become a singer.'

**What she says about Alagna:** 'We work together, in the same room; we are quick learners. We talk about music for hours. We are in love with this profession. We are one with each other, we try to help each other be our best. We have so much in common.'

**Student B:** You write for *Stage and Opera*, a magazine read by theatre and opera enthusiasts of all ages. You have interviewed Roberto Alagna. Read the notes about him below, which were made during the interview. Using the information in the article on pages 94 and 95 and your imagination, add some more notes about your impression of the opera singer, including his appearance and personality.

■ 2  You both have to write an article about the famous couple for your magazine. Ask each other questions about the person you *did not* interview, in order to build up a profile of both the singers for your article. Take notes.

Your article should include the following topics:
- the development of their early careers
- their appearance and personality
- their attitude to life
- what the critics think of them
- what they said during the interview
- their personal relationship
- their working relationship and the future

■ 3  When you have enough information, plan your article. Look back at Unit 1 at the Help with Writing section. Think about the style and the layout of your article. Who will read the article? What will interest your readers?

Now write your **article** in **300–350** words.

■ 4  Now work with your partner. Your articles will both be written in very different styles; compare them together. Comment on the good points about your partner's article.

### ROBERTO ALAGNA: The Inside Story

**Discovered:** In a Paris pizzeria, where he sang eight hours a night for tips.

**Main roles:** *La Traviata* at La Scala, Milan in 1993; Romeo in London in 1994

**What the critics say:** 'Will he be spoilt by instant success?' 'Is he just another example of our hunger for the instant star?'

**What he says about himself:** 'Like any other singer I want my own identity. I wonder if I please people because I'm like another singer or because I'm me. There's nothing calculated in my interpretation. I sing what I feel. My style isn't new, it's just mine.'

**What he says about Gheorghiu:** 'We'd like to build a career together. We don't accept offers to sing together for the sake of it. With our rapport we could do great things. Angela is more prudent than me. I'm a bit exuberant. I have to do everything at once. She's calmer; she has serenity.'

UNIT 5 *All Right on the Night*

**HELP WITH LISTENING: THREE-WAY MATCHING TASKS**

In Part Four of the Listening Test, you hear a conversation between two people, usually a man and a woman, who are discussing a topic and giving their opinions. There are six statements on the page and you have to decide whose opinion the statements reflect. There are three possible answers: the statement may reflect the man's opinion, or it may reflect the woman's opinion, or it may be a point about which they both agree.

**1** The following exercises will help you to develop the listening skills you need to do this task.

1 Listen to these extracts from conversations about the cinema and decide whose opinion the statement reflects; the man's (**M**) or the woman's (**W**).

| | | |
|---|---|---|
| **Extract One** | Certain aspects of the film lacked originality. | ☐ |
| **Extract Two** | The film went on for too long. | ☐ |
| **Extract Three** | The actress seems to have a limited range. | ☐ |
| **Extract Four** | The film didn't really deal with challenging ideas. | ☐ |

2 Listen to some more extracts from conversations about music. This time decide whether only one of the speakers agrees with the statement (**O**), or whether they both agree (**B**).

| | | |
|---|---|---|
| **Extract Five** | I agree with the critic's assessment of Marina Lovinia. | ☐ |
| **Extract Six** | I was disappointed with the singer's performance. | ☐ |
| **Extract Seven** | The CD is exceptionally good. | ☐ |
| **Extract Eight** | It can be a bad thing for a band to attract too much publicity. | ☐ |

3 Look at the expressions in the box. Decide whether each one is generally used to express agreement or disagreement.

| | |
|---|---|
| absolutely | be that as it may |
| exactly | I take your point |
| hardly | you must be joking |
| surely | I can't go along with that |
| perhaps, but I still think | there may be something in that |

*All Right on the Night* **UNIT 5**

## REMEMBER

- Before you listen, look at the rubric to see who is speaking and what the topic is.
- Read the questions and underline the main ideas in the statements.
- Remember that both speakers will talk about the points raised in the statements, so you are not listening for who talks about it, but rather for whose point of view these actual words reflect.
- Think about the exact meaning of the statement.
- Remember the questions follow the order of information in the text.
- Listen for typical ways of agreeing and disagreeing.
- Listen for clues in the speakers' intonation and tone of voice.

**2** Now try this Part Four Listening task.

You will hear two reviewers, John and Lynn, talking about a book they've both been reading. For questions **1–8**, decide whether the opinions are expressed by only one of the speakers, or whether the speakers agree.

Write **J** for John,
**L** for Lynn,
or **B** for Both, where they agree.

1  The plot is inadequate.

2  The situation described is not very original.

3  It's difficult to relate to the characters.

4  The subject matter is thought provoking.

5  The book is well-suited to a film version.

6  The film raises important issues.

7  The book is quite frightening in parts.

8  Generally my opinion of the book is favourable.

**3** Listen again and write down expressions that mean:

1  to be precise (Lynn)
2  in my opinion (Lynn)
3  Really? You must be joking! (Lynn)
4  it's a normal situation (John)
5  there are many of them (Lynn)
6  with lots of noise and action (Lynn)
7  very involved and excited (Lynn)
8  a very readable book (John)

UNIT 5 *All Right on the Night*

## READING 3
*Reading for main points and specific information*

■ 1   Look at this varied selection of reviews. Read them quickly and decide which branch of the arts each review is dealing with.

■ 2   Now read again more carefully and decide if each passage gives a positive or negative review of the performance or product. Underline the words or phrases which indicate the writer's opinion.

■ 3   Match each of these statements **1–8** with one or more of the passages **A–F**.

1   It was better than I expected. ____ ____

2   It is becoming increasingly popular. ____

3   It is an adaptation from another medium. ____

4   You can never be sure what you'll see. ____

5   It's an opportunity to see some masterpieces. ____

6   It is less explicit than some works. ____

7   One performance stands out. ____

8   It is faithful to the original artist's ideas. ____

**A**

### Perlman Joins the Party

There can be few more unpleasant musical experiences than listening to someone whose performances you have respected make a fool of themselves with unfamiliar repertoire. The classical disc catalogue is littered with embarrassing examples of this particular folly. Thankfully, on his latest release, Perlman has collaborated with some of the best exponents of the form – the excellent *Klezmatics* who add a modern jazz approach and the more traditional *Brave New World*, redolent of paprika and strong coffee. Perlman is totally within style, part of the band, part of the party, not the star turn.

## VOCABULARY 2
*Using your dictionary*

■ 1   Look up these words from the reviews in your dictionary. Which meaning of the word is used here? What other meanings are there?

1   turn (A)
2   fluid (B)
3   threads (B)
4   celebrated (C)
5   bunch (D)
6   quiet (E)
7   gems (E)
8   hoot (F)
9   frothy (F)

## B

### STREET FIGHTER

Like many before him, director de Souza falls foul of transferring a necessarily repetitive computer game to the big screen: instead of a fluid cinematic narrative, we have a stop-start plot with too many heroes, multiple plot threads, and virtually no suspense or excitement. Having taken hostage 63 aid workers and a handful of Allied Forces soldiers renegade warlord General M Bison (Raul Julia) demands a hefty ransom. Colonel Guile (Jean-Claude van Damme) and more than a dozen multi-ethnic heroes then try to penetrate the defences of Bison's hi-tech fortress. The late Julia hams it up shamelessly as the camp commandant, but not even his suave presence and throw-away quips can save this noisy, brainless mess.

## C

### MORE TALES FROM THE ATTIC

If you love horror stories but blanch at sex and violence, Diana Guest's new work, *Forbidden Garden* could be what you've been waiting for. One night, journalist Patrick Kaiser hears the sound of sobbing coming from the end of his garden. Going outside to investigate, he swiftly becomes involved with a family whose two children, Hildy and Christian, live in mortal terror of their monstrous father, the celebrated pianist Julian Ferrare. What unnatural hold does this man have over his family? And what binds Hildy and Christian so tightly to the attic at the top of the house? Kaiser's attempts to discover the secrets of this mysterious foursome and his fight to protect the children from the evil around them lead us into a nightmarish world that simply can't fail to grip and compel. Read it if you dare.

## D

### Fortnight Club

The latest in a series of fascinating fortnightly shows where a large bunch of experienced comics try out new material and play around with new ideas in a friendly and relaxed atmosphere. Go for the surprises, go for the fun, but don't expect performers to trot out their regular acts. Above all – go early, as word is getting round! The quality can't be guaranteed but it makes for a fascinating night out.

## E

### BRUCE CRASTLEY

CRASTLEY'S REPUTATION as a master of light and shadow is certainly borne out in this generous twenty-year retrospective. Most of the quiet, warm-toned views here – of fireworks over the Brooklyn Bridge, sculpture fragments at the Met, a window of the Louvre – are impeccably balanced, meditative studies. But *For Lisette* (1976) and *Waiting Grand Central* (1983), push further into the poetic and daring, fragile compositions and a wealth of black tones that produce complex, nearly flawless gems. Through March 23.

## F

### THE RIVALS

R B Sheridan's sparkling eighteenth century comedy of moneyed manners **The Rivals** is a production which could have been showy, flouncy and self-satisfying beyond endurance. But it's actually quite a hoot, not least because, as well as carrying off the play's formidable wit, most of the performers manage to reflect Sheridan's redeeming undercurrent of generosity, even towards his most absurdly affected characters. This is the kind of show that might well give frothy costume comedies a good name.

UNIT 5 *All Right on the Night*

## WRITING 2
### Reviews

A review is an evaluation of a film, book or event, giving a description and overall impression, using vivid, colourful language. A review could be in a formal or informal style, depending on the publication it is written for and the intended readership.

**1** Look back at the reviews on pages 100 and 101.
- Do they tell you all you want to know about the event?
- How is the information organized in each of them?
- In each case, comment on the style of writing. What type of publication do you think they were written for?
- Which tense is used most of the time in each of the reviews? Underline any other tenses used. Why have they been used in each case?

**2** Think about the layout of a review. What information should be included in each paragraph? The reviews on pages 100 and 101 are quite short. However, the length of the text and the number of paragraphs will depend on the task you are doing. The information could be organized as follows:

- **Introduction**
  Written in a style to gain the attention of the reader, this first paragraph should include the genre, the setting, the background, the main characters, etc.

- **Main paragraphs**
  Include your description and comments on the plot, the acting, the writing, the direction, etc. mentioning any particular aspects that you feel are significant.

- **Conclusion**
  Overall evaluation of the event with your recommendations to the reader.

**3** Which of the following points are essential to a good review?

> genre    plot    characters    style of director/writer    appeal
> performances    costumes    ideas    audience    visuals
> the writer's opinion    lighting    sound effects    acting

With a partner, think about a book review and also a film review and add any other aspects that you feel should be mentioned in addition to the above.

**4** Look at the following words and expressions. Would any of them obviously be used in an introduction? Which of them give the personal opinion of the writer?

> It deals with
> All in all, it is well worth seeing
> The plot revolves around
> It is produced/directed by
> I was particularly impressed
>     by/disappointed by
> It conveys a sense of
> It is a classic of its kind
> It will appeal to lovers/fans of
>
> It tells the story of
> This well-written/thought-provoking
>     book/play
> Don't miss it.
> It is set in
> On the whole I would(n't) recommend
>     it in view of the fact that
> It stars
> This lively, sparkling, comedy

**5** The language in a review should be descriptive and evocative, creating an image of the event in the mind of the reader. Some reviews are positive in tone; others are critical.

Decide which of the following words and phrases were used in a favourable review, and which in a critical one.

| moving | rather underrated | extremely perceptive | intricate |
| trivial | highly sophisticated | totally compelling | spectacular |
| rather wooden | disappointing | quite subtle | phoney |
| rather overrated | utterly predictable | highly entertaining |
| terribly unconvincing | clichéd |

**6** Look at the following Writing tasks. With a partner discuss how you would plan both the reviews. Think about the following points:

- What information would you include?
- What layout would you choose?
- What style would be appropriate?

✎ Remember to use the Writing Checklist on page 11.

1 You see this notice on your college notice board.

---

### WRITING COMPETITION

'The book I would take with me if I were stranded on a desert island.'

Describe the book that is so special to you, that you would not want to be without it. Tell us why it has had such a great influence on you and your life.

The winner will be presented with £100 in book tokens and the winning entry will be published in the college magazine.

---

Write your **competition entry**.

2 You are a member of a Film Club. Each month members are asked to write a review of a film they have seen recently for publication in the Club Newsletter. The secretary has asked you to submit a review for next month's newsletter.

Write your **review**.

**7** Now choose one of the questions and write your **review** in **300–350** words in an appropriate style.

**UNIT 5** *All Right on the Night*

### EXAM PRACTICE 5

**1** For questions **1–5**, think of **one** word only which can be used appropriately in all three sentences.

**1** I may be old-fashioned, but I can't understand the fashion for wearing colours that clearly _____ with one another.

When arranging meetings with overseas companies, it's important not to _____ with their local public holidays.

Samantha has decided to pull out of the filming because her views always seemed to _____ with those of the director.

**2** I don't think the actor who plays the _____ in that new film has been miscast.

The projector _____ stretched right across the floor and it was clear that somebody was going to trip over it.

Newcastle have gone into the _____ with 30 points, and it looks as if they will win the tournament.

**3** Before I joined the local film club, time used to really _____ at weekends.

Look, I don't want to get involved in your family problems, so please don't _____ me into this argument.

In their search for the case of missing diamonds, the police sent frogmen to _____ a nearby pond.

**4** This is a very delicate _____ , so I think we'd better discuss it in private.

The latest _____ of *Music Magazine* contains an article about child prodigies.

I don't want to make an _____ of it, but I was very disappointed by the way you behaved at the cinema last night.

**5** Although Clara doesn't have many lines to say, she appears in almost every _____ in the film.

I know you were annoyed with me, but there was no need to make such a _____ in front of all my friends.

The police sometimes ask victims to return to the _____ of a crime in the hope that they will remember some further details of what happened.

## 2
For questions **1–10**, read the text below. Use the word given in **capitals** at the end of some of the lines to form a word that fits in the space in the same line. There is an example at the beginning (**0**).

### Ancient Music

In ancient Greece, which is usually considered to be the (**0**) _birthplace_      **BIRTH**
of Western civilization, music was both ubiquitous and (**1**) _____      **SUPREME**
important. Although we know little about how ancient Greek music
actually sounded, classical scholars refer to it as 'an art which was
(**2**) _____ into the very texture of people's lives'. As in modern      **WEAVE**
European culture, elaborate instrumental skills were the preserve of
(**3**) _____ musicians; but the ancient Greeks considered that instruction      **PROFESS**
in singing and in the playing of musical instruments such as the lyre should
be an (**4**) _____ part of education for every citizen. Music was an      **ESSENCE**
important feature of domestic celebrations, (**5**) _____ rituals and feasts,      **RELIGION**
and musical competitions were held alongside (**6**) _____ contests.      **ATHLETE**

For the ancient Greeks, music and poetry were (**7**) _____ . The      **SEPARATE**
poet and the composer were frequently the same person, so that often
words and music were created together. It is worth noting that, in spite
of its (**8**) _____ connections, music was regarded as the natural      **MATHEMATICS**
(**9**) _____ to the subjective language of poetry rather than the      **ACCOMPANY**
objective language of (**10**) _____ argument.      **INTELLECT**

## 3
Read the text again and answer the following short-answer questions.

1 Which word from the text tells us how commonly something was found?
2 Which word from the text tells us how complicated something was?
3 In your own words, explain the meaning of the phrase 'the preserve of'. (paragraph 1)
4 In your own words, explain why the writer seems surprised that poetry and music were created together.

UNIT 6

# Tip of my Tongue

**SPEAKING 1**
*Talking about personal abilities*

1   Do you have a good memory? Are you better at remembering some things than others? Talk to your partner about the words in the box.

> numbers
> names
> lists of points
> appointments
> messages
> jokes
> songs/poems/quotations
> English vocabulary

A

*Tip of my Tongue* **UNIT 6**

■ 2  Do you know any good methods for memorizing things?

■ 3  Choose one of the two pictures labelled **A** or **B**. Look at your picture for one minute then close the book. Tell your partner as many things about the picture as you can remember. Your partner can look at the picture to check. Change roles and repeat for the other picture.

B

UNIT 6  *Tip of my Tongue*

### READING 1
*Reading for specific information*

**1** How important is memory in learning a language?
Does this affect your approach to studying English?

**2** Read this extract from a book about memory. Use the words given in **capitals** at the end of some of the lines to form a word that fits in the space in the same line. There is an example at the beginning (**0**).

## TYPES OF MEMORY: PART ONE

Most readers will be familiar with the experience of looking up a telephone number and then repeating it to themselves for the time it takes to sit down and dial the number. As luck would have it, this is (**0**) *invariably* the occasion for someone to ask a distracting question with the result that the number is forgotten and has to be looked up all over again. (**1**) _____ familiar and irritating is when you need the same number 24 hours later and find that you are quite incapable of remembering it. These experiences reflect the (**2**) _____ recognized view among psychologists that with verbal learning the ability to hold information for brief periods (usually up to 30 seconds in duration) demands fairly constant (**3**) _____ , and any distraction or interruption is likely to severely impede that ability. Moreover, it has been established that our capacity for short-term (**4**) _____ is remarkably consistent, and that most people experience some (**5**) _____ in memory as soon as the number of items or chunks of information (**6**) _____ seven.

VARIABLE

EQUAL

WIDE

REPEAT

RETAIN
BREAK
EXCESS

This type of memory, known as 'short-term memory', is clearly different from 'long-term memory', which is our capacity for recall of information minutes, weeks and years after the original (**7**) _____ . Furthermore, the difference is not simply one of duration. Unlike short-term memory, which is limited in capacity, long-term memory is seemingly (**8**) _____ and can accommodate any amount of new information. Not (**9**) _____ , this new information can be stored at a price; it is generally acknowledged that we need to work much harder to commit information to long-term memory, and the type of strategy we described as being (**10**) _____ to short term memory may not be adequate in the long term.

PUT

EXHAUST
SURPRISE

ESSENCE

**3** Try this experiment in groups of three. Decide who is Student A, Student B and Student C. Read **all** the instructions before you begin.

> Spend 30 seconds trying to memorize a telephone number.
> Then close the book and follow *your* instructions.
>
> **Student A:** Keep repeating the number in your mind.
>
> **Student B:** Think about what you had for dinner yesterday.
>
> **Student C:** Count to 20 out loud. First in your own language and then in English.
>
> When Student C has finished counting, each try to write down the telephone number.
>
> The telephone number to remember is: 0136-227-8359615

Check with your partners to see how well each of you has remembered the number.

**4** Discuss these terms and expressions with your partner. What do you think each one means?

a short-term memory
b long-term memory
c the mental lexicon
d low-frequency vocabulary
e on the tip of my tongue

**5** Read another extract on page 110 from the same book and decide if the statements **1–7** are true or false.

1 The speed at which we can recognize and recall words suggests that the 'mental lexicon' is very organized.

2 It is likely that there are similarities between the organization of our 'mental lexicon' and the arrangement of a dictionary.

3 In the Brown and McNeil experiment, some people could describe a sextant, but couldn't remember the name for it.

4 In the Freedman and Loftus experiment, the results show that the second question was more difficult to understand than the first one.

5 Words which are connected in meaning can be remembered together more easily.

6 Words used often are more easily remembered than words used recently.

7 Knowing about memory is important for language learners because of the limited time which they have for study.

## TYPES OF MEMORY: PART TWO

Our 'mental lexicon' is highly organized and efficient. Were storage of information haphazard, we would be forced to search in a random fashion to retrieve words; this simply is not feasible when one considers the speed at which we need to recognize and recall. Furthermore, it is extremely improbable that we organize words in the brain as a dictionary does. Imagine you were trying to recall the word 'nozzle' for instance. It is unlikely that you would retrieve the word 'noxious' (which appears next to 'nozzle' in the dictionary) in place of the target word.

Some very interesting experiments carried out by Brown and McNeil exemplify this point forcefully and give us clues about lexical organization. The experimenters gave testees definitions of low frequency vocabulary items and asked them to name the item. One definition was 'a navigational instrument used in measuring angular distances, especially the altitude of the sun, moon and stars at sea'. Some testees were able to supply the correct answer (which was 'sextant'), but the researchers were more interested in the testees who had the answer 'on the tip of their tongues'. Some gave the answer 'compass', which seemed to indicate that they had accessed the right semantic field but found the wrong item. Others had a very clear idea of the 'shape' of the item, and were often able to say how many syllables it had, what the first letter was, etc. It seems, then, that these systems are interrelated; at a very basic level there appears to be a phonological system, a system of meaning relations and a spelling system.

One way in which researchers investigate how the mental lexicon is organized is by comparing the speed at which people are able to recall items. It is generally accepted that if certain types of prompts can be answered more quickly than others, then this will reflect the lexical system. Freedman and Loftus asked testees to perform two different types of tasks: e.g.
1 Name a fruit that begins with a 'p'.
2 Name a word beginning with a 'p' that is a fruit.

Testees were able to answer the first type of question more quickly than the second. This seems to indicate that 'fruits beginning with p' are categorized under 'fruit' rather than under a 'words beginning with p' heading. Furthermore, experimenters discovered in subsequent tests that once testees had access to the 'fruit' category, they were able to find other fruits more quickly. This seems to provide further evidence that semantically related items are 'stored together'. Most researchers appear to agree that items are arranged in a series of associative networks.

We also have to consider other variables which affect storage. One important factor here is 'word frequency'; items which occur most frequently are also easily recognized and retrieved. Imagine a pile of cards, each representing an item of vocabulary. In this system the most frequently used words are 'at the top of the pile', and therefore easier to retrieve. 'Recency of use' is another variable, and, to return to the analogy of the pile, one can imagine words most recently used being at the top. These variables are concerned with the use of items, but it is also important to consider when items were first learnt. Imagine a pile of words organized chronologically: the words learnt on the first day of a language course would be at one extreme and those most recently learnt at the other.

Clearly, native speakers do not acquire all their vocabulary in lexical sets, but rather acquire items in a haphazard, chronological fashion, generally in a fairly predictable order of frequency. However, native speakers have many years in which to build up a comprehensive lexicon, whereas foreign learners are limited in this respect. Exploiting our present knowledge of storage systems to the full should allow us to attempt to speed up the learning process and facilitate storage.

*Which is the odd one out?*

## WRITING 1
### Summary skills

■ 1 Look back at the second extract and complete this summary of one of the experiments.

> **BROWN AND McNAIR'S EXPERIMENT**
>
> People were given _____ of low-frequency words and asked to say the word. Some people gave the name of an object used in a similar situation to the one described. This proved that their mental lexicon was divided into _____ .
> Other people, who couldn't remember the word, could give the number of _____ or the _____ . This proved that the mental lexicon is also organized according to _____ and _____ .

■ 2 Now write a similar summary of the second experiment, saying:
- what people had to do
- what results there were
- what the experiment proved

■ 3 How will what you have read influence how you study and how you keep vocabulary records?

## VOCABULARY 1
### Collocation

■ 1 Complete each sentence with one of the words from the box.

| widely | highly | deeply | broadly | closely |

1 It is _____ recognized that short-term memory requires repetition.
2 The effects of age on memory were studied _____ in this piece of research.
3 _____ respected scientists have been doing research in this area.
4 Researchers are _____ in agreement as to the best way of conducting this sort of research, although differences of opinion exist.
5 The performance of individuals in memory tests is _____ unpredictable.
6 The findings of the research group have been _____ reported in the press both here and overseas.
7 The results of one series of experiments must be seen as _____ unreliable, given the problems encountered with the volunteers.
8 The _____ held view is that long-term memory has no limits.
9 We are _____ unlikely to remember certain facts unless we write them down.
10 The old man was _____ troubled by his inability to remember dates and names.

UNIT 6 *Tip of my Tongue*

## GRAMMAR 1
### Conditionals

**1** Look at this sentence from the passage.

*Were storage of information to be haphazard, we would be forced to search in a random fashion to retrieve words.*

1 What type of sentence is this?

2 What is the usual sequence of tenses in this type of sentence?

How is the example sentence different to this?

3 What other words can be used to begin this type of sentence?

4 Rewrite the example sentence so that the meaning is the same, but begin with the word *if*.

If _____

**2** For questions **1–4**, complete the second sentence so that it has a similar meaning to the first sentence, using the word given. **Do not change the word given.** You must use between **three** and **eight** words, including the word given.

1 If you wrote that number down, you wouldn't keep forgetting it.

**to**

Were _____ number, you wouldn't keep forgetting it.

2 If he planned his experiments properly, he wouldn't keep getting into such a mess.

**to**

Were _____ , he wouldn't keep getting into such a mess.

3 As long as Linda continues to give me a lift to work, I shan't learn to drive.

**stop**

Were _____ to work, I would learn to drive.

4 Providing his theory isn't disproved, the professor will win the prize.

**someone**

Were _____ not win the prize.

**3** Look at this sentence. How is it different to the example sentence in exercise 1?

*Had it rained, the ceremony would have been held indoors.*

1 What is the normal sequence of tenses in this type of sentence?

2 What other words can be used to begin this type of sentence?

3 Rewrite the example sentence so that the meaning is the same, but begin with the word *if*.

If _____

112

## 4 Now answer questions 1–4.

1 If I'd been able to contact you, I'd have told you about it.

**possible**

Had _____ , I'd have told you about it.

2 Only John's decisive intervention saved the project from being a complete disaster.

**so**

Had John _____ , the project would have been a complete disaster.

3 If there hadn't been enough snow, a dry ski-run would have been made available.

**insufficient**

Had _____ , a dry ski run would have been made available.

4 As you didn't notify the company of your intention to cancel the holiday, they will not refund your deposit.

**given**

Had _____ your intention to cancel the holiday, they would have refunded your deposit.

## 5 Look at this sentence. How is it different to the previous example sentence?

*Should it rain, the ceremony will be held indoors.*

1 What is the normal sequence of tenses in this type of sentence?
2 What other words can be used to begin this type of sentence?
3 Rewrite the example sentence beginning with the word *if*.

If _____

## 6 Now answer questions 1–4.

1 As long as nobody notices the error, we shall not make an apology.

**at**

Should _____ point we will make an apology.

2 If your CD proves to be faulty, please return it to the address on the box.

**asked**

Should your CD _____ to return it to the address on the box.

3 Were you to lose your ticket, no duplicate would be issued.

**it**

Should _____ possible to issue a duplicate.

4 In the event of a complaint from a customer, the manager must be called directly.

**make**

Should _____ , the manager must be called directly.

UNIT 6  *Tip of my Tongue*

## USE OF ENGLISH 1
### Cloze passage

■ 1  Before you complete the cloze passage answer these questions.
1. What are usually recognized as the five senses?
2. What type of things often get referred to as 'sixth sense'?
3. Have you ever had any experiences of this type?
4. Look at the words in the box. What does each one mean? In what context is each word generally used? Use your dictionary to help you if necessary.

| surveillance | orthodox | phenomenon | ambush | telescopic | ludicrous |

■ 2  Fill each of the numbered blanks in the passage with **one** suitable word from the box below. The first one has been done for you as an example.

| by | no | in | only | on | as | out |
| get | means | are | other | who | being | taking |
| to | have | ~~at~~ | far | around | not | which |

### Sixth Sense

The idea that some people can sense when they are being stared (**0**) __at__ has so (**1**) _____ been rejected as ludicrous (**2**) _____ orthodox scientists. But now researchers are (**3**) _____ the claims more seriously.

According (**4**) _____ Cambridge University biologist Dr Rupert Sheldrake, the phenomenon has long been recognized (**5**) _____ fields such as wildlife photography and military surveillance. The security manager of a large store in London, for example, has caught thousands of people (**6**) _____ his surveillance cameras, and he is in (**7**) _____ doubt that some people have a 'sixth sense'; in (**8**) _____ words, they know when they are being watched. They can (**9**) _____ their backs to the camera, which may also be hidden, yet still (**10**) _____ agitated when the camera is trained on them. Some move on, whilst others look (**11**) _____ to try and spot the camera.

Some police teams (**12**) _____ said to have a rule about (**13**) _____ keeping people in telescopic sights too long because suspects may sense they are being watched. And the experience of a soldier (**14**) _____ had a strong sense of being watched as he patrolled along a dark alley one night (**15**) _____ to find later that he had narrowly missed (**16**) _____ ambushed is by no (**17**) _____ an uncommon one.

Dr Sheldrake is now gathering data on the staring phenomenon (**18**) _____ part of a scientific study and will be carrying (**19**) _____ experiments designed to measure staring sensitivity by monitoring skin resistance, (**20**) _____ he hopes will throw further light on the question.

## VOCABULARY 2
### Prefixes

**1** What does the prefix *re* in front of a word often indicate?

**2** Match each of the words in the box with one of the definitions **A–I**.
Note: two of the words have the same definition.

| retrieve | repeat | recall | retain | record |
|---|---|---|---|---|
| remember | recognize | revise | remind | research |

A  Bring back into the memory          _____

B  Identify/acknowledge                _____

C  Set down in permanent form for reference  _____

D  Say or do over again                _____

E  Make or help someone remember something  _____

F  To collect facts by scientific study  _____

G  Succeed in not losing or forgetting  _____

H  Find given information again in the memory  _____

I  Read or look at again to improve familiarity  _____

**3** Complete each sentence with a noun form of one of the verbs from the box in exercise 2. Use each verb only once, then mark the stressed syllable of the noun.

1  The _____ of numbers can help you to commit them to memory.

2  They made a _____ of the interview so that it could be broadcast later.

3  He was sent a _____ because he hadn't returned a library book.

4  She is working as a _____ at the local university.

5  He started a programme of _____ four weeks before the exam.

6  He said, 'Hello again', but there was no look of _____ in her eyes.

7  Long-term _____ of information requires more work than short-term.

8  Giving the first letter of a word speeded up its _____ from memory.

9  The statue was erected in _____ of the country's greatest writer.

10  I had no _____ of the events he described.

UNIT 6  *Tip of my Tongue*

## SPEAKING 2
*Talking together about a visual prompt*

■ 1  Look at the two photographs. Make a list of the similarities and differences between them. Think about:

The setting:
  where it is
  why it's happening

The people:
  their appearance
  their relationship with one another
  their feelings

The subject:
  how the photograph has been taken
  why the photograph has been taken
  where/how the photograph might be used

■ 2  Talk to your partner about the photographs. Use the language in the box to compare and contrast them.

> they are both
> they both show
> whereas
> on the other hand
> while
> it makes me think of
> I think they must/can't/could/may/might be...

■ 3  What is the relationship between people, memory and computers? Discuss your ideas with your partner.

## LISTENING 1

*Three-option multiple choice*

You will hear two different extracts about the Internet. For each question 1–4, choose the answer (**A**, **B** or **C**) which fits best according to what you hear.

**Extract One**  (a news report about an Internet business)

1  What is surprising about the business?
   **A**  the number of people who run it
   **B**  what you can buy from it
   **C**  where it is located

2  The website is useful to record companies because it
   **A**  provides them with market information.
   **B**  pre-selects potential recording artists.
   **C**  promotes their products at no cost.

**Extract Two**  (part of a documentary about the Internet)

3  What does the speaker find most disturbing about the trend he describes?
   **A**  the number of people involved
   **B**  the attitude of the people surveyed
   **C**  the particular group of people affected

4  The speaker regards the researchers' conclusions as
   **A**  exaggerated.
   **B**  predictable.
   **C**  irresponsible.

## READING 2
### Lexical cloze

**1** Read this article about the Internet and for questions **1–8**, decide which answer (**A**, **B**, **C** or **D**) best fits each gap.

### Postal System Holds its Own

You might think that the dear old postage stamp is well and (**1**) _____ licked. And the culprit is easy to find. It's e-mail. These days it seems you can send just about anything over the Internet. And if it can't be written or (**2**) _____ to an e-mail you can bet there are half a dozen e-businesses only too willing to send it for you. But according to Britain's Post Office, you'd be wrong. Predictions of a paperless society, (**3**) _____ by computers, appear to be way off the (**4**) _____ . At least that's what the postal services are telling us: business is booming. 'There's something particularly attractive about holding something in your hand. The first thing most people do with an e-mail is print it', says a spokesperson.

And at a first (**5**) _____ , things do indeed look good for postal services, despite the emergence of new technologies such as the Internet and mobile phones, which actually (**6**) _____ to bulk out the mailbag. For example, your average annual mail drop increases by 14 extra letters a year when you buy a mobile phone, and when people start to buy online (**7**) _____ going to the shops in person, it's often the Post Office that gets to deliver the goods. But this growth of surface mail arising out of technological advance may not, on (**8**) _____ inspection, prove to be sustainable in an ever-changing world.

| | | | | | | | |
|---|---|---|---|---|---|---|---|
| **1** | **A** surely | **B** truly | **C** keenly | **D** wholly |
| **2** | **A** assigned | **B** ascribed | **C** attached | **D** attributed |
| **3** | **A** brought about | **B** caught on | **C** put aside | **D** shown up |
| **4** | **A** course | **B** target | **C** spot | **D** mark |
| **5** | **A** scan | **B** glance | **C** peep | **D** glimpse |
| **6** | **A** cause | **B** due | **C** tend | **D** lead |
| **7** | **A** instead of | **B** apart from | **C** except for | **D** on behalf of |
| **8** | **A** sharper | **B** closer | **C** deeper | **D** tougher |

**2** What do you think is the future of the Internet?
Talk about:
- areas where the use of the Internet will expand
- limitations to the use of the Internet
- how the world will change as a result of the Internet

UNIT 6 *Tip of my Tongue*

## LISTENING 2
### Part One
## *Listening for specific information*

1. Talk to your partner about the Internet. Discuss these points:
   - what experience you have of it
   - your understanding of how it works
   - how important you think it is
   - the implications for English and other languages

2. You will hear the beginning of a radio programme about the language used on the Internet. As you listen, choose the two main points Bob Elman makes.

   A  The Internet should use a variety of languages.
   B  The English used on the Internet is nothing like everyday English.
   C  Human interaction would be easier if everyone spoke the same language.
   D  The jargon used on the Internet will soon develop into a whole new language which English speakers won't be able to understand.
   E  It's inevitable that languages change to meet new conditions.

3. Before you listen to the rest of the programme, make a list of words and expressions which are commonly used in relation to the Internet.

4. Listen to a continuation of the programme. How many of the words on your list are used by the speakers?

### Part Two
## *Note taking*

Listen to the rest of the radio programme again and complete the table on page 119.

## VOCABULARY 3
## *Record keeping*

1. Read this list of ways of organizing a vocabulary book. Discuss the advantages and drawbacks of each method with your partner.

   a  Chronological – like a diary, organized according to when you first came across them.
   b  Alphabetical – like a dictionary with words listed according to the letter they begin with.
   c  Under topic headings – e.g. sport, crime, Internet, etc.
   d  Grammatically – according to the type of word, e.g. verbs, nouns, etc.
   e  Another way?

2. Which of the following do you think it might also be useful to record?
   - Examples of how the word was used, e.g. 'to post a contribution'.
   - References of where you heard/saw it so that you can look at the context again.
   - The prepositions that are used with the word, e.g. 'in the context *of*'.
   - The appropriate register/situation in which to use the word.
   - How the word is pronounced and stressed.

3. When you have organized your vocabulary records, what is the best way to memorize the words it contains?

## INTERNET LANGUAGE

Familiar words with a new meaning in the context of the Internet.

| Word | Part of speech | Literal meaning | Meaning in this context |
|---|---|---|---|
| _____ | verb | watersport | moving around net - you don't know where you're going |
| _____ | verb | make a noise | making choices on the net by pressing a button |
| _____ | noun | place/location of something | one user's contribution to the net |
| _____ | verb | to send something | to put some material on the net |
| _____ | noun | novice/newcomer | new user of net |
| _____ | verb | exist unobserved | surfing without contributing to the net |
| _____ | verb | to burn | to tell off |

Examples of greetings and salutations:

_____ = abbreviation of _____

_____ = abbreviation of _____

Computer terms that are entering the common language:

_____ = still used though it no longer describes the object.

_____ = a noun that is now widely used as a verb.

_____ = has a wider range of meanings than the equivalent common words.

_____ = new meanings of this word seem likely to be used more widely.

UNIT 6 *Tip of my Tongue*

## READING 3
*Gapped text*

**1** Read this article about the way computers are affecting the English language. Six paragraphs have been removed from the text. Choose from the paragraphs **A–G** on page 121 the one which fits each gap (**1–6**). There is one extra paragraph which you do not need to use.

# Computers and Language

One evening in 1945, a luckless moth flew into a huge government computer in Virginia, USA. Computers were then largely mechanical, and the insect was crushed instantly between two metal blades, shutting down the machine and providing English with its first widespread bit of computer slang: *bug*.

| 1 |

On the timeline of technology, computers are, if not exactly in their infancy, perhaps barely in their teens. Their real impact on English is yet to come: ultimately, computers will profoundly alter the way that language itself is written. Before the flood tide of computers, however, only engineers and scientists came into contact with computer terminology. Now, a large part of society is exposed to the jargon, either in the home, office, through schools, or in the media.

| 2 |

Discoursing on RAM and ROM at social gatherings, of course, is in the end no different from carrying on about power-steering or carburettors. More compelling is the way computer jargon is increasingly applied to other concerns. It is perhaps emblematic of technology that, as with *bug*, the most successful linguistic crossovers thus far are all inspired by computer failure.

| 3 |

Other computer borrowings abound, not all originating from the idea of technical failure. Some, such as *programmed*, to describe behaviour, have been enriched by their computer association but are ultimately not far from their pre-computer meanings. The business world, for instance, has appropriated words like *network* and *interface*.

Such borrowing simply replaces existing words with rather graceless jargon.

| 4 |

For example, computers offer fresh meaning for the word *background*. When powerful computers are given more than one job to do, they relegate the lesser task to 'background' – processing that problem only when the more important 'foreground' task is momentarily at rest. Computer buffs have found background an attractive metaphor for a certain level of thought. Instead of 'I'll sleep on it,' one may say, 'I'll keep that in the background' – implying that the thought will not only be stored but some additional, probably subconscious, thinking will be done.

| 5 |

Such obscure usages remain mostly confined to technical communities, such as Silicon Valley. At the same time, some commentators are concerned that these and other computer metaphors are dangerous. In her book *The Second Self*, a study of computers and culture, sociologist Sherry Turkle warns that when children take computers too literally as models of human thought, they may devalue the subtlety of their own minds.

| 6 |

In the end it is the very ubiquity of computers which will bring far more profound changes to language than merely fresh vocabulary. Soon the computer will fundamentally alter the way people write. While the current adult population has largely adopted computers for writing, few will use the machines the same way as their children will, who have never known anything else.

**A** Another new and exotic arrival which illustrates this link between thought and computers is *munge*. This describes the state of being delayed while the computer performs a particularly complex task. Normally delays are sources of irritation, but *munge* implies they are forgiveable because of the difficulty of the task. *Munge* is also applied to difficult human mental tasks, expressing regard for the difficulty of the task and at the same time sympathy for the thinker.

**B** *Crash*, which is a major system shutdown, has found broad acceptance. One story goes that *crash* arose with the first student computer enthusiasts at the Massachusetts Institute of Technology, most of whom also belonged to the MIT biking club, where crashes were of the conventional variety.

**C** Broadening access to computers will place an additional premium on the ability of writers to create original thought and diminish the value of well-schooled but merely glib expression. The most elegant, evocative, and revolutionary creations of language will still spring directly from human inspiration.

**D** Since that incident, computers have proliferated at an astounding rate, culminating in the past decade's barrage of bits and bytes, servers and hosts, chat rooms and websites. Yet thus far, the computer's influence on general language still lags quite considerably behind the jargon of, say, sports or commerce.

**E** Though research has shown that conventional computers operate differently from the human brain, the newer 'neural network' computers more closely imitate the brain's structure, and may well some day offer even more enticing mental associations to those millions of people all over the world who use computers as a fact of life.

**F** There is, however, a more intriguing class of computer-inspired language. This derives from the fact that some aspects of computers seem so similar to human thought that they provide new words with which to describe our own mental processes.

**G** Even polite conversation is not immune: anyone trapped at dinner with voluble new computer owners knows that the little machines can easily become an obsessive topic. Small wonder then, that tales abound of hosts and hostesses who ban computer speak from the table altogether.

**2** Look back at the main part of the text and find words or phrases that mean (paragraph numbers in brackets):
 a on the whole (1)
 b used everywhere/by everyone (1)
 c very informal spoken language, used by particular groups of people (1)
 d special words used by particular groups of people (2)
 e interesting/fascinating (3)
 f typical (3)
 g occur in great numbers (4)
 h taken/adopted (4)
 i demote/put into a lesser rank (5)
 j limited/restricted (6)

**3** There are several collocations with 'computer' in the text. Look back at the text to complete the following word partnerships.

Words such as *crash* and *bug* are examples of computer…  s_____
t_____
j_____
l_____

People who use a computer might be described as computer…  b_____
e_____
o_____

UNIT 6  *Tip of my Tongue*

## LISTENING 3
### Sentence completion

■ 1  Discuss these questions with your partner.

At what age do children learn to talk?

What things do they learn first?

How do they learn?

■ 2  You will hear part of an interview with a woman who has written a book on the subject of feral children, children growing up without the company of other human beings. For questions **1–10**, complete the sentences with a word or short phrase.

Many feral children are believed to have been brought up by _____ **1**.

Lorna says that she finds many of the stories told about feral children _____ **2**.

The sounds made by the wolf girls of Midapur were described as _____ **3**.

In eight years one of the girls only managed to learn _____ **4**.

Lorna describes the way a baby learns language as a process of _____ **5**.

Lorna says it's wrong to liken our language ability to a _____ **6**.

Feral children joining human society as teenagers failed to learn _____ **7**.

People who learn foreign languages _____ **8** are always identifiable as non-native speakers.

Feral children seem to learn vocabulary by means of _____ **9**.

Genie failed to learn the language necessary to _____ **10**.

■ 3  What does the evidence of feral children tell us about:
- language learning in general?
- learning a foreign language?

## PHRASAL VERBS 1
### With 'up'

■ 1  Look at these two sentences from the listening text. Underline the phrasal verbs in each one.

*We all know people who have taken up foreign languages in adulthood.*

*It will always be possible to pick up that these are not native speakers.*

■ 2  Which of the verbs in the box are closest in meaning to the two phrasal verbs in exercise 1?

| started doing | notice | collect | mention | raised | tired | filled |

■ 3  Complete each sentence with a suitable verb. Then match the meaning of the phrasal verb you have formed to one of the verbs in the box in exercise 2.

1  I'm _____ up with hearing you complaining, can't you be more positive?

2  Sorry I didn't phone you, but my time has been completely _____ up with a crisis at work.

3  I was _____ up to believe that language learning was about remembering words.

4  Sorry to _____ this up, but didn't you say I might expect a salary rise?

5  I've got to go now because I promised to _____ the children up from school.

## WRITING 2
### Narratives

■ 1  Think about a day in your childhood when something strange or unusual happened.

1 How much do you remember about each of the following? Make some notes about:
- the weather/time of year
- the place/the event
- the people who were there
- how you felt before anything happened

2 Use your notes to tell your partner about what happened. Ask your partner questions about his/her day.

3 Write a paragraph to introduce the story. This paragraph should describe the background. What will the tense of the main verbs be in this paragraph? What other tenses might you need to use?

■ 2  How much do you remember about the events leading up to this strange or unusual event?

1 How can you make the story more interesting for the reader by building up the scene? Think about:
- what you/others expected to happen that day
- how you were feeling
- the normal things that were happening

2 Write a paragraph that sets the scene for the strange event. What will the main tense of the verbs be in this paragraph? What other tenses might you need to use?

■ 3  How much do you remember about the strange event itself?

1 Do you remember the details that made it strange? Think about:
- how well your readers will understand what happened
- how well they will understand why it was strange
- how well they will understand how you or others felt
- how to tell the story so that the strange thing is surprising

2 Write a paragraph explaining what happened. What will the main tense of the verbs be in this paragraph? What other tenses might you need to use?

3 Think about how you want the story to end. It could be:
- an explanation
- a result
- how you feel now
- what you understand now that you didn't understand then, etc.

■ 4  Write the end of your account.

■ 5  Read through what you have written, checking that the story flows and making any changes you think are necessary.

📖 N.B. The Workbook has further work on narrative tenses.

UNIT 6  *Tip of my Tongue*

**6** Look at the following Writing tasks. Discuss with your partner how you would plan each piece of writing and then make outline notes for the story and the article.

✎ Remember to use the Writing Checklist on page 11.

1   You see this writing competition in a literary magazine. Write a **story** as an entry for the competition.

> # WRITING COMPETITION
>
> Would you like your writing published?
>
> We invite all would-be authors to submit a story for the competition.
>
> Your story will begin or end with the words;
>
> 'I had thought it was going to be a perfect day. How wrong I was.'
>
> The winning story will be published in our magazine and the writer will be given a personal introduction to Hancock Mills, one of our largest publishing houses. In addition they will win £50.00 in book tokens.

2   A travel magazine has invited readers to contribute an article for a special edition entitled 'An unforgettable journey'. Write an **article** describing a memorable journey you have made, and explain why it was so special.

**7** Now choose one of the Writing tasks in exercise 6 and write your answer in **300–350** words in an appropriate style.

*Tip of my Tongue* **UNIT 6**

## EXAM PRACTICE 6

**1** For questions **1–5**, think of **one** word only which can be used appropriately in all three sentences.

**1** After turning off the motorway, take the Bristol road and continue to _____ left until you get to the roundabout.

After spending four whole days looking for information on the Internet, I couldn't _____ to look at the screen for another moment.

Although operations in that hospital are free, patients have to _____ the cost of medicines themselves.

**2** If you eat in the hotel restaurant, give the waiter your room number and he will _____ the cost of the meal to your account.

After they'd spent five days indoors with their computer games, it was good to see the children _____ across the sand and dive into the sea.

The police have intercepted the computer hacker and will _____ him with a number of offences.

**3** I think they were rather rash to _____ quite so much money to that e-commerce venture.

Although Amanda appeared to agree with the proposal, she clearly wasn't going to _____ herself to anything yet.

Harry kept repeating the secret code number under his breath in an attempt to _____ it to memory without writing it down.

**4** Although the boys talked about football every evening, they never seemed to _____ the subject.

There's no point in studying until the early hours of the morning, you only _____ yourself and so impair your performance the following day.

I'm afraid that in order not to _____ our supplies of that particular printer ribbon, we are rationing each customer to one only.

**5** For the moment, demand for traditional postal services is _____ up, despite the advent of e-mail.

The computer may have retained the lost document somewhere in its memory, but I'm afraid we're not _____ out much hope of finding it.

Although the concert has been cancelled, people are _____ on to their tickets in the hope of getting a refund.

125

# UNIT 6 *Tip of my Tongue*

**2** For questions **1–15**, read the text below and think of the word which best fits each space. Use only **one** word in each space. There is an example at the beginning (**0**).

### Deep Blue

Can people build machines capable of evolving (**0**) __*into*__ something better, something able, perhaps, to invent solutions that go (**1**) _____ the boundaries of human imagination? Using brute-force methods of calculation, computers can nowadays play (**2**) _____ passable game of chess. In 1997, an IBM supercomputer (**3**) _____ as 'Deep Blue' defeated the reigning world chess champion Garry Kasparov. In (**4**) _____ doing, Deep Blue appeared to satisfy (**5**) _____ least some of the criteria for artificial intelligence, for Kasparov described the experience as being every (**6**) _____ as gruelling as playing a top-notch human challenger.

Yet Deep Blue's victory (**7**) _____ the world's artificial-intelligence community unimpressed. That was because the machine performed its feat merely by crunching numbers faster than (**8**) _____ other computer had managed before. Its enormous processing power enabled it to predict a game's possible course (**9**) _____ to 30 moves ahead, while its clever programming allowed it to work out (**10**) _____ of the millions of possible moves (**11**) _____ strengthen its position best. (**12**) _____ its own, all that Deep Blue could do, no matter (**13**) _____ brilliantly, was the mathematics. (**14**) _____ it could not do was devise its own strategies for playing a game of chess, thus confirming conventional wisdom that (**15**) _____ long held that a machine's abilities are limited by the imagination of its creators.

**3** Read the text again and answer the following short-answer questions.

1. Which phrase in the second paragraph reinforces the idea introduced by 'brute-force methods of calculation' in paragraph 1?

2. In your own words, explain how Garry Kasparov found playing chess against the computer.

3. What does the phrase 'its feat' (paragraph 2) refer to?

4. In your own words, explain what is meant by the term 'conventional wisdom'. (paragraph 2)

UNIT 7

# A Matter of Taste

**LISTENING 1**
*Matching*

**1** Discuss these questions with your partner.

What is good taste?
- how can you tell?
- who decides what is good taste?
- is good taste important?

**2** Read the words in the box. Discuss how they relate to ideas of what is and isn't considered to be good taste.

| art | culture | fashion | individuality |
|---|---|---|---|
| design | elegance | originality | style |

**3** Before you listen answer these questions.

1 How important do you think each of the following factors is in determining our taste in things?

| age | class | education | gender | experience |
|---|---|---|---|---|
| aspirations | occupation | race | nationality | wealth |

2 Look at the pictures. Which objects appear feminine to you, which masculine and which seem to have no particular gender?

3 Why do some of these objects have strong gender connotations? Is this something which is changing?

127

UNIT 7   *A Matter of Taste*

■ 4   You will hear part of a radio programme in which two designers are asked their views on the subject of gender and taste. For questions **1–8**, decide whether the opinions are expressed by only one of the speakers, or whether the speakers agree.

Write   **V** for Vivian,
         **D** for Darren,
or       **B** for Both, where they agree.

1   Gender is probably the most important factor influencing a person's taste.   ☐ 1

2   We immediately recognize objects as either masculine or feminine.   ☐ 2

3   Many of our ideas about the gender of objects have their roots in the very distant past.   ☐ 3

4   These days our stereotyped ideas are changing fast.   ☐ 4

5   In the past, feminine taste was held in high esteem.   ☐ 5

6   Ideas of 'design' rather than 'taste' have challenged women's traditional roles.   ☐ 6

7   People are now more likely to make personal choices rather than follow stereotypes.   ☐ 7

8   We cannot say whether the relationship between gender and taste will change in the future.   ☐ 8

■ 5   How did the speakers express agreement and disagreement? Listen again to these phrases from the listening. In each case, is the speaker agreeing or disagreeing? The first one is an example.

1   *agree*_____        2   _____
3   _____               4   _____
5   _____               6   _____
7   _____               8   _____
9   _____              10   _____

■ 6   Do you think goods will continue to have gender connotations? Use some of the words and expressions from the listening in your discussion. Agree and disagree with your partner as appropriate.

A Matter of Taste  UNIT 7

## VOCABULARY 1
### Part One
*Adjectives*

**1** Look at these words from the listening. Which would you use to talk about:
- men?
- women?
- places?
- objects?
- language?

| cluttered | cosy | flowery | efficient | eclectic | imaginative |
| rational | pretentious | original | superficial | fluffy | |

### Part Two
*Synonyms*

**1** Darren believes the issue of gender is 'central to' ideas of taste. What would be a good synonym for 'central to' in this context?

**2** For questions **1–6**, find a suitable synonym for each of the highlighted parts of these phrases.

1 gender is **ingrained in our consciousness**
2 gender differences have become **blurred**
3 everything's **up for grabs** these days
4 fixed **stereotypes** remain actually
5 you can no longer **generalize** like that
6 people don't feel so **hidebound** by these images any longer

### Part Three
*Compound words*

**1** Compound words are formed by joining two words together to form a new word which has its own meaning. For example:

*work + place = workplace*

**2** Take one word from box **A** and join it to a word from box **B** to make a new word that matches one of the definitions **1–12**.

| A | black | come | draw | hand | B | all | back | back | down |
| | hold | show | straight | sun | | fall | forward | land | out |
| | view | waste | wind | work | | out | place | point | rise |

1 somewhere you work
2 a large bag
3 a gift of money to the poor
4 a power failure
5 a disadvantage
6 return to fame or power
7 a sum of money received unexpectedly
8 place where nothing lives
9 start of the day
10 uncomplicated
11 personal opinion
12 crisis or confrontation

UNIT 7  *A Matter of Taste*

## HELP WITH SPEAKING: PART TWO

Remember that in Part Two of the Speaking Test, you have to speak to your partner, not to the examiner. This part of the exam tests your ability to take part in an informal discussion on a fairly serious topic.

## REMEMBER

- Look at and talk to your partner, not the examiner.
- Listen to what your partner says and respond naturally.
- Ask your partner questions to find out what he or she thinks, don't just give your opinions.
- Agree or disagree politely.
- Pick up on points your partner makes by adding your own ideas.

■ 1  Part Two has two phases. During the first phase, which lasts one minute:

- the examiner will tell you which photo(s) or aspects of the visual material to look at.
- listen to the instructions carefully and make sure that what you say is relevant.
- remember that you both need to talk in this minute, so ask each other questions and respond to what your partner says.
- don't talk for too long without involving your partner.

■ 2  The second phase lasts three minutes. During this part:

- the examiner will tell you the context of the discussion.
- listen to the instructions carefully in order to make sure what you say is relevant.
- work systematically through the visual material, discussing the issues raised by each image and considering all possibilities.
- bring in other ideas which are relevant to the task.
- you should work towards a conclusion, but you don't have to agree with each other!
- don't come to a conclusion too soon.

■ 3  Now try the following Speaking Part Two task.

1  Look at photograph A.
   Why might some people regard this is as bad taste? Talk to your partner for one minute.

2  Now look at all four photographs.
   A new book by a leading popular psychologist entitled *What is Good Taste?* is about to be published. The book is aimed at a non-specialist market. These four pictures are being considered for the cover. Talk together about the aspects of taste raised by each photograph and then decide which one would make the most appropriate cover.
   (three minutes)

A Matter of Taste  UNIT 7

B

D

C

131

UNIT 7 *A Matter of Taste*

## USE OF ENGLISH 1
*Summary skills*

**1** You are going to read two short texts which discuss the subject of taste.

1 Read the articles through once quickly and decide:
  - Which writer is in favour of a recent change and which is against?
  - Which article is the more serious in tone?
  - Which writer uses irony to make a point?

2 Where would you expect to find each of these texts?
  Who is the target reader in each case? What tells you?

3 From the alternatives in the box, choose the title which bests suits the content and style of each text.

> A Taste of Things to Come        In the Best Possible Taste
> There's no Accounting for Taste   A Taste for the Unreal
> Something to Appeal to the Taste Buds

**2** Now read the two texts again more carefully and answer questions **1–5** which follow.

> In his 1991 book entitled 'Taste', Stephen Bayley, former museum director and academic, observed that the 'urban hotels of the 19th century introduced a new, literate class of consumers to the experience of interior design'. Then as now, leading hotels tended to be either 'museums of taste', preserving the luxuries of a bygone age, or 'laboratories of taste' that act as the test bed for the latest ideas in decoration and comfort, the most successful of which will eventually percolate down into the domestic environment.
>
> Bayley's assertion is perfectly reasonable. Indeed, many of today's affluent, professional, educated people see the inside of many more hotels than they do museums. The hotel has become the conduit through which cultural stimulae are relayed to the wider populace. And if hotels are the litmus of taste, then the keen observer can come to but one conclusion; the minimalism that was so fashionable through the 1990s is now definitely on the wane. Based on the idea that 'less is more' this fashion led to interiors that were little more than empty halls in pastel colours with clean lines and no surface clutter. The latest round of hotel refurbishments have seen a move away from this principle, and in its place is a resurgence of detail and decoration. As this trend spreads out from the hospitality industry into homes across the country, individuals can again rejoice in the clutter of everyday life.

*line 19*

1 What does the phrase 'this principle' (line 19) refer to?

2 What synonym for the hotel business is used in the second paragraph?

> Television has had an incalculable effect on the brains, the habits and the values of modern people. You may welcome this fact or deplore it, but you cannot deny it. Less often noticed is the effect of television on the eyes and in particular on the ability to notice the muted shapes and colours of the natural world. The moving image commandeers the eyes and overrides the faculty of judgment.
>
> The purpose is to hold your attention, regardless of your rational powers. Everything is devoted to this end: the electric shapes of the studio; the glitter and glitz of the furnishings; the saturated colours; the faces that gaze with ready-made hilarity into the passive eyes of millions. Ludicrous, luminous clothing, in garish reds and greens, gives to the giggling stars the jerky, stenciled quality of cartoons. Natural colours and organic shapes are driven into the background and the foreground is filled with artifice.
>
> The effects of this on viewers can be seen in their clothes: what were once unthinkable combinations of fluorescent colours – supermarket green and luminous orange, electric blue and neon purple – are now commonplace sights in the high street.
>
> Perhaps, when our eyes are fully accustomed to these assaults, the natural world will be perceived as only a fading and colourless background to the human reality; a shapeless grey-green sea, glimpsed through the car window as we speed by.

*line 11*

*line 18*

**3** Which word in the first paragraph provides the opposite image to that created by the word 'garish' in line 11?

**4** In your own words, explain what the writer is referring to in the phrase 'these assaults' in line 18.

**5** In a paragraph of between **50 and 70** words, **summarize in your own words as far as possible**, the examples given in the two texts of the ways in which people's taste has been influenced by commercial developments.

**3** In your own words, explain the meaning of these phrases from the first text.

   **a**  a bygone age
   **b**  a test bed
   **c**  percolate down into
   **d**  the conduit through which
   **e**  the litmus of taste
   **f**  on the wane

**4** Underline all the adjectives in the second text. Divide them into three categories:

   - those with a positive connotation
   - those with a negative connotation
   - those which are used in a neutral way

# UNIT 7 A Matter of Taste

## READING 1
### Multiple choice

■ 1  What type of person do you imagine owning works of art?

Do you think works of art are worth the money that people pay for them?

Why do people buy works of art?

■ 2  Read this text about the owner of a picture by the late 19th century French painter, Cézanne, and answer the questions 1–5 which follow it.

### HOW TO LIVE WITH YOUR OWN CEZANNE

Walking around the Cézanne exhibition in London, one starts to wonder, after the eighth room of masterpieces, where all these pictures come from. One knows *Les Grandes Baigneuses* from the National Gallery, but some of the paintings are complete strangers, flown in from São Paolo, St Petersburg, Ohio, Canberra and Cardiff. And then there is a smattering of works marked 'private collection'. Despite their being 226 works in the show, there is only one belonging to a private owner that actually reveals the name on the label. This is *Le Bassin du Jas de Bouffan* in gallery 4. It is a small to medium-sized work, painted between 1878 and 1880, and it is owned by Madame Dupont.

It is not a particularly crowd-pleasing work, as many of Cézanne's landscapes are. Painted in winter at his father's grand but neglected weekend retreat, it has a stark, geometric quality that could be overshadowed by the more brightly appealing views of *L'Estaque* hanging on either side. But *Le Monde* has run a half-page appreciation of this Cézanne and the exhibition picks it out as pivotal in the artist's 'constructive' phase. Yet, it usually hangs in a small dining-room.

Madame Dupont has never given an interview about her Cézanne before. In an age when art thieves treat security systems with contempt, you can't blame her. But after the intervention of a chain of five people, she and her husband agree to meet me in a hotel.

People who own big pictures tend to have big hair, big coats and shoes that aren't made for walking, but for separating their feet from the limousine carpet. By contrast, Madame Dupont, a medium-sized woman in her late thirties, has mousey hair and is wearing a well-cut, but hardly arresting black jacket. Her husband, Arturo, looks equally low-profile in a green coat, although he is wearing a bow-tie for identification purposes, which is lucky. Otherwise we'd still be circling the hotel lobby.

1  What first attracted the writer to this particular painting in the exhibition?

   A  the place where it is usually kept
   B  the period in which it was painted
   C  its location within the exhibition
   D  the information provided about it

2  Which word from the text underlines the writers view that this painting is not a 'crowd-pleasing work'? (line 15)

   A  smattering (line 8)
   B  neglected (line 17)
   C  stark (line 18)
   D  pivotal (line 23)

3  What does the writer imply about Madame Dupont in the third paragraph?

   A  she is obsessively secretive
   B  she is flattered by his request
   C  she is understandably cautious
   D  she is unnerved by his approach

4  The writer's tone in describing typical owners of works of art is

   A  admiring.
   B  neutral.
   C  ironic.
   D  dismissive.

The first thing to be negotiated was what I could say and what I couldn't say 'for security reasons'. In interviews one usually (1) _____ from mentioning the street in which someone lives, but the Duponts would rather I brushed over which continent they come from. 'We don't have sleepless nights about security... really we don't, (2) _____ there would be no pleasure in owning it.'

They have owned the picture since 1992 when Madame Dupont spotted it (3) _____ up for sale at an auction. For her, the effect was instant. 'I'd seen it in reproduction, but when I saw it close up, I thought, "I love this painting." It wasn't just because it was by Cézanne, it was the atmosphere in the work that is so amazing, you can really feel the air and lightness. There have been few things that have (4) _____ me in that way... not for years and years.'

At the auction, she (5) _____ for it herself, and the hammer went down at £1.4 million, which she clearly thinks is quite cheap for a Cézanne. The *International Herald Tribune* described it as the best buy of the year. The Duponts think, in a typically understated way: 'We were quite lucky. With auctions one never knows.'

(6) _____ to say, you need more than cash to buy a Cézanne. One also needs considerable courage to (7) _____ a vast sum for what Madame Dupont calls 'just paint on a bit of canvas'. Almost inevitably, she comes from a dynasty of art dealers while she herself is a paper restorer.

The refreshing feature of the Duponts is that they seem to have bought their Cézanne because they genuinely loved it. This is rarer than one might think. All too often works of art are regarded as an investment which also serves to (8) _____ status on its owner. When I ask them if they take people around their flat like sightseers, Mme Dupont gives a (9) _____ uncomprehending frown. 'We don't have the painting for a social reason, it's so that we can (10) _____ up a personal relationship with it.' They don't hold cocktail parties in front of it then? 'Oh no, many of our friends don't even realize it's there. It's good that lots of people can see it in the exhibition, but without it our house has a different atmosphere. It's like being without a good friend.'

5 The writer regards the Dupont's appearance as

A highly inappropriate.
B surprisingly unpretentious.
C slightly disappointing.
D unwisely indiscrete.

### A Matter of Taste UNIT 7

3 Now read a continuation of the text. For questions **1–10**, decide which answer (**A**, **B**, **C** or **D**) best fits each gap.

1  A renounces      B refrains
   C resists        D recoils

2  A providing      B albeit
   C nonetheless    D otherwise

3  A coming         B showing
   C putting        D turning

4  A stretched      B touched
   C reached        D fetched

5  A haggled        B dealt
   C bargained      D bid

6  A Pointless      B Worthless
   C Useless        D Needless

7  A cast off       B lay out
   C set down       D hand in

8  A accord         B allow
   C confer         D concede

9  A blank          B bald
   C blunt          D bare

10 A draw           B bring
   C build          D make

4 Now read the continuation of the text again, and answer these questions.

1 In your own words, describe the two things you need in order to buy a Cézanne, according to the writer.

2 Why do you think the writer begins the sentence about Madame Dupont's family with the words 'almost inevitably'?

3 What is Madame Dupont keen to deny in the final two paragraphs?

5 Look back at both parts of the article. In a paragraph of between **50 and 70** words, **summarize in your own words as far as possible**, the reasons why, in the writer's view, Madame Dupont is unlike many other owners of works of art.

**UNIT 7** *A Matter of Taste*

## SPEAKING 1
### Developing a topic

■ 1  Look at these pictures. Talk to your partner about why you like or dislike each one.

Think about:

> subject matter
> images portrayed
> use of colour
> skill of the artist
> what it makes you think of
> how it makes you feel
> who it might appeal to

■ 2  Imagine that you have to choose a picture or poster for either your wall at home, your classroom or the place where you work. Talk about how important some of the following points would be when choosing a picture. Which points would be more important in the different situations?

- size
- colour
- subject matter
- style of drawing/painting/graphics
- reputation of the artist
- how fashionable it is
- what your family/friends think of it
- how much you like it
- the message/idea it communicates
- how much it costs

## WRITING 1
### Letters

■ 1  Look at the following Writing task.

*A modern art statue has been positioned in a prominent position in the centre of the town where you live. You feel that this statue is ugly and unpleasant to look at. Write a letter to the editor of the local newspaper explaining why you think the statue is inappropriate and asking for it to be removed.*

Write your **letter** in **300–350** words in an appropriate style.

■ 2  Before you write, think about the following points:
- Who will read the letter?
- Who do you want to influence?
- What style should the letter be written in?
- Make a note of all the points you are going to include in your letter.

✎ Remember to use the Writing Checklist on page 11.

A Matter of Taste  UNIT 7

## USE OF ENGLISH 2
### Cloze passage

**1** Before you complete the cloze passage discuss these questions with your partner.
1. What do you know about the artist John Constable?
2. Why do you think his work is popular?
3. What do you think about famous artists' work being used on souvenirs or for advertising?

**2** For questions **1–15**, read the text below and think of the word which best fits each space. Use only **one** word in each space. There is an example at the beginning (**0**).

### The Naffing of Constable

To (**0**) ____my____ mind, 'At home with Constable's Cornfield' is the worst exhibition to be put (**1**) _____ at the National Gallery in years. It would be an eyesore anywhere, but in the context (**2**) _____ Britain's finest picture collection, it is nothing (**3**) _____ of a scandal. Constable's original, and highly popular, painting is surrounded (**4**) _____ poor imitations reproduced on china, tea-trays, wallpapers, biscuit tins, etc., (**5**) _____ to mention the copied daubs of Sunday painters.

(**6**) _____ its defence, some may be tempted to say things like 'Why not show the love ordinary people have (**7**) _____ this picture?' or 'It brings in people (**8**) _____ otherwise might not come.' But this is not the purpose of the National Gallery. Its function is rather (**9**) _____ banish sentimental thinking and maintain the highest standards.

For what other comparable national institution would seek to (**10**) _____ away with such a drop in standards? (**11**) _____ football, for example. It would be like letting the canteen staff represent Manchester United in the Cup – no football fan would tolerate the integrity of the club (**12**) _____ compromised by such a sacrilege.

Indeed, engulfed in such trash, *The Cornfield* itself no (**13**) _____ looks quite so good. What's (**14**) _____ , by including photographs of the offending objects' owners in their homes, insult is (**15**) _____ to injury. The very people the exhibition intends to please are made to look silly.

**3** Which of the following words do you think best describes the writer's attitude?

| | | | |
|---|---|---|---|
| arrogant | indignant | patronizing | scornful |
| condescending | exasperated | disappointed | measured |

**4** Talk for two minutes on the following subject, using the ideas below to help you.

What do you think the role of public art galleries and museums should be?
- education
- making art accessible to all
- promoting young artists and new ideas

UNIT 7  *A Matter of Taste*

## READING 2
### Part One
*Multiple choice*

■ 1 You are going to read part of a novel about a large house in the country where a group of artists live. People interested in learning artistic skills come for short residential courses at the house. The novel is set in the 1970s.

1 What styles do you associate with the 1970s? Think about: music, art, fashion, design, etc.

2 What type of people do you think the artists are?

■ 2 Read this extract from the novel.

### FRAMLEIGH HOUSE

Two hours later, the visitors have been allocated their rooms, have unpacked their bags and learned their way about the place. They have met Toby, the owner, Paula and other members of the Framleigh Artistic Community; they have discovered the studios and the Common Room and the refectory, wandered out onto the terrace and along the prospect and back along the overgrown paths of the old kitchen garden. They have been impressed, bemused or affronted by the place according to age, inclination and experience. None of them remains unmoved, since Framleigh is, in its way, unique.

Designed by William Kent, the house itself is perhaps not outstanding. There are other eighteenth century country houses of equal or greater grace and elegance. But the park has always been considered a masterpiece, transcended only by Rousham and Stowe, the perfect manifestation of the picturesque: Hogarthian lines of beauty, sham ruins, cascades, grotto, the lot. Twenty-five acres in which the disordered was cunningly turned into a contrivance, in which the physical world was made an artistic product, in which nature became art.

All that, though, was a long time ago, and since then much has happened including the misfortune of several generations of Standishes. Toby's father failed to take advantage of the opportunities offered by mass tourism and Framleigh has gone to seed. What the course members see, as they wander about the place, is a lamentable ruin of what was, overlaid by the tastes of subsequent generations: by Victorian brick, by Edwardian insensitivity, and above all by weeds.

Elegance is now at so many removes as to seem not so much irretrievable as barely to be imagined. In the Common Room – once the drawing room – hangs an oil painting of the house in its hey-day, spruce and sparkling in a landscape clean as a whistle, the trees and grass manicured, the parterre precise as an architectural diagram. Indeed, there is something diagrammatic about the whole painting, not least the bewigged and beribboned figures parading in the foreground, doll-like men and women, impossible to think of as flesh and blood. Thus, too, the house's own previous persona seems fictional, a mythical thing from the pages of a book, its present blurred and muted state far more real and apposite.

In the painting, the houses and park appear as a contrived and ordered island amid the green ocean of the countryside. In contrast, today, the shaggy woodland of Kent's landscaped grounds is an unexpected tumult amongst the disciplined squares and oblongs of agricultural Warwickshire. Many of the trees, of course, have far outgrown the intended scale; elsewhere undergrowth

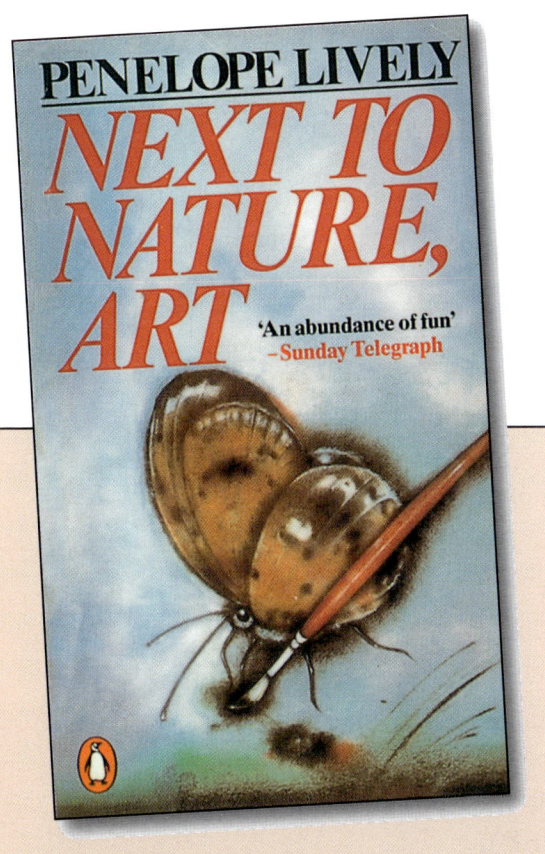

and copses have blunted the original layout; the serpentine lake has all but vanished in thickets of unquenchable rhododendron. The whole place appears to be held in check only by the estate wall: a disorderly raffish presence alongside the innocent council houses and bungalows
80 displaying their washing, greenhouses and prams where village and the entrance to Framleigh Park meet at the road.

In the same way, the inside of the house has an atmosphere not so much of graceful decay as an insensitivity to change, a kind of deafness and blindness to the world that saddles it now with peeling wallpapers, old flooring shivered into a spider's web of cracks, wheezing
90 pipes, clanking sanitation and a pervasive smell of damp. Since Toby, when up against it, has sold off most of the remaining paintings and the better pieces of furniture, the rooms are furnished with thirties stuff giving way to modern in the 'visitors' bedrooms and an element of ethnic cushions, rugs and covers introduced lately by Paula.

From *Next to Nature, Art*

■ 3  For questions **1–6**, choose the answer (**A**, **B**, **C** or **D**) which you think fits best according to the text.

1  What is the visitor's first reaction to Framleigh House?

   A  They are all equally impressed by it.
   B  They have each felt a strong reaction to it.
   C  They have all found it difficult to appreciate.
   D  They have each found different things to admire.

2  Why is the writer so impressed by the park?

   A  It is better than any other.
   B  It is in perfect harmony with the house.
   C  It shows the beauty of natural things.
   D  It was designed as a work of art.

3  What has caused Framleigh to lose its original elegance?

   A  changes of ownership
   B  tasteless alterations
   C  poor maintenance
   D  the effects of tourism

4  How does the writer feel about the painting in the Common Room?

   A  It is not well painted.
   B  It doesn't seem realistic.
   C  It seems out of place there.
   D  It may be genuine.

5  How does Framleigh Park now look different from the painting of it in the Common Room?

   A  It no longer looks so well proportioned.
   B  It no longer contrasts with the surrounding countryside.
   C  It is no longer isolated from the village.
   D  It no longer has a clearly defined boundary.

6  Why has Toby changed some of the furnishings at Framleigh House?

   A  to reflect its new use
   B  to bring it up to date
   C  for aesthetic reasons
   D  for financial reasons

UNIT 7  *A Matter of Taste*

**Part Two**
*Comprehension*

■ 1  Now read the extract again and answer these questions.

   1  Which three words in paragraph 1 indicate ways in which the visitors are different to one another?
   2  Which two nouns in paragraph 2 describe the house?
   3  Why are 'Rousham' and 'Stowe' mentioned in paragraph 2?
   4  What is 'All that' referred to in line 32?
   5  Which word in paragraph 3 tells us most about the history of the Standish family?
   6  Which idiomatic phrase in paragraph 3 describes what has happened to Framleigh in recent years?
   7  Which word in paragraph 3 gives us a sad impression of Framleigh?
   8  What do you think is meant by Framleigh's 'hey-day'? (line 49)
   9  Which idiomatic phrase in paragraph 4 is also a simile?
   10  Explain what the writer means by 'flesh and blood'. (line 58)
   11  Which word in paragraph 4 means 'in the right place'?
   12  What metaphor is used for Framleigh and the surrounding countryside in paragraph 5?
   13  In what sense do you think the rhododendrons are 'unquenchable'? (line 75)
   14  Which phrase in paragraph 5 means 'kept under control'?
   15  The estate wall is described as 'disorderly' and 'raffish' in line 78. What do you think it looks like?
   16  Which two adjectives in paragraph 6 describe noises?
   17  In what sense do you think the cushions, rugs and covers are 'ethnic'? (line 97)

## VOCABULARY 2
*Prefixes*

■ 1  Look at these three words from the extract. What do they have in common?

   **a**  overgrown (line 10)
   **b**  outgrown (line 71)
   **c**  undergrowth (line 72)

   Which is a noun? Which is an adjective? Which is a verb?

   Can you find any other examples of words formed in this way in the text?

■ 2  Complete each sentence with a word formed with *out*, *over* or *under*.

   1  There has been an _____ of food poisoning amongst the hotel's guests.
   2  She always says what she thinks; she's very _____ .
   3  The accident happened when the car was trying to _____ a lorry.
   4  The factory's _____ has more than doubled in the past eighteen months.
   5  Your landlady will wash small items like _____ , larger things must go to the laundry.

   📖 N.B. The Workbook has further work on prefixes.

## GRAMMAR 1
### Inversions

**1** Look at this sentence from the passage.

*Designed by William Kent, the house itself is not outstanding.*

1 What is the subject of the sentence?
2 Why did the writer decide to begin the sentence in this way?
3 Rewrite the sentence so that it begins with the subject.
4 How many ways are there of writing the sentence so that the subject comes first?

**2** Rewrite the following sentences so that they do not begin with the subject.

1 Bob, who is a competent potter, would be equally good at making chairs or clocks.

2 The pottery group, which is by far the most popular, meets on Mondays.

3 Paula, who feels at ease with all kinds of people, is a mixture of successful businesswoman and artist.

**3** Now, look at these sentences.

*So happy was Toby feeling that he forgot about his troubles.*
*Beautiful as the garden may be, it doesn't compare with Rousham.*

1 What is the subject in each of these sentences?
2 Rewrite them so that they begin with the subject.

3 How are they different from each other?

**4** Rewrite each of the following sentences so that they do not begin with the subject.

1 Nick was so interested by the course, he decided to change his career.

2 Valerie's work was so impressive that she was offered a pay rise.

3 John's painting may be attractive, but it's not in the same class as Paula's.

4 The course may have been enjoyable, but I'm afraid it wasn't worth the money.

N.B. The Workbook has further work on inversions.

UNIT 7  *A Matter of Taste*

## LISTENING 2
*Sentence completion*

**1** Before you listen discuss these questions with your partner.

1 What type of work do graphic designers do?
2 How is the work of a graphic designer different to that of a portrait or landscape painter?
3 How much are you influenced by the design of products and packaging when you buy things?

**2** You will hear part of a radio programme about the designs which appear on disposable kitchen towels. For questions **1–7**, listen to Part One and complete the sentences with a word or short phrase.

*A few words on kitchen towels*

The design appearing on kitchen towels influences around _____**1**_____ per cent of purchasers.

The presenter describes the market for disposal paper products as _____**2**_____.

Tests show that _____**3**_____ often feature in the designs most favoured by housewives.

Kevin Marks describes the process of getting ideas for designs as _____**4**_____.

Kevin says that in recent years, _____**5**_____ have become more popular.

Kevin says that increasingly, designs are no longer confined to the _____**6**_____ of the towels.

Most of the designers interviewed said that they preferred _____**7**_____ kitchen towels.

**3** Each of the designers goes on to talk about one design found on paper towels. As you listen to Part Two, look at the five designs below and write the speaker's name under the picture each is referring to.

1
2
3
4
5

## USE OF ENGLISH 3
*Word-building cloze*

■ 1  Read this extract from a review of a new exhibition in an art gallery. Use the words given in **capitals** at the end of some of the lines to form a word that fits in the space in the same line. There is an example at the beginning (**0**).

### Art for the Sleepless

| | |
|---|---|
| The local art gallery has (**0**) _reorganized_ its exhibits, getting rid of some of | **ORGANIZE** |
| its less successful displays to make way for new surprises. By far the | |
| most fascinating of these is the room hung with the drawings which | |
| one highly (**1**) _____ 20th-century artist did when she was unable to | **CLAIM** |
| sleep. Insomnia is a terrible affliction and (**2**) _____ get used to staring | **SUFFER** |
| at the gloomy but precise outlines of objects in the darkness with the clock | |
| (**3**) _____ stuck at 3am. At moments like this, Louise Bourgeoise would | **SEEM** |
| turn on the light, and doodle. | |
| Drawing is said to be the most personal art form and great artists (**4**) _____ | **SUPPOSE** |
| have a distinctive drawing style which is (**5**) _____ . Picasso was Picasso even | **MISTAKE** |
| in his doodles. But Bourgeoise makes no attempt, in these nocturnal jottings, | |
| to distinguish herself as an artist; to make art. Although you do (**6**) _____ | **EVENT** |
| notice the (**7**) _____ with which she weilds a biro, these sketches otherwise | **SUBTLE** |
| look exactly what they are; the spontaneous productions of a mind delirious | |
| from lack of sleep. Whether or not these doodles, done in biro on lined paper, | |
| envelopes, whatever came to hand, should really be (**8**) _____ as art, let | **CATEGORY** |
| alone put on public display, is (**9**) _____ . They do, nonetheless, provide a | **ARGUE** |
| fascinating (**10**) _____ into the mind of an important artist. | **SIGHT** |

■ 2  Which word best describes the writer's attitude towards the drawings she describes?

A  defensive
B  supportive
C  dismissive
D  derisive

■ 3  Would you be interested in seeing such an exhibition?

Would you consider it to be worthwhile art?

UNIT 7  *A Matter of Taste*

## SPEAKING 2
### Comparing and contrasting

■ 1  Look at these pictures of rooms.

Describe the rooms labelled **A** and **B** by saying what is similar and what is different about them. Talk about:

- choice of furniture/fabrics/ornaments/decorations, etc.
- arrangement of furniture, etc.
- choice of colours, textures, etc.
- lighting

■ 2  Who do you think lives in such a room?

Would you like to live there?

What are the advantages/disadvantages of the room?

What changes would you make to the room?

## WRITING 2
### Giving opinions

The Writing Paper of the examination sometimes includes a question which asks you to take two ideas and relate them to each other as you write. This type of writing needs careful planning. The following exercises are designed to help you.

**1** Think of someone you know very well, for example your best friend, a family member, your partner, or even yourself.

1  Make a list of words to describe this person under these headings:

   Physical appearance    Character    Lifestyle

2  Now think of something which reflects that person's taste, for example:
   - their taste in clothes
   - their room, flat or house
   - their car or other prized possession
   - a picture or other artistic object

   Make a list of words and phrases to describe the thing(s) you have chosen.

3  Look for connections between the two lists. In particular things which may be surprising, unexpected or interesting.

**2** Read this Writing task.

*You have read the extract below as part of a magazine article entitled 'You are what you Buy' which your teacher gave you to read. She has now asked you to write an essay entitled:*

'To what extent does the choice of the material things we surround ourselves with reflect our personality and attitude to life?'

*You should address the points raised in the extract in your essay.*

> There is no easier way to form a judgement about a new acquaintance than to be invited to visit the person concerned in their domestic environment. For people tend to surround themselves with objects that reflect their personality and attitude to life.
>
> It's true that some people are good at presenting a false picture of themselves to the outside world. They select their clothes, even cars, with a view to enhancing whatever image they would like to project.
>
> But this is not something they can keep up within the confines of their own home. A quick look at the contents of a student's bedroom or study area, therefore, will tell you everything you need to know about that individual's personality and attitude to life.

This type of task is asking for your opinion and needs to include examples to support the points you make. Before you write the essay, answer the following questions.

## UNIT 7 A Matter of Taste

1. First think about the basic idea presented in the question and decide whether you wish to:
   - agree with it
   - disagree with it
   - discuss it without coming to a conclusion

2. Now think about how to use your examples which should be taken from your lists in exercise 1 on page 145. You could, for instance:
   - compare yourself with another person/other people
   - give real-life examples of someone/people you know
   - use your ideas to talk about people in general/types of people

3. Now think about the structure of your essay. It will need an introduction, three to four paragraphs and a conclusion.

   What will you include in your introduction?
   What main point will you have in each paragraph?
   What examples will you include to support this point?

   Remember that your paragraphs should be leading to your conclusion.

   What will you include in your conclusion?

4. Think about the language that you will use in the composition. For example:

   **Exemplification**
   My brother is a good example of this. He…
   Consider the example of my cousin, Louisa. She…
   You only have to look at the average teenager to see…

   **Concession**
   Although we tend to think that…
   Despite the fact that…

   **Surprising/Unsurprising information**
   Far from being conservative in his choice of music, X is rather adventurous.
   As I had expected, she chose the…
   Strange as it may seem, his room is actually quite…
   Her choice of X was exactly what I would have expected/predicted.
   Contrary to my expectations, Jill chose…

   **Useful words and expressions**
   It's the exception which proves the rule.
   stereotypes
   generalize
   keen on
   fond of
   a (great) fan of
   to do what is expected
   to follow fashion

▶ 3  Now write your composition. Use the words and expressions in the boxes to help you. Write no more than 350 words.

✎ Remember to use the Writing Checklist on page 11.

UNIT **8**

# Go your own Way

**SPEAKING 1**
*Advertising*

■ 1  Talk to your partner about advertising. Think about:
- different types of advertising
- the best way/place to advertise the following products and services

| | | |
|---|---|---|
| food | banking services | detergents |
| clothes | children's toys | cosmetics |
| local events | music concerts | insurance |

- an advertisement you think is effective – say why
- an advertisement you especially like or dislike – say why

149

UNIT 8  *Go your own Way*

■ 2   What are the responsibilities of advertisers? Talk about:
- honesty/good taste/accuracy
- effects on people's lifestyles
- effects on people's expectations
- effects on people's expenditure
- effects on children

■ 3   What do you understand by these terms?

| merchandising | marketing | brand loyalty | trade marks | spin-offs |

■ 4   Look at these advertisements.

How effective do you think each one is?
How does it achieve its effect?

## READING 1
### Lexical cloze

**1** For questions **1–6**, read the text below and decide which answer (**A**, **B**, **C** or **D**) best fits each gap.

### Best Friend Lookalikes

Like so many commonly (**1**) _____ beliefs, the idea that dog owners look like their pets is, apparently based on fact. (**2**) _____ , one South American dog food manufacturer has based its entire advertising strategy on the theory. Of course, some dogs (**3**) _____ a much closer resemblance to their owners than others, and earlier this year, a poll of 8,000 television viewers identified the closest link in the case of collies. Examples of this breed were correctly (**4**) _____ with their owners by twice as many people as the poor bloodhound. The King Charles spaniel and golden retriever also (**5**) _____ to have a higher than average correlation. And it's not just that owners look like their dogs. According to research into facial perception (**6**) _____ by the University of St Andrews, women with big dogs tend also to have human partners weighing on average 9lbs more than the partners of women who own small dogs.

| | | | | |
|---|---|---|---|---|
| 1 | **A** kept | **B** held | **C** felt | **D** seen |
| 2 | **A** Thereby | **B** Nonetheless | **C** However | **D** Indeed |
| 3 | **A** bear | **B** catch | **C** become | **D** draw |
| 4 | **A** fitted | **B** twinned | **C** paired | **D** joined |
| 5 | **A** got round | **B** turned out | **C** brought about | **D** came across |
| 6 | **A** conducted | **B** achieved | **C** discharged | **D** fulfilled |

**2** Why do you think the dog food company chose this campaign? Do you think it will have worked? Why (not)?

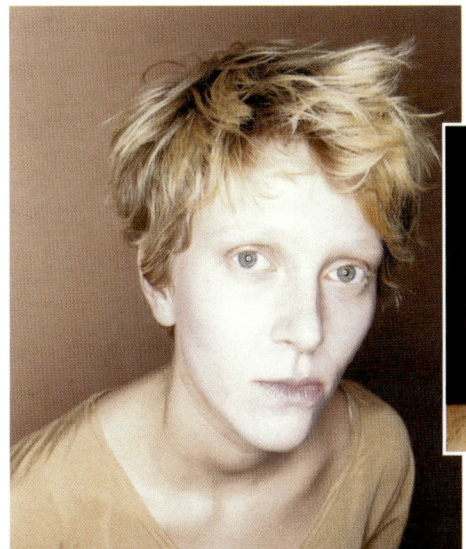

UNIT 8 *Go your own Way*

## USE OF ENGLISH 1
### Word-building cloze

■ 1  For questions **1–10**, read the text below. Use the word given in **capitals** at the end of some of the lines to form a word that fits in the space in the same line. There is an example at the beginning (**0**).

### Not quite what they seem

| | |
|---|---|
| The (**0**) _marketing_ campaigns of leading companies have long | **MARKET** |
| targeted what are known as the 'gatekeepers' in society – the select few | |
| who can drive a trend or establish a brand. Whether through advertising, | |
| (**1**) _____ or product placement, they have had such people in their | **SPONSOR** |
| (**2**) _____ as the one in ten who the rest will follow. | **SEE** |
| | |
| Now a more insidious method, pioneered in the USA, is set to take | |
| hold as advertising companies send out (**3**) _____ agents – smart | **COVER** |
| young people with charisma and (**4**) _____ talents – to market | **PERSUADE** |
| products directly in social situations. This new breed of trendsetter | |
| is paid to covertly hand out wares under the guise of (**5**) _____ | **FRIENDLY** |
| and (**6**) _____ , as in 'Would you like a cigarette – why not try | **GENEROUS** |
| one of mine?' Advertising agencies view the process as a cost- | |
| (**7**) _____ way of targeting a niche market, using the tried and tested | **EFFECT** |
| method of word of mouth. Whether or not the strategy is successful | |
| in boosting sales remains to be seen, but there may be (**8**) _____ side | **FORTUNE** |
| effects. One likely (**9**) _____ , for example, could be an increase in | **COME** |
| psychologists' waiting lists as a new neurosis grips the nation. 'But I | |
| thought he really liked me. After all, he bought me a drink/perfume/CD | |
| etc…' could become a common (**10**) _____ in consulting rooms up | **CONFESS** |
| and down the country. | |

■ 2  Which phrase from the text reinforces the idea that the companies' representatives will be acting 'covertly'? (line 10)

A  under the guise of (line 10)

B  a niche market (line 13)

C  tried and tested (line 13)

D  word of mouth (line 14)

3  How does the writer regard this new marketing method?

   A  as unlikely to succeed

   B  as something of a joke

   C  as a threat to the innocent

   D  as a cynical exercise

4  What do you think of this form of marketing?

   What type of people are likely to be influenced by it?

## SPEAKING 2
### Long turn

1  Try to speak on your own for two minutes on the topic of advertising. Choose one of these prompt cards and use the ideas on the card to help you. If you practise with a partner, remember to listen and ask a question after his/her turn.

   **Card A**

   > To what extent does advertising influence the purchasing decisions of young people?
   >
   > - images in the media
   > - branding and lifestyles
   > - information about products

   **Card B**

   > Why are some forms of marketing more effective than others?
   >
   > - target age group
   > - nature of the product
   > - new and established products

2  With a partner, continue to discuss the general theme of advertising. Talk for about four minutes, using these questions as a guide.

   - Do you think the Internet has affected advertising in any way?
   - How do you think advertising might change in the future?
   - Do you think the controls on advertising should be tighter?
   - How far do you think advertising influences your own choice of products?

UNIT 8 *Go your own Way*

## LISTENING 1
## *Matching*

**Part One**

**1** Have you ever played computer games? Talk to your partner:

- What games do you like/dislike?
- What images/stereotypes are portrayed in games? For example:
  good/bad
  male/female
  winning/losing
  competition/collaboration
- Who do you think designs the games?
- What type of people are the games designed for?
- What, if any, is the educational value of games?

**2** You will hear three young people talking about computer games. Which of the statements **A–F** best summarizes the main point each person is making?

| | | |
|---|---|---|
| **A** the games are too violent | Person 1 | _____ |
| **B** the games are improving | Person 2 | _____ |
| **C** the games are very predictable | Person 3 | _____ |
| **D** the games allow no choice of hero | | |
| **E** the games reflect real life | | |
| **F** the games use unfair stereotypes | | |

**Part Two**

**1** You will now hear two people being interviewed: Claire, a mathematics professor, and Nick, a computer game designer. They will be talking about computer games. For questions **1–9**, decide whether the opinions are expressed by only one of the speakers, or whether the speakers agree. Write **C** for Claire, **N** for Nick or **B** for Both, where they agree.

1 The students' attitudes matched my predictions.

2 Some attempts have been made to make games more attractive to girls.

3 Some people doubt the value of the games in any case.

4 The nature of the games may be a factor affecting people's career choices.

5 The makers of the games have found a very lucrative market.

6 Attempts to make a special game for girls seem appropriate.

7 Women fighters in games are a welcome development.

8 Computer games should have an educational purpose.

9 The best games are those which everyone can play equally.

## VOCABULARY 1
### Writing definitions

**1** Look at these words and expressions from the listening. In your own words, explain what each of them means in the context of the discussion.

1. a male-dominated industry
2. a subtle influence
3. counter-productive efforts
4. the odd woman
5. a token girl fighter
6. secluded market
7. lifeskills
8. to target
9. a successful formula
10. an honorary man

## WRITING 1
### Proposals

**1** In Paper 2 you may be asked to write a proposal. This will usually involve imagining yourself in a situation. Look at this example task:

*You are working for a company which makes computer games. The company is planning to introduce a new range of games that will appeal especially to young women. Write a proposal for the company recommending the type of game that should be produced and how this might be marketed.*

Write your **proposal** in **300–350** words.

**2** Using information from the listening text, plus your personal knowledge of the market for computer games in your own country, make notes under the following headings.

- The type of games on the market at the moment.
- The attitude of young women to computer games.
- The type of product your company should develop.
- How the product should be marketed and advertised.

**3** Compare your notes with your partner. Add any good ideas that your partner has to your notes.

**4** Look at the Help section on Reports and Proposals on pages 156 and 157.

**5** Now use your notes to write your proposal. Think about:
- Who will read it?
- Why they will read it?
- When and how it might be used?
- What the information will be used for?

📖 N.B. The Workbook has further work on writing proposals.

UNIT 8 *Go your own Way*

## HELP WITH WRITING: REPORTS AND PROPOSALS

Reports and proposals are both formal pieces of writing, in which the information should be well-organized, clearly laid-out and written in a style appropriate to the reader. Although reports and proposals are similar in some ways, there are important differences.

**1** Read and compare the following two Writing tasks. What are the main differences in the information that you are being asked to provide?

1 You are a member of the student committee at a large college. The college authorities have asked the committee to prepare a detailed report on the use of study facilities in the college. As secretary of the committee, you must write the report. This should give information about the use of areas provided for private study and comment on the availability of computers, as well as mentioning any other relevant factors regarding student study habits.

Write your **report** in **300–350** words.

2 You are a member of the student committee at a large college. As part of a sponsorship deal, a multinational company has donated a large sum of money to improve study facilities in the college. The college authorities have asked the committee to submit a proposal outlining how the money could be spent most effectively for the benefit of all the students.

Write your **proposal** in **300–350** words.

**2** Now discuss the following points with a partner:

- Who is the target reader in each case?
- What is the most appropriate style and layout for each text?
- How should each text be organized to reflect its content?
- What grammatical tense would you expect to use most in each text?
- What should the focus of each concluding paragraph be?

**3** The extracts from paragraphs on page 157 were written in response to each of the writing tasks in exercise 1. Give each paragraph a suitable heading.

**4** Now look carefully at the extracts from the proposal. Underline the phrases and words which can be used specifically for making recommendations in the different sections of the text.

**5** Look at the Writing task on page 155. Discuss with a partner how you would plan this proposal. Then write your **proposal** in **300–350** words.

✎ Remember to use the Writing Checklist on page 11.

Here are some more phrases which could be used in a proposal.

| | |
|---|---|
| The purpose of this proposal is to… | This scheme intends to… |
| This would be of considerable benefit to… | We feel certain that… |
| Subject to permission being granted… | We hope to develop… |
| This course of action would be… | I trust these recommendations… |

**1**

_____

As requested, this report outlines the range of study facilities currently available in the college. The information about study habits has been collected through interviews with 60 students studying at a range of levels within the college.

_____

At present, there is a large library situated in a building separate from the main college. The library contains a range of books and cassettes, in addition to a video library with a viewing room…

_____

The computer room is situated on the floor above the library and houses ten computers, all with access to the Internet. This area is very popular with the students…

_____

The main study area available to the students is within the library itself. As this is a multi-purpose area, it is frequently very crowded. This does not always create an atmosphere that is conducive to studying…

_____

The majority of students choose to study in the library as this is the largest area. The peak period for private study is between 4pm and 6pm and this is when space in the library is insufficient to meet student demand. However, not all students wish to…

_____

On the whole, the current study facilities are adequate. However, the main drawback is…

**2**

_____

This proposal is submitted by the student committee to present our recommendations for the future development of the study facilities in the college…

_____

The library is currently well-used by the students although many of the books are out of date. Some areas require supplementing and developing to reflect new courses which are now being offered. In particular, the area of science…

_____

The use of computers is now an essential part of many courses, yet the ten computers now available for student use are wholly inadequate to meet demand from students. By increasing the number of computers it would…

_____

At present, the communal study area within the library is often over-crowded, mainly because there is very little space available in the college for individual study. It would be of great benefit to the students if an area could be provided for undisturbed private study…

_____

Problems of space are most acutely felt in both the computer room and library. These areas are essential to students, but are over-used. We would recommend the conversion of the existing computer room into a private-study area. As the number of computers is presently inadequate, we would strongly suggest that a purpose-built computer room be built, capable of accommodating the increased capacity required…

_____

The above recommendations have been made after full consultation with a range of students. If carried out, these proposed improvements will have a very positive effect on the working environment in the college. We hope that our suggestions will receive your serious consideration…

UNIT 8 *Go your own Way*

## READING 2
*Gapped text*

■ 1  You are going to read an article in which a man talks about the relationships between people in the laboratory where he works. Nine sentences or phrases have been removed from the article. Read carefully and decide which of the sentences or phrases **A–I**, fits in each of the blanks **1–9**.

A  But not all lab coats are identical
B  But the hierarchy of the coat doesn't end there
C  but with a certain difference in the cut
D  my clothes are too poor to be troubled by pollution
E  protective coats come in several colours
F  take it off only to go to the refectory for lunch
G  the fact that I'm wearing it at all means that today is a lab day
H  the more senior the technician, the less likely to wear a lab coat
I  the white coat singles me out

# Lab coats

Most days, depending on the trains, I get in about nine o'clock. I dump my coat and bag in the office, pull on a white coat and head for the laboratory. The white coat is important; it has a strong symbolic value. First, **(1)** _____ , I'm running an experiment, not to be disrupted with meetings and administrative queries. Second, **(2)** _____ , separates me from the rest of the world of non-researchers, who wear no coats. It begins to envelop me in the aura of being a scientist, ready to perform mysterious – almost priestly – labours.

**(3)** _____ , there is a subtle hierarchy amongst them in which their primary function – to keep chemical and biological goo from polluting one's day clothes – has become overladen with symbolism. You don't have to be long in the lab to notice it. First, **(4)** _____ ; if you're a workshop technician, the coat is likely to be blue, if a porter, brown. There's no real reason why a researcher shouldn't wear a blue or brown coat, but the colour difference, like an army uniform is an unspoken indication of rank. If you are a lab technician, you'll wear a white coat too, **(5)** _____ – it will button differently at the neck. What's more, you'll be likely to keep it properly fastened at the front. We researchers, on the other hand, leave ours more casually open, swinging around us as we sprint down the corridor from office to lab, though the tradition is fading a bit now as biologists spend less and less time amongst chemical reagents and living things and more in the computer room watching complex multicoloured displays on screens.

**(6)** _____ . Even if they are given them free, graduate students won't wear lab coats unless they are actually doing something rather hazardous – handling radioactivity, say, when the regulations get quite severe, or a bit bloody, like a minor piece of dissection. The jeans, open collars or tee-shirts that the students wear may also be saying: **(7)** _____ and anyhow I don't want to be fenced in by regulations. At the other end of the hierarchy the rules shift again; **(8)** _____ . Here the message is that I have graduated from lab to office, away from the manual towards mental labour.

Not true for the senior researchers; many who have not been near the lab in years nonetheless put on a spotless white coat each morning as they arrive, sit behind their office desk in it, **(9)** _____ and when they leave for home at 5.30. They'll even go to committee meetings in their lab coats. Again the message is pretty clear: I would like to be down in the lab actually doing experiments with all you guys, I'm just too busy at the moment with a paper, a grant, a committee; but I haven't lost touch with what really matters, and I can still make a scientific contribution, not just an administrative one.

## 2

The article describes a hierarchy. Complete the grid with information about this hierarchy.

| Position in hierarchy | Type of person | Type of coat worn | Their attitude towards the coat |
|---|---|---|---|
| | | | |

## 3

Now read the article again and answer these questions.

1. Which verb in paragraph 1 means 'arrive at work'?
2. What impression is given by the use of the word 'dump'? (line 1)
3. Which verb in paragraph 1 means 'go towards'?
4. In your own words, explain the meaning of the phrase 'envelop me in the aura'. (lines 5–6)
5. Why has the writer chosen the word 'priestly' in line 6 to describe the scientist's work?
6. Which word in paragraph 2 means 'a dirty substance'?
7. What impression does the writer give by using the word 'sprint' in line 16?
8. Which word in paragraph 3 is used to mean 'for example'?
9. Which word in paragraph 3 means 'restricted'?
10. In what way have some scientists 'graduated'? (line 25)
11. Which word in the last paragraph means 'clean'?
12. What does the phrase 'what really matters' in lines 31–32 refer to?

UNIT 8 *Go your own Way*

## SPEAKING 3
### *Expressing opinions*

■ 1   The article on page 158 talks about symbols of hierarchies. Discuss these questions with your partner.

1  What hierarchies do you see around you?

2  Talk about the following areas and the status symbols related to them. Think about:

- rich/poor people
- young/old people
- students/employees
- work/leisure

in relation to:

> houses    cars    clothes    hobbies    sports
> food and drink    consumer durables

■ 2   Look at the three photographs. Talk about the people in them in terms of:

- where they stand in a hierarchy
- where they stand in relation to the people around them
- how you think they feel about their situation.

*Go your own Way* UNIT 8

UNIT 8 *Go your own Way*

## USE OF ENGLISH 2
*Cloze passage*

**1** Look at these idiomatic phrases. What do they have in common?

a keep to the straight and narrow
b take a short cut
c step out of line
d follow in someone's footsteps
e toe the party line
f he didn't put a foot wrong

Now match each of the expressions **a–f** to one of the definitions **1–6**.

1 follow official policy
2 find a quicker way
3 don't deviate from the norm
4 repeat another's experience
5 mistakes were avoided
6 do something unacceptable

**2** For questions **1–15**, read the text below and think of the word which best fits each space. Use only **one** word in each space. There is an example at the beginning (**0**).

### Strolling by Numbers

Public parks might be more user-friendly if planners (**0**) ___took___ a mathematical look at their designs. A team of researchers has shown that when left to their (**1**) _____ devices, pedestrians create a complex pattern of paths across grassy areas.

The team was intrigued (**2**) _____ the fact that in many parks, the trails left by walkers do not usually mirror the direct routes (**3**) _____ entry and exit points. So, they set (**4**) _____ to predict how the trails in a new park would evolve as pedestrians chose their favourite routes.

Several factors influence such choices. People usually choose a direct route to their destination, taking any available short cuts, but they also prefer walking on worn trails to trampling over rougher ground. In (**5**) _____ words, it's more convenient to take existing trails than to create new ones. Also, the closer a segment of an existing trail is to an individual, the more tempting it appears to be.

Using these assumptions, the team came (**6**) _____ with a computer simulation in which they opened a square park with a gate at (**7**) _____ corner to a crowd of virtual pedestrians. Each pedestrian had a fixed starting point and destination, and started at a randomly chosen time.

At (**8**) _____ , when the land was uniformly green with no worn trails, the pedestrians took the six possible direct routes to their destinations. (**9**) _____ , not every route was used by the (**10**) _____ number of people, and this (**11**) _____ to some paths becoming clearer than others.

As later walkers started to gravitate (**12**) _____ these well-trodden routes, the trails started to bunch together, eventually leaving a circuit with an island in the centre – a pattern that naturally appears time and (**13**) _____ in city parks. In effect, the path system shortens (**14**) _____ use, until the pattern matches the (**15**) _____ compromise for comfort and brevity for the largest number of people. Most people are quite happy to follow in each others' footsteps after all, it seems.

**3** What conclusions about human nature might you make from the results of this research?

## WRITING 2
### Newspaper articles

**1** What makes people want to either:
   **a** follow society's conventions?
   **b** rebel against society's conventions?

**2** You are going to read an article about people who have dropped out of society in the USA. These people, who describe themselves as 'gutter punks', live on the streets. What do you expect to read about:
   - their appearance/clothes?
   - their lifestyle/attitudes?
   - the reasons for their lifestyle?
   - other people's opinion of them?

**3** Now read the article and answer the questions that follow.

## BOHEMIA HOSTS ALIENATED TRIBE

**As evening falls, the tribe gathers by the river to forage for something to eat, drink or smoke. There is safety in numbers. Wearing studded dog collars, their mohawk haircuts dyed orange and green, their lips and nipples pierced, the tribe lives on the streets, rejecting mainstream America as inane, materialistic and hypocritical.**

They call themselves 'gutter punks', and they are a new kind of homeless person: white, middle class, often bright, politically militant and homeless by choice. Few are older than 21. Their appearance and their lifestyle may seem a nightmare to their parents and much of society, as if all the promise of youth in America had been turned inside out, producing nihilistic, angry ironic spawn dressed in black – the result of decades of family disintegration, suburban boredom and cynicism.

America has always had its rebels, but where hippies espoused peace, love and a return to the land, today's punks are different. Their world is dark, urban and dangerous. Many drink and do drugs not to have visions, but to black out. 'I only live for three reasons,' says Eric, aged 20, stumbling around the French quarter of New Orleans. 'To drink, to fight and to screw. I'm an escape artist.'

Yet earlier on Hippie Hill that looks out on the quarter's picturesque Jackson Square, Becca, aged 18, who is sober, sweet-faced and carrying a sleepy puppy said: 'People are afraid of us, but we're not the ones who are scary.'

'Tribe' is a word many of them use to describe their sub-culture, complete with ritualistic piercing, tattooing and adornment. New Orleans, a winter haven, probably has thousands in the street at any one time. 'But numbers are really hard to guess', says Paul Rigsby, a private detective who tracks runaways. 'These kids are as migratory as Canada geese.'

New Orleans has everything that punks want: abandoned buildings to squat in, a Bohemian atmosphere and opportunities to pick up food and drink in the street. The number of punks in New Orleans has grown so large that traders and politicians in the French quarter have begun to complain about public urination, drunkenness and fights. Traders circulated a picture of punks entitled: 'Don't feed the animals'. The punks say they are hassled by the police all the time. Homelessness campaigners say the punks are often 'swept' from the streets before big local events.

1   Circle all the words used in the text to describe the punks.

2   Underline the parts of the passage where the punks talk about themselves.

3   Underline the parts of the passage where the writer gives his explanation of why the punks behave as they do.

4   Underline the parts of the passage where we hear other people's opinion of the punks.

5   What style is the article written in? Who do you think is the intended audience?

6   How would the article have been different if it had been written for:
    - young people?
    - local people?
    - people who want to help the punks?

**4**   Using information from the article, but in your own words and in an appropriate style, write either:

1   An article for a local newspaper complaining about the punks and suggesting what should be done about the problem.

2   An article for a young people's magazine that describes the life of the punks in a more positive way.

3   An article for a serious magazine read by people who want to understand and help solve such social problems.

Write your **article** in **300–350** words.

## LISTENING 2
### Part One
### *Three-option multiple choice*

**1**   Look at the expressions in the box below. They are from the extracts you are about to listen to. Which expression suggests feelings of:
   - modesty?
   - embarrassment?
   - enjoyment?
   - anger?
   - ability?
   - weakness?
   - uneasiness?

| | |
|---|---|
| to avert one's eyes | to be adept at something |
| to have qualms about something | to relish something |
| to be livid | to give in to temptation    to feel shabby |

## 2
You will hear three extracts from a radio programme about personal integrity. For questions **1–6**, choose the answer (**A**, **B** or **C**) which fits best according to what you hear.

**Extract One**

1 What is the woman talking about?

   A other people's letters
   B other people's diaries
   C other people's conversations

2 How does feel about what she does?

   A unembarrassed
   B indifferent
   C contrite

**Extract Two**

3 What is the man talking about?

   A letters
   B diaries
   C conversations

4 What feeling does he express?

   A anger at his own weakness
   B regret about his past actions
   C shame at giving in to temptation

**Extract Three**

5 What is the woman doing when she speaks?

   A justifying a form of social behaviour
   B questioning an accepted practice
   C criticizing a common attitude

6 In her view, what she calls 'controlled dishonesty' is

   A unattainable.
   B unacceptable.
   C unavoidable.

## 3
Listen to Extracts One and Two again and answer the following questions.

1 Which of the speakers used which of the expressions in the box in exercise 1 on page 164?

2 How do you feel about invasions of privacy like these?

## 4
In what situations do you think honesty is important? Talk about:

- friends and acquaintances
- parents and children
- doctors and patients
- politicians
- research scientists

UNIT 8 *Go your own Way*

**Part Two**
***Sentence completion***

■ 1  You are going to hear part of a radio discussion on the subject of scientific deception. Before you listen, look at the list of words and phrases in the box. These are from the listening text. Use them to discuss these questions.

- What do you think scientific deception is?
- What types of activity do you think it includes?
- What problems do you think might be associated with scientific deception and its discovery and investigation?

| | | | |
|---|---|---|---|
| deceit | fiddling | fraud | misconduct |
| proof | reputation | trust | sloppiness |
| to falsify something | to point the finger | to blow the whistle | |
| to cut corners | to turn a blind eye | to make an honest mistake | |

■ 2  You will hear part of a radio discussion on the subject of scientific deception. For questions **1–10**, complete the sentences with a word or short phrase.

*Scientific deception*

Derek says that tackling scientific deception is made more difficult by the absence of ⬚ **1** .

Derek describes ⬚ **2** as a mild form of scientific deception.

The most common form of scientific deception involves ⬚ **3** existing pieces of research.

Derek explains that ⬚ **4** plays an important role in all science.

Heather explains that successful science often involves an element of ⬚ **5** .

Heather explains that fraud cannot always be distinguished from an ⬚ **6** .

'Whistle-blowers' often find themselves accusing their ⬚ **7** of deception.

It's important that those exposing scientific deception have what Derek calls ⬚ **8** .

Heather explains that, in most cases, it's difficult to prove that there is what's termed ⬚ **9** to deceive.

Derek and Heather advocate the setting up of ⬚ **10** to look into the problem.

**3** What do you think about the problem of scientific deception? Look at these comments different people have made about the problem and say to what extent you agree with them.

- it's a scandal that should be exposed publicly
- it's not a problem as long as it does no harm to anyone
- it's not fair to blame individuals if everyone's doing it
- it's an inevitable result of human nature
- it's a serious crime which should be punished severely
- I'm sure there are much worse things going on that we don't know about

## GRAMMAR 1

**1** What is the difference between *deceit* and *deception*? What are the adjectives and adverbs formed from each word?

**2** Complete each of these sentences with a verb, noun, adjective or adverb formed from the verb *to deceive*.
1 The puzzle looked _____ easy, but proved very difficult to solve.
2 I don't really trust Lucy; I think she's a really _____ person.
3 That young scientist is not as naive as he seems, you know, appearances can be _____ .
4 I'm afraid Polly is only _____ herself if she thinks her work looks original.
5 It's the quickness of the hand that _____ the eye.

## PHRASAL VERBS 1

**1** Look at this sentence from the listening. Underline the phrasal verb.
*Young scientists are often the ones who come across these things.*

**2** Complete each sentence with a suitable preposition.
1 John burst _____ the room and told everybody what he had discovered.
2 In the course of the investigation, the scientists came up _____ a number of problems.
3 Whistle-blowers cannot necessarily count _____ the support of their colleagues.
4 It's unlikely that anyone would get _____ with copying whole pieces of someone else's work.
5 A committee is being set _____ to look _____ the whole area of scientific deception.
6 His story was very convincing to the layman, but other scientists saw _____ it immediately.
7 The team came _____ with four simple equations to illustrate their point.
8 The researchers set _____ to predict how trails in a new park would work.

# UNIT 8 Go your own Way

## EXAM PRACTICE 8

**1** For questions **1–12**, read the two texts below and decide which answer (**A**, **B**, **C** or **D**) best fits each gap.

### The Whole Truth

Pay their wages but don't tell researchers what to write. That is the message to drugs companies from the medical establishment this week. Several leading medical journals announced that they are taking a tougher (**1**) _____ on publishing the results of clinical trials funded by the pharmaceuticals industry. Their action has been (**2**) _____ by concerns that companies sponsoring the research are trying to influence the design and interpretation of trials, and that unpalatable results are being (**3**) _____ under the carpet. (**4**) _____ the pharmaceuticals industry may protest, these concerns are well founded. Surveys show that company-funded trials are more likely to (**5**) _____ positive results than independent studies. From now on, many journals will publish papers only if the main authors, not the sponsor, make the final decision on publication. To achieve this, the journals will ask authors of papers to sign a statement declaring that they had access to all the data, and accepting full responsibility for the (**6**) _____ of the trial and its findings.

| 1 | **A** view | **B** bearing | **C** posture | **D** stance |
|---|---|---|---|---|
| 2 | **A** pressed | **B** prompted | **C** urged | **D** implored |
| 3 | **A** swept | **B** held | **C** dusted | **D** hidden |
| 4 | **A** Despite | **B** As regards | **C** Notwithstanding | **D** However much |
| 5 | **A** pay | **B** yield | **C** earn | **D** gain |
| 6 | **A** comportment | **B** demeanour | **C** conduct | **D** behaviour |

### The Commercial Persuaders

These days, advertisers seldom attempt to sell *things*; rather they sell lifestyle images. There was a time when adverts were used to (**7**) _____ the quality of a product. If they were trying to sell you a spade, they would tell you that the spade was well balanced and durable, that it (**8**) _____ the functions of a spade as well as possible. Now if you buy the spade you are promised, by (**9**) _____ , a whole new lifestyle. (**10**) _____ , the advertisers seem to think they can buy anything and anyone to promote their products. That's probably because they can. They pay fortunes to people we admire so that those people will do the persuading. When a great sportsman achieves some extraordinary (**11**) _____ , the only question he has to ask is which products he will sponsor and how much they will pay him. When Michael Jordan announced he was retiring from basketball he (**12**) _____ tens of millions off the value of shares in the American firm whose trainers he advertised.

| | | | | | | | |
|---|---|---|---|---|---|---|---|
| 7 | **A** spotlight | **B** climax | **C** highlight | **D** focus |
| 8 | **A** performed | **B** satisfied | **C** rendered | **D** accomplished |
| 9 | **A** connection | **B** association | **C** affiliation | **D** correlation |
| 10 | **A** On the contrary | **B** Instead | **C** Otherwise | **D** What is more |
| 11 | **A** feat | **B** effort | **C** deed | **D** upshot |
| 12 | **A** brushed | **B** cleaned | **C** wiped | **D** swept |

**2** For questions **1–5**, think of **one** word only which can be used appropriately in all three sentences.

**1** The scientists only managed to _____ the problem after months of painstaking research.

Although they had sophisticated computer equipment, the police were unable to _____ the gang's secret code.

I think you should take a holiday Frank, I'd hate to see you _____ under the pressure of all this work.

**2** During the _____ of her research, Tanya uncovered some disturbing information about her boss.

The local football team are well on _____ for their third championship victory in four years.

The accuracy of all the available data is checked as a matter of _____ .

**3** I tried to _____ from my mind the memory of that awful day.

Sam was inclined to _____ as unimportant the complaints of the colleagues working under him.

After discovering that money had gone missing from the cashbox, Teresa had no choice but to _____ her dishonest assistant.

**4** The two organisms are very similar and can only be reliably _____ with the aid of a microscope.

Sir Peter is a very _____ looking old gentleman, who had a long career in the diplomatic service.

A very _____ firm of lawyers has been engaged to advise the company on contractual matters.

**5** Enthusiasm for the new project tended to _____ away after the initial burst of enthusiasm.

Before the new building can be constructed, the contractors will need to _____ the site, which is in an area of wetland.

The central heating engineer said he would need to _____ the hot water system before he could mend the pipes.

# UNIT 9

# Nose to the Grindstone

**SPEAKING 1**

*Talking together about a visual prompt*

1. Look at the four pictures of people working and for each one talk about:
   - the skills required for the job
   - the financial rewards
   - the job satisfaction
   - the advantages and disadvantages

2. How important are the following factors when choosing a career?

   | | |
   |---|---|
   | money | job security |
   | convenience | challenge |
   | prospects | social aspects |
   | variety | status |

   opportunities for travel, training, creativity, etc.

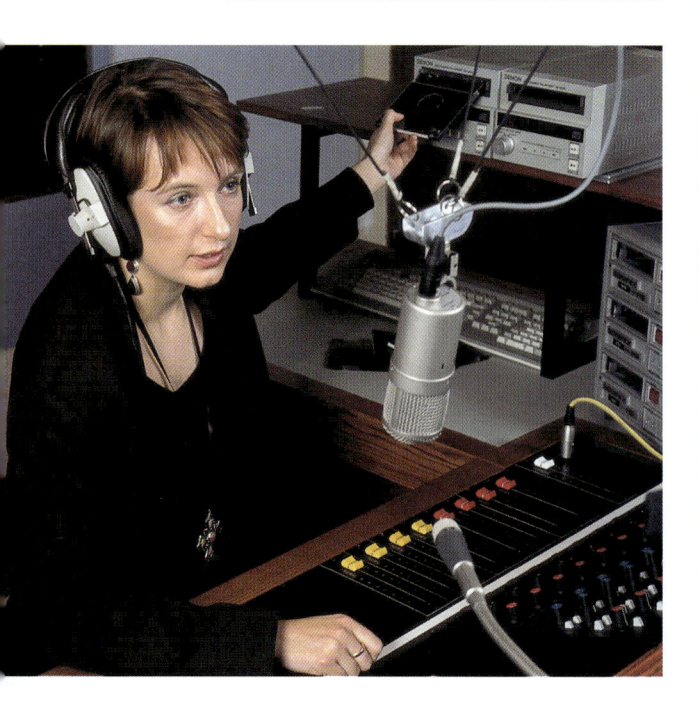

Nose to the Grindstone  **UNIT 9**

## READING 1
*Lexical cloze*

■ 1   For questions **1–12**, read the two job advertisements below and decide which answer (**A**, **B**, **C** or **D**) best fits each gap.

■ 2   Both passages are job advertisements which were placed in a scientific magazine by large companies. Compare and contrast them in terms of:

- the style of writing
- the use of language
- their effect on the reader

> **The post of**
> **Operations Engineer**
> **has been created following the restructuring of the department.**
>
> The post requires excellent management ability (1) _____ with a high level of scientific competence.
> Applicants must (2) _____ a minimum of four year's experience as a B grade clinical scientist and have a solid (3) _____ in electronic engineering, together with substantial experience of equipment management and development.
> Applicants must have a first degree in a relevant scientific subject and (4) _____ a higher degree or management qualification.
> Essential personal (5) _____ are self-motivation, commitment to working as part of a team and the ability to communicate well with other staff at all levels.
> The (6) _____ date for applications is 15th June.

1  **A** linked         **B** joined       **C** coupled      **D** added
2  **A** gain           **B** hold         **C** do           **D** have
3  **A** grounding      **B** setting      **C** footing      **D** upbringing
4  **A** arguably       **B** preferably   **C** actually     **D** eventually
5  **A** qualities      **B** aspects      **C** traits       **D** features
6  **A** stoppage       **B** completion   **C** terminal     **D** closing

171

UNIT 9 *Nose to the Grindstone*

## COME AND JOIN US

As a formulation chemist, you'll be right at the (7) _____ of the things we do here, working with equally able people from many different disciplines and with the latest lab equipment at your (8) _____ .

You will apply chemistry to the design and preparation of samples and use a range of techniques to analyse them. It's work that will use and (9) _____ the knowledge you gained in your degree course and it will test and develop your ability to work (10) _____ others, responding to their great ideas as well as developing your own.

Finally, if you want to see acres of green (11) _____ tonnes of concrete, you'll feel totally at home working with us in Berkshire.

**Please apply in writing with a full CV and (12) _____ letter.**

| | | | | |
|---|---|---|---|---|
| 7 | A essence | B entity | C gist | D heart |
| 8 | A use | B disposal | C ease | D perusal |
| 9 | A count in | B build on | C stand by | D draw off |
| 10 | A alongside | B sidelong | C adjacent | D besides |
| 11 | A by choice | B in preference | C opposed to | D instead of |
| 12 | A enclosing | B attendant | C covering | D supplementary |

### SPEAKING 2
*Giving opinions*

■ 1  What makes a good employee? Make a list of the personal qualities you would look for if you were employing someone.

■ 2  What is the best way to recruit staff? Talk about the advantages and disadvantages of each of the following as a way of selecting people:
- application form
- references
- interview
- trial period
- personality test
- personal recommendation

Nose to the Grindstone **UNIT 9**

# USE OF ENGLISH 1
## Cloze passage

■ 1  For questions **1–15**, read the text below and think of the word which best fits each space. Use only **one** word in each space. There is an example at the beginning (**0**).

### When Caruso Met Puccini

The story of how Enrico Caruso, the great operatic tenor, first met composer Giacomo Puccini (**0**) ___could___ easily have come from a Hollywood musical, if (**1**) _____ from opera itself.

Imagine (**2**) _____ scene. A young man and woman are in love. She is to star in a show; he wishes to play opposite her, (**3**) _____ he is unknown. She challenges (**4**) _____ to audition before the composer himself; he accepts, overrides all obstacles of protocol, and performs with (**5**) _____ stunning artistry and style that the part (**6**) _____ instantly his.

Unfortunately, our lover did not quite (**7**) _____ the part. He was short and tubby, with an undistinguished moustache and an undesirable accent. It was the composer (**8**) _____ was handsome and debonair.

What our lover (**9**) _____ have, however, (**10**) _____ the optimism of youth. With all the engaging audacity of a film hero, Enrico Caruso, (**11**) _____ very badly to sing Rudolfo in *La Boheme*, arrived unannounced one day in June 1897, at the Tuscan home of Giacomo Puccini. He was admitted under protest. Puccini, a wide brimmed hat on his head, ushered him into a studio made stifling (**12**) _____ a roaring fire. Perspiring from heat and nervousness, Caruso asked to sing from the opera. Puccini obligingly sat down at the piano. It (**13**) _____ only a few bars for the composer to realize (**14**) _____ in tone and dramatic intensity here was the perfect, the ultimate, Rudolfo. With the final note, Puccini spun (**15**) _____ in genuine amazement. 'Who has sent you to me,' he asked, 'God?'

(Adapted from an article by Nancy Caldwell Sorel in *The Independent*.)

■ 2  Find words in the passage that mean:

a  official or accepted procedure
b  very best possible area
c  extremely impressive
d  rather overweight
e  trial performance by an applicant for a job in the performing arts
f  well mannered
g  daring
h  hot and airless
i  sweating

UNIT 9 *Nose to the Grindstone*

## LISTENING 1
### Three-option multiple choice

■ 1   You will hear three employers talking about recruiting staff through interviews. For questions **1–6**, choose the answer (**A**, **B** or **C**) which fits best according to what you hear.

**Extract One**

1  What area does the speaker work in?

   A  retailing
   B  telesales
   C  information technology

2  What does she advise interview candidates to do?

   A  prepare what you're going to say
   B  do some research
   C  ask lots of questions

**Extract Two**

3  What field does the speaker recruit for?

   A  book publishing
   B  newspaper journalism
   C  current affairs broadcasting

4  He says that applicants need to show that they can

   A  respond to the needs of the situation.
   B  remain cool in the face of criticism.
   C  work within a hierarchical structure.

**Extract Three**

5  This speaker explains that she's looking for people who

   A  have a broad range of skills.
   B  can demonstrate a flexible approach.
   C  are clearly focused on the needs of the job.

6  What job does she recruit for?

   A  market research interviewer
   B  raw materials buyer
   C  personnel manager

## VOCABULARY 1
### Definitions

■ 1   Look at these expressions used in the listening texts. In your own words, explain what each one means:

   a  to go down well or badly
   b  to let themselves down
   c  to go over the top
   d  to get you down
   e  to back down
   f  to get something going
   g  to go against someone
   h  to get down to the nitty gritty

## WRITING 1
### Formal letters 1

■ 1   Imagine you have to interview someone for each of the jobs advertised below. With your partner, draw up a list of questions you would want to ask each person applying for each of the jobs.

> We are looking for a reliable person to look after William (aged 3) and Sophie (aged 2). Only experienced nannies or au pairs with good references need apply. We provide clean accommodation, full board, plus every Sunday off. Competitive salary. We are based in London and would offer a 4-month contract to the right person; renewable by mutual consent.
>
> Please apply in writing, giving full personal details and enclosing a photograph to:
>
> Mr & Mrs Sloane, P.O. Box 251, London W1

> **Are you: patient? flexible? responsible? reliable? good in a crisis? and fun?**
>
> If so, you could be the type of person we are looking for. We need someone to spend time with Paul (8), Samantha (11) and Jason (13) over the summer holidays. They like computers, animals and mountain bikes. We like peace and quiet. Full board provided, plus some time off. Rural location. If you think this sounds like you, write telling us all about yourself to:
>
> Simon & Kate Freeman, Forest Cottage, near Mowtown, England.

■ 2   Imagine that you are interested in applying for one of these two jobs.

Write a letter to the employer in which you:
- introduce yourself
- say why you think you would be suitable
- ask for more information about the job

You may write about your real self or invent the information if you prefer.

■ 3   Before you write anything, talk to your partner and make notes. Think about:
- the information you should include (e.g. family background, education, experience, hobbies, personality, etc.)
- the order in which things are presented
- the layout and organization of the letter
- the appropriate style for the letter

■ 4   Use your notes to plan your letter. Then write it in **300–350** words.

UNIT 9 Nose to the Grindstone

## READING 2
*Multiple choice*

**1** Discuss these points with your partner.

What are the advantages and disadvantages of:
- working mothers?
- nannies?
- nursery schools?

**2** Read the article about nannies.

# DOES MUMMY KNOW BEST?

**FOR WORKING WOMEN,** entrusting children to a stranger is often a necessity. But, the subject of nannies, like hunting, is guaranteed to turn the most mild-mannered person into a ranting omniscient fiend.

When I first hired a nanny, three years ago, half my friends were appalled. What is the point of having children, they said, if you're not prepared to look after them? They cited Sigmund Freud's widely accepted theory about the first five years of life being the ones that determine behaviour throughout life. Was I really willing to leave this most onerous of tasks to a stranger? Was I prepared for the hideous eventuality of having my son love his nanny more than he did me?

The other half, old nanny hands themselves, whooped for joy. I had seen the light, they said. I would now be fulfilled by my work as well as by my child, and would as a result be a better mother. You need adult company sometimes, they said, and intellectual stimulation. Children are lovely, but lovelier still if you have the odd break from them. They'll always love you more, because you are their mother – thinking otherwise is simply paranoia. And you need to earn your own money to keep your self respect. What do you want to be – a housewife? Pull the other one.

Judge not, lest you be judged. The first rule of parenting is not to cast aspersions on the way other people bring up their children. But with the best will in the world, it is hard to watch *Quality Time*, a documentary about working mothers, nannies and children to be screened on *BBC2* next week, without getting angry. It isn't that all three women – Janis, who works in public relations, Caroline, a beauty PR, and Dominique, a clothing executive – employ nannies. Nannies, after all, are a fact of life for many working women.

What is so shocking, in a programme that will surely go down as one of the great TV stitch-ups, is the women's apparent disregard for their children's emotional well-being. One gets the impression that not one of them knows her child, or even wants to. 'I'm not used to children,' deadpans one of the mothers. 'After all, I've only had them for five years.' And if that little admission doesn't make your jaw drop, I don't know what will.

Dominique has two nannies on duty 24 hours a day, one for each little daughter. And a weekend nanny too, of course. And a holiday nanny. According to one nanny, Dominique has never – not once – got up in the night to comfort her crying child. You get the picture? Her daughters do: they see their mother so little that they take her photograph to bed with them to talk to.

Heartbroken sobbing permeates the programme, as almost all of the children featured learn that their beloved nanny – the one who plays, kisses, comforts, gets up in the night – has gone away for a long 'holiday'. Again. 'So far we've had sixteen nannies,' says Caroline's five-year-old daughter. Actually it has only been six, but out of the mouths of babes…

What's so grotesquely compelling about the documentary is the casual, systematic way that the children – outwardly privileged – are emotionally bludgeoned before our eyes. They evidently have only a minimal attachment to their absentee mothers: that privilege is reserved for their nannies. And the nannies keep disappearing. No one explains why, so the bewildered children just cry, harder each time, as any sense of security they might once have enjoyed becomes ever more eroded.

That this will result in emotionally damaged children would be blindingly obvious to an amoeba – but not, apparently, to this trio of mothers in their power suits. But what if this style of parenting isn't bad, just honest? Should we admire Caroline for admitting she's 'not very good with children' despite having two of her own? 'I was getting on', she says in the film, 'I thought I might as well have them'. When I speak to her later she says, 'I had them very late. I'm a career woman!'

It is, conceivably, brave to identify your weak spot – children – and let others take care of it, while you concentrate on what you are good at: work. Of her weak spot, Caroline says, 'I know I wouldn't be much fun with them all day every day. I'm not motherly in that way.' Janis meanwhile, sees nothing amiss in her two-year-old daughter having had six nannies, including a maternity nurse. 'Because she has been looked after by so many people, she is very independent,' says Janis, 'On her first day at school, she just breezed in'. Caroline agrees. 'The girls are amazingly unfazed by the succession of nannies. They know we are coming home at the end of the day.'

I suggest that it must be nice for the girls to know that their mother will be there to give them breakfast and put them to bed. 'Actually, the nanny gives them breakfast – I'm busy getting ready,' is the reply. 'Sometimes I don't see them at all in the mornings. It doesn't bother me or the girls.'

Since I have given the three women featured in *Quality Time* a hard time, perhaps I should give them a chance to do it to me. I packed my job in – and the £50,000 a year that went with it – to become a housewife. Because I believe that little children need their mothers. And the best nanny in the world is no substitute for the worst mother. Basically, I think that if you have children you should look after them.

**3** Now answer the questions **1–7**. Choose the answer (**A**, **B**, **C** or **D**) which you think fits best according to the text.

1 When the writer first employed a nanny

   A   most of her friends disapproved.
   B   some of her friends deserted her.
   C   none of her friends were surprised.
   D   all of her friends reacted strongly.

2 The friends described in the third paragraph are women who

   A   have worked as nannies.
   B   had nannies themselves as children.
   C   have employed nannies themselves.
   D   have no children of their own.

3 In the writer's opinion, parents watching the programme should not

   A   get angry at the three women.
   B   expect other families to behave like them.
   C   take the programme too seriously.
   D   criticize the lifestyle of other families.

4 What does the writer feel most strongly about with regard to the TV programme?

   A   The women's attitude to their children.
   B   The TV company's attitude to the women.
   C   The level of responsibility given to nannies.
   D   The intrusion of the programme into private affairs.

5 What causes most problems for the children seen in the film?

   A   lack of affection
   B   turnover of staff
   C   inconsistent discipline
   D   poorly trained nannies

6 How do the children's mothers feel about the situation?

   A   They are aware of the problems.
   B   They refuse to accept any criticisms.
   C   They try to justify their decisions.
   D   They blame their staff for any difficulties.

7 The writer's general attitude towards working mothers, as revealed in the last paragraph is

   A   critical.
   B   sceptical.
   C   indifferent.
   D   sympathetic.

4  Find these expressions in the article. In your own words, explain what the writer means by each of them.

1  pull the other one (line 28)
2  to cast aspersions (line 30)
3  the best will in the world (lines 31–32)
4  make your jaw drop (lines 47–48)
5  you get the picture (lines 53–54)
6  outwardly privileged (line 67)
7  getting on (line 83)
8  sees nothing amiss (line 93)
9  breezed in (line 98)
10  unfazed (line 99)
11  packed... in (lines 111–112)

5  Discuss these questions with your partner.

- Do you have any sympathy with the women in the programme?
- In what way might the programme have been unfair?
- What style of writing has the writer adopted? Why?
- Where would you expect to find this article?
- What type of person would read it?
- Would they agree with it?

## WRITING 2
### Formal letters 2

1  Write one of the following letters to the journalist.

1  A letter from one of the mothers defending yourself and complaining about how the programme was made.

2  A letter from a working mother or a nanny pointing out that not all children with working mothers suffer in the ways described in the article.

3  A letter from somebody who agrees with the points made in the article, quoting personal experience.

## SPEAKING 3
### Discussing proverbs

1  Look at these two proverbs which the writer quotes in the article.

*judge not lest you be judged*
*out of the mouths of babes...*

Why did the writer choose to use these expressions?

2  Look at these proverbs and sayings and discuss the extent to which they reflect truths about the society in which we live. Do they have equivalents in your language?

a  one man's meat is another man's poison
b  like father like son
c  clothes maketh the man
d  people who live in glass houses shouldn't throw stones

## USE OF ENGLISH 2
### Nouns formed from phrasal verbs

**1** Look at this phrase from the article on pages 176 and 177.

*The programme will surely go down as one of the great TV stitch-ups.*

What is a *stitch-up*?

This compound noun is formed from the phrasal verb *to stitch (someone) up*. Notice that this noun is hyphenated. Other nouns of this type are single words, e.g. *feedback*, although the order of the words may change, e.g. *an outbreak of flu*.

**2** Complete each sentence with a noun formed from a phrasal verb. Use the verb in brackets.

1 Police are on the _____ for a man with dark hair and a grey moustache. (look)
2 John apologized for his angry _____ during the discussion. (burst)
3 Mr Smith was delayed as he had a _____ on the motorway. (break)
4 Sally is responsible for cleaning, repairs and the general _____ of the building. (keep)
5 The meeting finished without reaching a satisfactory _____ . (come)
6 Scientists have announced a _____ in their search for a cure for the disease. (break)
7 The company has reported an _____ in its profits this year. (turn)
8 I am not working this evening, but I can't go out because I am on _____ . (stand)

**3** Phrasal verbs can also be used to form adjectives. Look at the example.

*The breakdown truck moved slowly because it was towing a damaged car.*

**4** Complete each of these sentences with an adjective formed from a phrasal verb. Use the verb in brackets.

1 Louise looked in the mirror, sighed, and reached for her _____ bag. (make)
2 Mary couldn't be bothered to cook, so she bought a _____ pizza on her way home. (take)
3 Jim found the interviewer's abrupt manner very _____ . (put)
4 Dawn is an _____ tennis player who has won many championships. (stand)
5 Mr Thomas, flying to Miami, is asked to return to the _____ desk where his boarding card is ready for collection. (check)
6 The family business was the subject of a _____ bid by a large multi-national company. (take)

UNIT 9 *Nose to the Grindstone*

## HELP WITH THE WRITING PAPER

In the exam you will have two hours to complete Paper 2, the Writing Paper. There are two parts to the paper. Part One is a compulsory task which involves writing an article, essay, letter or proposal. In this part, you are given a short text to respond to or base your piece of writing on. In Part Two, you have to answer one question from a choice of four. You may be asked to write an article, letter, proposal, review or report. Remember that question five always relates to the set books, so do not attempt to answer this question unless you have studied one of the set books in detail. It is up to you to use the available two hours wisely so that you allow enough time to plan, write and check both of the answers you write. Be careful not to spend too much time on just one of the tasks.

Look at the following Part One and Part Two example tasks. They are similar to the ones you will find in the exam.

### Part One

You **must** answer this question. Write your answer in **300–350** words in an appropriate style.

1 You see the following writing competition in an International magazine. Write an article for the magazine expressing your views on the questions raised about language learning.

---

### WRITING COMPETITION

**Media Language Learning – the Best Way?**

Many people are successfully learning a language using Distance Learning Programmes on their computers and through the Internet. Does this mean that classroom learning, and visiting a country to learn the language, will soon be a thing of the past?

We want to hear from you about your experience of language learning.

- Have you used a Distance Learning Programme?
- Is it necessary to converse with native speakers to become fluent in a language?
- Is the expense of a classroom-based language course really worth it?
- Is it possible to become a competent language user through independent learning?

Write to us with your views. The winning article will be published in next month's issue. The winner will receive a Distance Learning Programme on CD-Rom for the language of his/her choice.

---

Write your **article**.

## Part Two

Write an answer to **one** of the questions **2–5** in this part. Write your answer in **300–350** words in an appropriate style.

2 You work for an international magazine. You have been asked to write a review of a restaurant for a feature entitled 'Tastes around the World'. Write about a restaurant that you know well, describing all aspects, and say why you would recommend it.

Write your **review**.

3 A travel magazine has invited readers to contribute articles for a feature entitled 'An Unforgettable Visit'. Write an article describing a place you have visited, saying why you think the place is so special and what made your visit memorable.

Write your **article**.

4 You are secretary of an environmental protection society. Your area has a range of environmental and social problems. The local authorities have asked you to submit a proposal suggesting ways of dealing with these problems which will involve the whole community.

Write your **proposal**.

5 Set book questions – a choice from **(a)**, **(b)** and **(c)**.

### How do I choose the question in Part Two?

No one type of writing task is easier than another. However, it is important to choose the question that *you* can answer most easily.

- First, read all the tasks carefully.
- Underline the main points in each task to remind yourself of: the text type, the target reader, the context and your purpose in writing.
- Choose the one you think you have enough ideas and information to write about. Think about the most appropriate style to write in.
- Make a plan and include notes on the points to include, text structure, and good examples of vocabulary and expressions to use.

Using these guidelines, choose one of the Part Two Writing tasks above. Time yourself as you plan and write your answer.

**REMEMBER**

- When you are writing, be aware of the time; leave a few minutes to check your work at the end.
- Make sure your answer is relevant.
- Make sure you cover all the points.
- Your handwriting should be clear enough to read easily.
- Check that your work does not exceed or fall short of the word limit.

UNIT 9 *Nose to the Grindstone*

## LISTENING 2
*Four-option multiple choice*

**1** What do you think are the advantages of a small family-run business:
- for the consumer/clients?
- for the owner?
- for the employees?

**2** You will hear part of a radio programme about a small business involved in tea-blending. For questions **1–5**, choose the answer (**A**, **B**, **C** or **D**) which fits best according to what you hear.

1 Mr Miles believes that his teas are popular because

A they are similar to those of larger companies.
B holidaymakers buy them as souvenirs.
C his company is able to maintain high quality.
D his teas are typical of that part of the country.

2 What is Mr Miles' opinion of teabags?

A He would prefer not to sell them.
B The tea in them is of inferior quality.
C Most of his customers prefer loose tea.
D They are not particularly convenient.

3 As Mr Miles' business has grown, what has remained the same?

A the number of people he works with
B the amount of time he spends at work
C the device he uses for measuring the tea
D the types of tea which he produces

4 What does Mr Miles do to ensure the quality of his tea?

A He experiments with different types of tea.
B He spends most of his time tasting tea.
C He adjusts the quantities of different teas used in a blend.
D He uses information passed on by his grandfather.

5 What is Mr Miles' view of the tea industry?

A He'd like to escape from it.
B It's in need of some new ideas.
C It is rather old-fashioned.
D Family ties are overstressed.

**3** Listen again and make a note of the words and phrases that tell us:
- two ways in which teas are sold
- how quality is maintained
- Mr Miles' attitude to his work

Nose to the Grindstone  UNIT 9

## READING 3
### Gapped text

■ 1  Before you read the article discuss these questions with your partner.

1  Would you prefer to work for yourself or a company?

2  In choosing a company to work for, which of the following factors would be important to consider?

| | |
|---|---|
| size of company | quality of staff |
| reputation of company | perks |
| quality of product | decision-making process |
| attitude towards staff | location |
| business methods | recruitment process |
| management structure | |

3  Look at the words in the box below. What does each of them mean in the context of an employee in a large company?

| | | | | |
|---|---|---|---|---|
| redundancy | cost-cutting | downsizing | efficiency | loyalty |
| bottom line | competitive | workload | profitability | |

■ 2  Look at this headline. What situation do you think the article is going to describe?

# WHO LOVES THE FIRM TODAY?

*Downsizing has turned workers into couldn't-care-less cynics. Even the companies are worried.*

■ 3  Read the article on page 184 about a business phenomenon known as 'downsizing'. Six paragraphs have been removed from the text. Choose from the paragraphs **A–G** on page 185 the one which fits each gap (**1–6**). There is one extra paragraph which you do not need to use.

Downsizing became one of the key business concepts of the 1990s. For some it represented all that was good, efficient and forward-looking, but for others it signalled the end of all they had worked for. Downsizing is defined as the 'energetic pursuit of cost-cutting as a means of survival or a route to greater profitability'. Put simply, a company could make more money if the same amount of work could be done by fewer people.

**1**

Exponents of downsizing, however, failed to predict the effects of the process on both the attitude of the staff who held on to their jobs and on the attitudes of the workforce in general. The theory had been that the survivors of downsizing, fearful for their own jobs, would keep their heads down, work harder and cling enthusiastically to the wreckage. If their endurance failed, there would always be plenty of others only too ready to take their place.

**2**

But things have not worked out quite as anticipated. Unexpected outcomes of the cutbacks in white-collar jobs have been outlined in a recent book, *The Loyalty Effect* by Frederick Reichheld. The victims of these layoffs, he argues, can have a tough time regaining their balance. They also carry an important lesson: never, ever to give that kind of blind dedication and loyalty to a company again.

**3**

Indeed, research has found a great deal of anger among retained staff who made it through the upheavals of the cost-cutting measures. They felt tension between, on the one hand, the desire to hold onto their precious permanent jobs as experienced incumbents, and on the other, the feeling that they should be getting out, making contacts and acquiring skills that might be useful in the future; just in case they should be next on the list. They were the most fearful sector of all and somewhat aggrieved that values of loyalty and employer-related skills were being discounted against the bottom-line.

**4**

The big downside of this new attitude is now being felt by companies. All smart firms realize that healthy profits depend upon loyal customers. And the best way to keep them happy is through loyal employees who treat them well, who are a name and a voice in an otherwise faceless bureaucracy and who can build a long-term relationship with customers.

**5**

This has consequences for the business itself. Where there is a massive turnover of personnel, the staff dealing with sales often do not know either the product or the customer. Paperwork is often done in a sloppy way because employees, thinking they have no long-term future in the company, have no investment in getting it right.

**6**

Many companies have been slow to recognize the consequences of their own short-termist cost cutting. Some have begun to move back towards the notion of 'jobs for life' in an attempt to improve staff morale and thence the quality of service to customers. In others, managers are taking time to explain to employees how they could have a career with the company, whilst supervisors do simple things to build a team spirit, like going out for a drink with their staff. This seems like little more than common sense, and it is perhaps a comment on how bad things have become that even these basic measures are now being explained to companies by highly-paid consultants.

Adapted from an article by Jack O'Sulivan in *The Independent*.

A This view that allegiance to one's company is a thing of the past is gaining ground. More and more, the conventional wisdom is that employees must take full responsibility for their own careers and that the key to success is watching out for number one.

B Survivors have a tough time too. They have to cope not only with their natural anxiety about future rounds of cuts, they also have to take on the added workload of those who were laid off. And for this increased workload, they see little in the way of increased compensation.

C Even more serious than inefficiency, job insecurity accompanied by low wages and broken loyalties means that some employees decide to get the most out of the company while they are there. This leads to company secrets being sold to the highest bidder. The traditional controls which companies put in to stop this, and problems such as fraud, are based on a mutual trust that may no longer be there.

D The solution was to make line managers responsible for the recruitment and training budgets, so that if they lost someone, it was a cost to their department. Suddenly, managers who had little interest in whether people stayed or left, became very concerned about inspiring staff and working on their morale and sense of loyalty.

E After all, the argument went, any prospective employee, having previously been declared surplus to requirements, would have learnt a keen respect for a full-time job. Especially in today's ever more uncertain employment climate, where a full-time post must seem like gold dust to those in the process of searching the job market.

F Of course, in a competitive environment, once one company succeeded in doing it, they all had to jump on the bandwagon or go under. What it meant for many loyal, enthusiastic employees, along with a few dud ones, was that they were suddenly, inexplicably, made redundant.

G Company restructuring, however, has thrown this delicate balance into jeopardy. As a result of endless cost-cutting changes, US companies now lose half their customers in five years, half their employees in four, and half their investors in less than one year. The picture is not that different in Europe: loyalty is becoming a big problem, particularly among younger recruits. Research has found that only 37% of young workers describe themselves as loyal.

UNIT 9 *Nose to the Grindstone*

■ 4  Now answer the following questions.

**Main text**

1  What two synonyms of redundancy are used in paragraph 3?

2  Which word in paragraph 4 means 'disruptive changes'?

3  Which word in paragraph 5 is used to mean 'drawback' or 'disadvantage'?

4  In your own words, explain what the writer means by the phrase 'faceless bureaucracy' in paragraph 5.

5  Which phrase from paragraph 6 is used to describe the phenomenon of workers joining and leaving companies regularly?

6  Which word in paragraph 6 means 'careless'?

7  In your own words, explain the term 'staff morale'. (paragraph 7)

8  In your own words, explain the term 'team spirit'. (paragraph 7)

**Paragraph options A–G**

9  Which phrase in paragraph A is used to mean 'becoming more accepted'?

10  Compare the meaning of the word 'key' as used in paragraph A, with the meaning of the same word as used in the first line of paragraph 1 of the main text.

11  In your own words, explain the meaning of the phrase 'watching out for number one' in paragraph A.

12  What synonym of 'redundancy' is used in paragraph B?

13  Which crime is mentioned in paragraph C?

14  Which idiomatic phrase in paragraph F means 'to do what everybody else is doing'?

15  Which idiomatic phrase in paragraph G means 'put at risk'?

■ 5  Discuss the following questions with a partner.

1  What should companies do to make sure that, whilst remaining competitive, they retain the loyalty of their employees?

2  What advice would you give to a young person just about to start a career in a large multinational company which is known to have a large turnover of staff?

3  How can young people best prepare themselves for a world where there is less job security? Talk about issues such as: re-training, geographical mobility, pension planning, etc.

■ 6  Now read through the article again, in the correct order. In a paragraph of between **70 and 90** words, summarize **in your own words as far as possible**, the negative consequences of downsizing that are described in the article.

## GRAMMAR 1
### Reference skills

■ 1  You can use words or phrases of reference to help you in the gapped text task. Now that you have done the task, look back at paragraph F. The word 'it' refers back to 'downsizing' in paragraph 1 of the main text.

Now look at the following words and explain who or what they refer to in the other half of the text.

a  those in the process of searching the job market (paragraph E)
b  those who were laid off (paragraph B)
c  retained staff (paragraph 4)
d  allegiance to one's company (paragraph A)
e  watching out for number one (paragraph A)
f  This (paragraph 6)
g  inefficiency (paragraph C)


## USE OF ENGLISH 3
### Word-building cloze

■ 1  For questions **1–10**, read the text below. Use the word given in **capitals** at the end of some of the lines to form a word that fits in the space in the same line. There is an example at the beginning (**0**).

### A Real Chore

| | |
|---|---|
| Levels of job satisfaction amongst (**0**) _employees_ have plummeted during | **EMPLOY** |
| the past decade because of (**1**) _____ long working hours and mounting | **INCREASE** |
| levels of stress. 75% of office workers in the UK are fed up, according to | |
| recent research, because they feel (**2**) _____ and exhausted by the | **PRESSURE** |
| demands of their jobs. Only 20% of men expressed complete satisfaction | |
| with their working hours compared with 25% ten years ago. Amongst women, | |
| satisfaction levels were only (**3**) _____ better, with 29% saying they were | **MARGIN** |
| happy. The study showed that the most (**4**) _____ group were actually the | **SATISFY** |
| (**5**) _____ qualified professionals, who were more likely to be embedded | **HIGH** |
| in what has become known as 'long-hours culture'. Nonetheless, the | |
| (**6**) _____ of the 2,500 workers questioned, whether professional or | **MAJOR** |
| manual workers, said that they would not be prepared to take a pay cut | |
| in return for shorter hours. At the same time, people's (**7**) _____ to go on | **WILLING** |
| doing their best at work, (**8**) _____ of the consequences for their personal | **RESPECT** |
| lives, has also declined in direct proportion to their perceived level of job | |
| (**9**) _____ . And, according to one firm of consultants, the imminent arrival | **SECURE** |
| of computers fitted with an (**10**) _____ that can heat up food, thereby | **ATTACH** |
| obviating the need for office workers to take a lunch break, was hardly likely | |
| to improve the situation. | |

UNIT 9 *Nose to the Grindstone*

### LISTENING 3
Part One
### *Listening for specific information*

1 Have you ever played *Monopoly*? Tell your partner what you know about the game. Talk about:
- the idea behind the game
- how you play
- what skills you need to win
- why it is so popular

2 Listen to the beginning of a radio programme about *Monopoly*. Some numbers are mentioned in the programme. As you listen, note down what these numbers refer to.

2 =         36 =
3 =         1935 =
4 =         15,140 =
5 =         1,000,000 =
25 =        160,000,000 =

3 Listen again to check your notes, and then tell your partner how the tournament is organized.

Nose to the Grindstone **UNIT 9**

**Part Two**
*Sentence completion*

1. Now listen to another part of the programme which talks about how *Monopoly* was first introduced to Britain. For questions **1–7**, complete the sentences with a word or short phrase.

---

**Monopoly**

In order to assess the game, the chairman of Waddingtons played it with [    1    ].

The chairman was so excited that he decided to contact the USA via [    2    ].

Parker Brothers agreed to work with Waddingtons because they thought the company [    3    ].

In adapting the game for Britain, the chairman sent his [    4    ] to London.

The streets were chosen according to how familiar they would be to [    5    ].

One part of the board was named after a pub called [    6    ].

It is now possible to play a version of *Monopoly* [    7    ].

---

2. Match one phrase on the left with one on the right to complete a common expression used in the listening. The first one has been done for you as an example.

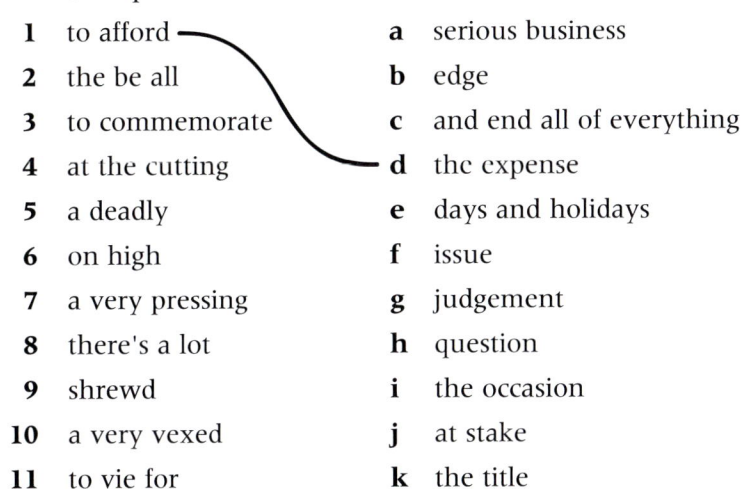

| | | | |
|---|---|---|---|
| 1 | to afford | a | serious business |
| 2 | the be all | b | edge |
| 3 | to commemorate | c | and end all of everything |
| 4 | at the cutting | d | the expense |
| 5 | a deadly | e | days and holidays |
| 6 | on high | f | issue |
| 7 | a very pressing | g | judgement |
| 8 | there's a lot | h | question |
| 9 | shrewd | i | the occasion |
| 10 | a very vexed | j | at stake |
| 11 | to vie for | k | the title |

3. Mark the stressed syllable on these words from the listening texts.

| | | | |
|---|---|---|---|
| monopoly | technology | telephonic | commemorate |
| championship | regulations | preliminary | property |
| engineer | competitors | tournament | opponent |

Now listen again to check your answers to exercises 2 and 3 above.

# UNIT 9 Nose to the Grindstone

## EXAM PRACTICE 9

**1** For questions **1–15**, read the text below and think of the word that best fits each space. Use only **one** word in each space. There is an example at the beginning (**0**).

### A Sticky Business

The post-it note is that rare thing; (**0**) __*a*__ genuine invention. New products constantly appear, but almost (**1**) _____ are refinements of earlier versions of the (**2**) _____ idea. In marketing terms, the post-it met an unperceived need because initially no one (**3**) _____ see the point of it.

One Sunday, Arthur Fry (**4**) _____ sang in a choir at his local church, was marking the pages of his hymn book in the time-honoured fashion with scraps of paper. (**5**) _____ usually happened, they soon fell (**6**) _____ . 'Why', he wondered, 'has no one ever invented a sticky bookmark?' Eureka!

For during the week, Fry worked for the 3M company as a chemist. The following Monday, he dug out the formula for an unusual adhesive developed by one of his colleagues, Dr Spencer Silver. The glue (**7**) _____ question had 'low tack', which meant that it stuck, (**8**) _____ didn't bond tightly. Its outstanding feature was that it could be peeled off (**9**) _____ leaving any trace. Until then, however, (**10**) _____ Dr Silver nor his colleagues had been able to think of a use for it.

Fry began to experiment. (**11**) _____ many hymn book pages had been glued inseparably together, he came (**12**) _____ with what we would recognize as a post-it note. Impressed, 3M (**13**) _____ ahead with test marketing. The first results were rather disappointing. Then someone noticed that once free samples had been given out, sales were very good. That observation probably saved the yellow sticker (**14**) _____ obscurity. Post-it notes are now (**15**) _____ the five top-selling 3M products.

(Adapted from an article by Rosalinde Sharpe in *The Independent*.)

**2** Read the text again and answer the following short-answer questions.

1 In your own words, explain why the post-it note is described as a 'genuine' invention. (paragraph 1)

2 What does the phrase 'time-honoured fashion' tell you about this method of marking pages? (paragraph 2)

3 What does the phrasal verb 'dug out' imply about the formula in paragraph 3?

4 Which phrase from the first paragraph could be used to explain why the first marketing trials of the post-it note were disappointing?

**3** For questions **1–9**, complete the second sentence so that it has a similar meaning to the first sentence, using the word given. **Do not change the word given.** You must use between **three** and **eight** words, including the word given.

1 Please call at once if you encounter any problems.

   **hesitate**

   Should you _____ call.

2 Doctors reported that cholera had broken out in remote villages.

   **outbreak**

   Doctors _____ cholera in remote villages.

3 The number of customers re-ordering goods from the company has increased.

   **upturn**

   There _____ customers re-ordering goods from the company.

4 The post requires a combination of management ability and scientific competence.

   **coupled**

   Management ability _____ is required by this post.

5 As part of its restructuring programme, the company is laying off some employees.

   **redundant**

   Some _____ as part of the company's restructuring programme.

6 The company intends to reduce spending on staff training.

   **cutbacks**

   The company has announced its _____ staff training.

7 If we hope to maintain profitability, there is no alternative but to cut costs.

   **have**

   Only by _____ maintaining profitability.

8 Mr Groves will not hesitate to dismiss you if your work does not improve.

   **have**

   Unless your work _____ in dismissing you.

9 Although we all expected Toby to apply for the job, he decided not to.

   **our**

   Contrary _____ applying for the job.

## UNIT 9 Nose to the Grindstone

**4** For questions **1–6**, think of the one word which can be used appropriately in all three sentences.

1 The _____ surrounding the disappearance of the money were extremely mysterious.

Helen decided that, given the _____ , she would decline Paul's offer of a lift home.

I think their financial _____ might affect any decisions the family might make concerning their children's education.

2 I don't think Judy is proving very suitable for the post because she seems unable to _____ any of the tasks I give her.

If you _____ this form, we will consider your claim for an extra allowance.

All Lance needed was a rare 19th century stamp to _____ his collection.

3 It has not _____ our notice that Glenys has been late for work every day this week.

Gas had _____ from the canister and the whole room stank of it.

Fortunately, we _____ the worst of the redundancies when the company went into recession.

4 If the lights should _____ , there are some candles in the cupboard in the kitchen.

It will be assumed that those who _____ to turn up for the meeting are not interested in joining the working party.

You can't _____ to notice Pauline's new hairdo; it's most unusual.

5 I can't _____ upon you strongly enough the need to maintain the firm's profitability over the coming year.

Hoping to _____ Sally, Paul took her to a very expensive restaurant.

The first candidate looked good on paper, but at interview she didn't really _____ .

6 Fatima's been to four interviews, but her poor keyboard skills always seem to _____ her down.

They decided to _____ off the celebratory fireworks at midnight.

Don't _____ anyone tell you that you can make a fortune without working hard, it's just not true.

UNIT 10

# The Road Ahead

## SPEAKING 1
*Talking together about a visual prompt*

■ 1   First look at photograph A. Talk together about the photo, saying who the people are, why they are in this place, and what might have happened just before the photo was taken. You have one minute for this.

■ 2   Now look at all the photos. A friend of yours wants to take a year off to see the world before going to university, but can't decide where to go and what to do. Talk together about the possibilities presented in the photographs, and decide which would be best for your friend. You have three minutes for this.

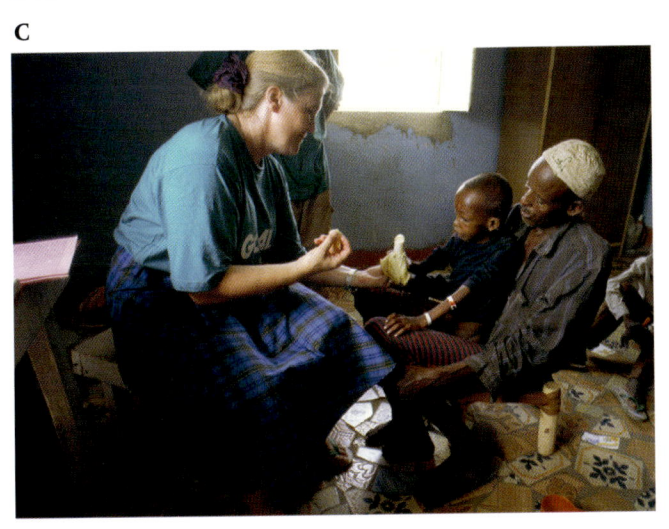

A

B

C

D

UNIT 10 *The Road Ahead*

## LISTENING 1
### Three-option multiple choice

**1** Discuss the following questions with a partner.

1 If you could take a year off from work or studying, what would you choose to do? Why?

2 What problems can young people encounter when they are travelling alone for the first time? How can these problems be avoided?

3 Does travel always broaden the mind?

**2** You will hear three different extracts in which people are talking about gap years. For questions **1–6**, choose the answer (**A**, **B** or **C**) which fits best according to what you hear.

**Extract One**

You hear a careers advisor talking to a group of students in their last year of school.

1 What is she discouraging?

   A an unstructured gap year
   B unpaid work during a gap year
   C doing career-related work during a gap year

2 What does she advise people to do?

   A make plans for the year in advance
   B let professional advisers plan the year
   C experience college life

**Extract Two**

You hear a girl talking about her gap year.

3 What led her to choose Canada for her gap year?

   A a romantic encounter
   B family connections
   C career opportunities

4 What aspect of her gap year did Kate find most difficult to cope with?

   A missing her family
   B being alone
   C living with another family

**Extract Three**

You hear a financial adviser talking about gap years.

5 What did she feel when she saw the families at the airport?

   A worried about her own son
   B unsure whether to give them advice
   C concerned in case they weren't fully prepared

6 What advice does she give regarding insurance policies?

   A check the details carefully
   B go for the most expensive
   C only pay for what you need

## WRITING 1
### Proposals

■ 1  What makes a good tourist resort? Talk to a partner about the things that you look for when you visit a place as a tourist. Make notes under the following headings:

- location/setting
- access to the countryside
- transport – how do you get around?
- accommodation
- requirements of different age groups – young single people/families with children/retired people
- facilities
- entertainment
- food and restaurants

■ 2  Imagine you work for a travel company. Your manager has asked you to write a proposal on how to increase the number of tourists visiting your country for their holidays. Give your suggestions about the resorts or areas in your country which would appeal to tourists, with recommendations on successful advertising and marketing of these areas.

✎ Use the Writing Checklist on page 11 to make your plan before you write.

When you have made your plan, show it to your partner. Exchange your ideas, and add any good ideas from your partner's plan to your notes.

Now write your **proposal** in **300–350** words.

**UNIT 10** *The Road Ahead*

## LISTENING 2
### Four-option multiple choice

■ 1  Before you listen, discuss these questions with your partner.

1  What are the benefits and drawbacks of tourism? Think about:
- mass tourism
- educational opportunities
- third-world economies
- employment opportunities
- the environment
- local cultures

2  How useful are guidebooks when you are travelling? What different types can you buy? What type would you choose?

■ 2  You will hear an interview with Wendy Toller, author of a popular series of guidebooks used by backpackers and other independent travellers. For questions 1–6, choose the answer (**A**, **B**, **C** or **D**) which fits best according to what you hear.

1  Wendy resents the suggestion that her guidebooks have
   - **A**  exploited certain types of people.
   - **B**  misled people about some things.
   - **C**  succeeded for lack of competition.
   - **D**  failed to provide realistic information.

2  Wendy admits that her guidebooks may
   - **A**  persuade people to visit unsuitable places.
   - **B**  fail to inform people of all dangers.
   - **C**  give a negative impression of some places.
   - **D**  influence people's choice of destination.

3  Through her guidebooks, Wendy hopes to make backpackers more
   - **A**  patient with local people.
   - **B**  informed about local agriculture.
   - **C**  aware of the needs of local wildlife.
   - **D**  respectful of the local way of life.

4  How does Wendy usually feel when she sees people using her guidebooks?
   - **A**  worried
   - **B**  indifferent
   - **C**  relieved
   - **D**  proud

5  What problem does Wendy see amongst some groups of young travellers today?
   - **A**  a dependence on her guidebooks
   - **B**  absence of a good reason for travelling
   - **C**  shortage of new places to discover
   - **D**  tendency to follow bad examples

6  How does Wendy feel about travel writing now?
   - **A**  She views it from a purely business perspective.
   - **B**  She's lost none of her original enthusiasm.
   - **C**  She tries to avoid personal involvement.
   - **D**  She's no longer interested in the travelling.

The Road Ahead UNIT 10

## PHRASAL VERBS 1

**1** Look at these two expressions used in the interview with Wendy Toller.

*to make money out of someone    to rip someone off*

**2** Look back at question 2.1 on page 196. Which word is closest in meaning to the expressions above?

**3** Are these two expressions synonyms? When would it be appropriate to use them?

**4** For questions **1–9**, write a new sentence as similar as possible in meaning to the original sentence but which uses one of the verbs from the box. You may need to change both the form of the verb and the structure of the sentence.

| discourage | agree | decide | disappoint | exploit |
| persuade | tease | enter | survive | surrender |

*Example:* The agency was accused of ripping tourists off.

*Answer:* The agency was accused of exploiting tourists.

1 Mark's father tried to put him off the idea of travelling to Africa.

_____

2 I put great faith in Anthea, but I'm afraid in the end she let me down.

_____

3 David was keen to do the exam and put his name on the list.

_____

4 James talked his friends into joining him on a camping holiday.

_____

5 Diana hasn't made her mind up whether to go on holiday or not yet.

_____

6 After five years on the run, the escaped prisoner gave himself up to the police.

_____

7 Dan tends not to go along with the idea of travelling for travelling's sake.

_____

8 Sue managed to live on $40 a week when she was travelling.

_____

9 Rebecca likes to wind up her little sister by commenting on her choice of clothes, etc.

_____

197

UNIT 10 *The Road Ahead*

## READING 1
*Gapped text*

■ 1  Before you read the article, discuss these questions with your partner.

1  What do you understand by the term 'cruise holiday'?
2  What kind of people go on cruises?
3  Why do they choose this type of holiday?
4  What sort of places do they visit?
5  Would you ever consider going on a cruise?

■ 2  Read the article about an unusual cruise. Six paragraphs have been removed from the text. Choose from the paragraphs **A–G** on page 199 the one which fits each gap (**1–6**). There is one extra paragraph which you do not need to use.

### Antarctica's Ancient Mariner

**Bill Glenton spent 17 days on board the 'Explorer', a specially adapted 'floating hotel' ship, cruising deep into the frozen continent of Antarctica.**

As Antarctic explorers go, we were poles apart from famous names like Scott and Amundsen. On their expeditions they never included septuagenarians whose only experience of pack ice was defrosting a fridge. We looked like fairly typical cruise passengers, except that ordinary seagoing holidaymakers don't pack thermal vests and woolly hats. Nor does a typical cruise begin in the remote islands of the South Atlantic.

| 1 |
|---|

Given their shaky sea legs, and the fact that this was a giant stride further than the original plans, I have to say the passengers took it remarkably well. All went well for several hours, until a strong opposing wind and a somewhat deflated captain turned us back. Drifting pack ice had blocked our pioneering way. The Explorer could have broken through, but the holy writ of a tight cruise schedule was more powerful still.

| 2 |
|---|

Tension rose as Captain Skog inched his ship backwards and forwards within feet of the gleaming blue-white giants. 'Titanic' was possibly the word in many minds, but happily, Skog brought us safely through. No, of course we were not rattled. That was only the engine vibration shaking the ice in our glasses.

| 3 |
|---|

This link with the rat race seemed peculiar in the uniquely unspoilt, silent wilderness. What noise there was we brought with us – mainly the clatter of the outboard engines on the landing craft. They ferried us every day to make wet landings at some of the endless penguin and seal colonies and to scale the steep snow-covered and rocky slopes to admire the expansive views.

| 4 |
|---|

Orally, and in print, we were given strict rules. No litter, graffiti or too-close contact with wildlife. We were also entering a complete no-smoking zone – cigarette ends make a poor diet for penguins. But keeping to the rules proved easier said than done.

| 5 |
|---|

Negotiating slippy rocks to avoid a sleeping seal just feet from our landing posed risks to it and us. And those deep holes in the snow made by our wellingtons could easily trap one of the many chicks. What looked to us like piles of pebbles were, in fact, the laboured efforts of penguins at nest building.

| 6 |
|---|

Yet to enjoy the most exciting of our wildlife adventures we did not even have to leave the ship – we watched the whales from on board. Killer and minke whales had accompanied us south but the finest moment came when Captain Skog hunted down a pod of humpbacks for us. Their flukes showered the crowd of watchers in the bow as the ship came within feet of the creatures.

**A** That was reassuring for the 80 passengers. However, it was not icebergs and pack ice that concerned us so much as the sea itself. Heading south after brief visits to various islands, the ship had to struggle across the extremely turbulent Drake Passage.

**B** Landing at some large colonies, for example, it was almost impossible not to disturb the thousands of penguins. Neither had anyone told the creatures to keep their distance. As we filmed, there was always the danger of stepping back on an unseen, over-curious penguin.

**C** Normally cruise ships keep to the western, more ice-free side of the Antarctic Peninsula, but our spirit of adventure was to be tested more than we had realized. We had not reckoned with our captain Peter Skog's long-held ambition to command the first cruise vessel to go deep into the usually ice-packed Wendell Sea. His chance had arrived: according to satellite reports, global warming had melted a passage through the ice.

**D** If the motor boats were an intrusion, so were we passengers. Visiting such unspoilt territory, virtually uninhabited by man, we were bound to impinge on the purity of the place. At our own peril, too, as we were firmly warned at the start of the cruise.

**E** Equally, we stumbled by chance on the well camouflaged, stony nests of skuas. But they, at least, could retaliate. We fled as they dive-bombed us, aiming their big, vicious beaks at our heads. The penguins had their own, if unintended, form of defence. Nothing stinks more than their accumulated droppings (except perhaps those of elephant seals).

**F** For some, remarkably, there were more pressing concerns than being squeezed by icebergs. One businessman kept up a conversation by mobile phone with his office. Electronic technology has certainly changed Antarctic exploration. Passengers were sending and receiving e-mails about everything from their investments to the welfare of their pets.

**G** Yet, if it was drama we needed to spice up our adventure stories for the folk back home, we were not to be frustrated. Resuming our voyage on the more conventional, western side, we found ice conditions thicker than usual. No more so than in the narrowest part of the seaway – the beautiful deep gorge called the Lemaire Channel. Halfway through we were blocked by icebergs.

■ **3** Look back at the main text on page 198. Find and underline examples of:

  **1** the writer joking about his unsuitability for the voyage.
  **2** the captain not wanting to lose time.
  **3** the writer pretending not to be afraid.
  **4** the writer describing the beauty of the place.

■ **4** Now look at options **A–G** above. Find and underline examples of:

  **1** the captain profiting from unusual circumstances.
  **2** the writer feeling guilty about his presence in such a place.
  **3** the writer being irritated by some of the other passengers.

■ **5** In the main text, circle the words or phrases which express the following ideas (paragraph numbers in brackets):

  **a** we were very different (1)
  **b** unaccustomed to being at sea (2)
  **c** moved something little by little, slowly and carefully (3)
  **d** in writing (5)
  **e** a place where smoking is forbidden (5)
  **f** turned out to be difficult in practice (5)

**UNIT 10** *The Road Ahead*

**6** In options **A–G** on page 199, circle the words or phrases which express the following ideas (paragraph letters in brackets):

a going in a southerly direction (A)
b not get too close (B)
c something the captain had always wanted to do (C)
d make something sound more exciting (G)

## USE OF ENGLISH 1

### Summary skills

**1** Before you read the texts, discuss these questions with your partner.

1 Have you ever been skiing?
2 Why are skiing holidays so popular in some countries?
3 What do skiers most like about the sport?
4 Why do some people not like the idea of skiing?

**2** Read the following texts about skiing. For questions **1–4**, answer with a word or short phrase.

---

**TEXT A**

Mountains that have been cultivated for skiing are a uniquely strange environment. The distant jagged peaks, snowy whiteness and eggshell-blue sky all speak of the sublime, and yet the skier's immediate surroundings are deeply domesticated. Every sharp edge, every reminder of danger, has
5 been ironed out from the piste down which he or she flies. The slopes are, in fact, as neatly carpeted and meticulously cared for as any suburban lounge. Skiing, too, is strange. Seen from one perspective, that of the sceptic, it represents human beings at their most preposterous. Clad in lurid colours, the creature with more time than sense slides repeatedly and
10 pointlessly downhill. Seen from another, that of the enthusiast, it represents people at their most elegant – only in such activities does our slow and unwieldy body come anywhere near the kind of grace exhibited in the animal kingdom.

Most images of skiing in the arts and the media are, however, generally
15 celebratory, enshrining the poet T.S. Eliot's words in *The Wasteland*: 'In the mountains, there you feel free'. And although this feeling of liberty is reportedly shared by most participants, skiing nonetheless encapsulates all the ambiguities of our relationship with the natural world. When people take to the wilderness en masse, what of the wilderness remains? Looking
20 at a ski poster, however, you can participate in the dream of moving swiftly through the peaks without actually inflicting your presence on the mountain, and with the value of antique posters rising by 50% in the past few years, it's an investment opportunity neither the enthusiast nor the sceptic can afford to overlook.

---

1 In your own words, explain what the writer means when she compares ski slopes to a 'suburban lounge'. (lines 6–7)

2 Which two words, used later in the paragraph, reinforce the idea that skiers might appear 'preposterous'? (line 8)

**TEXT B**

Why do it? Why slide down snowy mountains in freezing temperatures wearing vice-like boots clipped into high-tech planks? Is it worth all the effort? So say those uninitiated in the sport. I use the word 'sport' loosely, since you don't actually need to be that
5  sporty by nature to ski. Personally, aside from the occasional game of table football, I participate in no conventional sport from one year to the next. I have lousy co-ordination (I couldn't hit a tennis ball to save my life) and my general level of fitness is, I would have to say, poor. Yet, although there are certainly many highly-trained athletes
10 who enjoy skiing, I know many other people much like myself who are highly competent and passionate skiers.

So what motivates us? John Ruskin once said: 'Mountains are the beginning and end of natural scenery' and the canvas of white snow, blue sky and green pine is certainly worth the trip alone. Then there
15 is the air. The altitude is thinner and its powers of invigoration instant. Just watching your breath vaporize as you step outside first thing in the morning makes your heart leap. Naturally the temperatures are low, you simply can't have snow without them, but with the high-tech insulated clothing available today, there's no
20 reason for those with even the feeblest circulation to actually suffer. And, in any case, most of the time you are feeling the glow of the sun on your face, endowing you with a vibrant feeling that will last until bedtime.

3  Which word in the first paragraph of text B is used to identify people with similar ideas to the 'sceptics' in text A?

4  In your own words, explain why the writer mentions table football and tennis in the first paragraph of text B.

3  In a paragraph of between **50 and 70** words, summarize **in your own words as far as possible**, the reasons given in the two texts why people find skiing an attractive activity.

UNIT 10 *The Road Ahead*

### VOCABULARY 1

**1** Each of the passages on skiing includes a literary quote. In your own words, explain what point each of the quoted writers is making about mountains.

**2** Look back at the two texts and find words or phrases that mean:

**Text A**
a  very carefully
b  not very graceful
c  in large numbers

**Text B**
d  infrequent
e  very poor
f  very good at
g  weakest

**3** In your own words, explain the meaning of these words:

a  enshrining (text A, line 15)
b  encapsulates (text A, line 17)
c  invigoration (text B, line 15)
d  endowing (text B, line 22)

### LISTENING 3
*Matching*

**1** Before you listen, discuss these questions with your partner.
1  Is it better to go on holiday with family or friends? Why?
2  What are the advantages and disadvantages of going on holiday with a large group of people?

**2** You will hear two colleagues, Lucy and Gary, talking about their friend's holiday plans. For questions **1–11**, decide whether the opinions are expressed by only one of the speakers, or whether the speakers agree.

Write **L** for Lucy, **G** for Gary or **B** for Both, where they agree.

1  Rebecca's holiday sounds perfect.

2  It is a good idea going on holiday in a large group.

3  Rebecca may have been invited on the holiday for selfish reasons.

4  It's a risk going on holiday with people you don't know.

5  Rebecca's personality will help to make the holiday a success.

6  Rebecca may find the holiday boring.

7  There are likely to be tensions at the start of the holiday.

8  There are bound to be arguments amongst the children.

9  Rebecca may realize that this will be a different type of holiday for her.

10  There are likely to be disagreements over travel arrangements.

11  You have to admire Rebecca.

## READING 2
*Lexical cloze*

**1** For questions **1–12**, read the texts below and decide which answer (**A**, **B**, **C** or **D**) best fits each gap.

### Mauritius

On the island of Mauritius, crystal waters meet white sandy beaches fringed with palm trees. Its sub-tropical climate, (**1**) _____ with breathtaking natural scenery and first class accommodation, makes the island ideal for those in (**2**) _____ of rest and relaxation in the sun, with excellent sports facilities (**3**) _____ . Mauritius also (**4**) _____ wonderful sightseeing, both naturally and culturally; misty volcanic peaks tower above lush green forests and flower-filled villages that (**5**) _____ down to the sea. The islanders themselves are friendly by (**6**) _____ , welcoming visitors with enthusiasm.

| | | | | |
|---|---|---|---|---|
| 1 | **A** added | **B** combined | **C** counted | **D** joined |
| 2 | **A** probe | **B** hunt | **C** search | **D** scour |
| 3 | **A** on hand | **B** at will | **C** in stock | **D** by all means |
| 4 | **A** bears | **B** renders | **C** grants | **D** affords |
| 5 | **A** launch | **B** fetch | **C** stretch | **D** touch |
| 6 | **A** norm | **B** culture | **C** nature | **D** habit |

### Glasgow

In the late 19th century, when it was at the (**7**) _____ of an economic boom, the Scottish city of Glasgow was already at the (**8**) _____ edge of design, and this is reflected in the architecture surviving from the period. The city's 19th century citizens got rich very quickly, then (**9**) _____ the money they had made back into their city and its architecture. Like other boom cities, it looked to the exotic for inspiration; so it (**10**) _____ , for example, a wonderful gothic university building and a carpet factory that bears a (**11**) _____ resemblance to the Doge's Palace in Venice. Such fanciful architecture now forms the perfect backdrop for a city that has always taken the idea of having fun seriously. The old banks, courthouses and gentlemen's clubs have found a new (**12**) _____ of life in recent years as stylish bars and restaurants.

| | | | | |
|---|---|---|---|---|
| 7 | **A** height | **B** head | **C** tip | **D** crown |
| 8 | **A** biting | **B** shaping | **C** cutting | **D** carving |
| 9 | **A** flowed | **B** poured | **C** spouted | **D** gushed |
| 10 | **A** boasts | **B** claims | **C** brags | **D** prides |
| 11 | **A** striking | **B** discerning | **C** matching | **D** clashing |
| 12 | **A** turn | **B** bout | **C** birth | **D** lease |

**2** Which would you rather visit, Mauritius or Glasgow? Why?

UNIT 10 *The Road Ahead*

## WRITING 2
### *Describing a place*

■ 1  Talk to a partner. Describe one of your favourite places, a place that you love to visit.

- Why is it so special to you?
- How do you feel when you are in that place?

Now describe a place that you visited and you really disliked, a place you never want to return to.

- Why do you never want to revisit this place?
- How do you feel when you are in this place?

■ 2  Now read the following Writing task.

*An International travel magazine has invited contributions to a feature entitled 'Tourism – Heaven or Hell?' Write an article for the magazine describing a place that you know well that has been changed or may be changed by tourism. Give your opinion as to whether you think tourism has had or will have a positive or negative effect on the place you describe.*

■ 3  In order to create a clear picture of a place in the mind of the reader, you need to use descriptive words and phrases to depict not only what you can see, but also to create the atmosphere, and express your feelings about a place.

Think of the place on which you will base your answer to the question. Make notes under the following headings.

- facts and location
- your feelings about the place
- the atmosphere there in the past
- the atmosphere there now – has it changed?
- what happened/may happen to change the place?
- why the changes have happened/will happen?
- have the changes been/will they be for the better?
- your future predictions for the place

✎ Remember to use the Writing Checklist on page 11.

Now write your **article** in **300–350** words.

■ 4  After you have written your article show it to your partner. Read your partner's article and tell him/her whether you agree with his predictions about the place. Make a note of any good ideas, words, or phrases that you can see in your partner's article.

## USE OF ENGLISH 2
### Cloze passage

**1** What do you know about the Hawaiian islands? What type of holiday do you think people have there?

**2** For questions **1–15**, read the text below and think of the word which best fits each space. Use only **one** word in each space. There is an example at the beginning (**0**).

### How I lied my Way to the Top

I was on Big Island, the largest and (**0**) ___most___ southerly of the Hawaiian chain. Two dormant volcanoes dominate the island and between them runs the Saddle Road, a remote and rather frightening fifty-mile stretch of bumpy tarmac. The man from *Rent-a-Car* in Hawaii must have read adventure books as a child; as he (**1**) _____ over the keys to the four-wheeled drive vehicle, he provided a perfect dare. '(**2**) _____ you do, don't go on the Saddle Road,' he said.

Of course, he (**3**) _____ every reason to warn me (**4**) _____ taking this route. It is, after all, (**5**) _____ isolated and high that should you (**6**) _____ down, it would be difficult to (**7**) _____ to you with assistance. Then, there is the US military which (**8**) _____ use of the desolate landscape through (**9**) _____ the road passes, adding to the potential dangers.

Yet another reason is that a spur road off the Saddle leads to the very top of one of the volcanoes, and (**10**) _____ signs warn you not to, it is awfully tempting to swing the wheel over at this point and take the detour. I had two reasons for (**11**) _____ so; firstly, this volcano is taller than Mount Everest, or would be (**12**) _____ for the fact that its base is actually under water, and secondly, at the summit are some of the world's finest telescopes.

So, I lied, took the keys and headed (**13**) _____ the Saddle Road. As I (**14**) _____ off, the beaches were bathed (**15**) _____ warm sunshine. Yet on top of the volcano, maybe two hour's drive away, I could see snow.

**3** What is a dare? (paragraph 1, line 6)
Tell your partner about a time when you did something as a dare.

UNIT 10 The Road Ahead

## READING 3
*Multiple choice*

■ 1  What do you understand by the term 'stress'?
- what are the symptoms?
- who suffers from it?
- what causes it?
- how can it be remedied?

■ 2  Read the passage about stress carefully.

# Stress what stress?

**More than half the adult population claims to be suffering from it. From victims of rising crime to exhausted working mothers, from tightly-squeezed professionals to the despairing unemployed. It makes us tense, irritable and affects our concentration. Worse, it damages our health, causing everything from heart attacks to asthma, from chronic fatigue to spots.**

Cynics are quick to dismiss the phenomenon as fashionable hype. And they have a point. After all, we are living longer lives than any generation before us. Most of us have more cash, more holidays, more consumer durables, and more choices in our lives than ever before. Faced with the historical evidence of human survival, triumph and even happiness, against far greater odds than we experience today, talk of stress, the modern disease, just sounds like whingeing. Yet for many people stress is real enough. The effects of sudden and shocking events on physical and mental health have been well documented. But, crises are not the only things to damage our health. Professor Ben Fletcher, psychologist and Dean of the Business School at the University of Hertfordshire, argues that the work people do has a huge effect on their risk of physical disease. High demands, combined with low control, lack of support, and especially monotonous work, are stressful and increase our chances of an early death.

The evidence is persuasive. Danish bus drivers who faced the worst traffic lived shorter lives than colleagues on quiet country roads. Meanwhile, civil servants who feared unemployment during reorganization, were more likely to report health problems than more secure colleagues. And the unemployed – those with most boredom, least control over their lives, and greatest anxiety about finding new work – are more likely than any other group to commit suicide.

But does it make sense to sweep all these conditions under one title, 'stress'? The boredom of the unemployed is very different from the frustration of the bus driver, and the grief of the recently bereaved. Yet professionals, as well as the general public, persist in using the term. According to Carry Cooper, Professor of Organizational Psychology at the University of Manchester, it's an umbrella concept. While cause, context and response all vary, the underlying model is the same. Hans Selye, founder of modern research into stress, described it as 'the rate of wear and tear on the body'. The analogy emerges out of physics. Subject a bridge to repeated stress – perhaps the waves against the pillars, or steady vibrations from soldiers marching across it in step – and it will start to exhibit strain.

But stress is not entirely malign. A certain amount of pressure – Professor Cooper distinguishes pressure from stress – and we thrive. We keep going, we keep interested in the world, we stay alive. Too much and we get tense, troubled, breathless and run down. For example, the hormones produced by the 'fight and flight' mechanism – including adrenaline – while inspiring us to react properly to crises, can also damage our bodies. All it takes is one final stressful straw and the camel's back will crack.

Of course, it will crack in different ways depending on the form of stress we are exposed to, our own genetic make up and the support we have to help us cope. Personality matters too – even if scientists can't quite agree about which personality traits are at fault and why. In the late sixties, Dr Freidman and Dr Rosenman claimed that aggressive extrovert achievers were more likely to die of a heart attack than calmer people. Now the pendulum has swung the other way. Research reported in a recent edition of the *Lancet* shows that people who bottle up their emotions are more likely to die early, and in particular to have heart attacks.

So stress is real. The answer to our cynics who point to historical evidence is that our ancestors suffered from stress too. Richard Napier, a sixteenth century physician, recorded that around a third of his patients were 'troubled in the mind'. As psychologist, Dr Anthony Clare points out, this is almost exactly the same as the proportion of visitors at today's doctor's surgery who are recorded as experiencing stress-related problems. We are no more wimpish than our forebears, the stress they suffered probably contributing to their ill health and lower life expectancy.

Of course the stresses we face today are different – and may genuinely be greater for many people than thirty years ago. Compared with the fifties and sixties, we are all working far longer hours. The middle classes in particular are having to compete, where in the past their positions were guaranteed. Professor Cooper argues that we have less support today to help us deal with the inevitable stresses that arise. We no longer have the communities and extended families that acted as natural sources of moral support. So counselling networks and services have had to grow in their place. But the big test is to whether our futures will be consistently more stressful than our past, how will human beings manage to adapt to change? As we move from one job to another, acquiring new skills, meeting new people, we will always have to cope with constant fluidity in our lives. Will this always be tough to cope with or will the next generation, brought up on a diet of rapid movement, get used to continual change? No one knows, but the academics look forward to finding out.

*Adapted from an article by Yvette Cooper in The Independent.*

**3** For questions **1–7**, choose the answer (**A**, **B**, **C** or **D**) which you think fits best according to the text.

1 What is suggested by the 'cynics'?
   A Stress results from too many choices.
   B There is no historical evidence for stress.
   C As people live longer, so stress increases.
   D People always find something to complain about.

2 Ben Fletcher points out that stress
   A often follows traumatic events.
   B may be connected with boredom.
   C is a purely physical condition.
   D can result from other illnesses.

3 Professor Cooper thinks that stress
   A is overused as a term.
   B has its basis in positive responses.
   C is an aspect of personality.
   D has parallels in the physical world.

4 Contemporary theories discount the link between high levels of stress and
   A aggressive behaviour.
   B heart disease.
   C emotion.
   D personality.

5 The evidence of Richard Napier supports the idea that, in the past, people
   A used different terminology.
   B were also cynical about stress.
   C had similar symptoms to today.
   D suffered more acutely from stress.

6 Professor Cooper connects modern stress-related problems to a lack of
   A personal flexibility.
   B financial security.
   C social stability.
   D professional support.

7 Which word best describes the writer's general attitude towards the ideas put forward by those who study stress?
   A sceptical
   B receptive
   C indifferent
   D dismissive

# UNIT 10 *The Road Ahead*

## VOCABULARY 2
### Definitions

**1** Explain each of the following words and expressions from the passage, in your own words.

1. consumer durables (line 15)
2. far greater odds (line 18)
3. whingeing (line 20)
4. well documented (lines 22–23)
5. analogy (line 52)
6. run down (line 61)
7. the final straw (lines 65–66)
8. traits (line 71)
9. bottle up (line 77)
10. wimpish (line 88)
11. moral support (lines 101–102)
12. fluidity (line 109)

## USE OF ENGLISH 3
### Noun phrases

**1** Look at the text on pages 206 and 207 again.

1. Which two words in paragraph 1 of the passage on stress are joined by a hyphen?
2. Why has this type of punctuation been used?
3. Can you find another example of its use in the passage?

**2** Rewrite each of these sentences so that it includes a hyphenated noun phrase.

1. I am in favour of measures which cut costs.
2. This new deal will secure the prospects of the company in the long term.
3. The company employed some consultants who are paid extremely highly.
4. The plant grows best on slopes which face North.
5. The tournament is held every four years.
6. Production increased thanks to the introduction of machinery which allowed less labour to be used.
7. He has no difficulty in motivating himself.
8. The business is regarded as quite a small scale affair.
9. I bought the pullover from a company that sells via mail order.
10. The company called in an accountant with very good qualifications.

## HELP WITH THE SPEAKING TEST

**1** The Speaking Test is divided into three parts and is taken by pairs of candidates.

### Part One (3 minutes)

- The examiner will ask each of you questions in turn.
- Be ready to speak about yourself, including your present situation, childhood and future plans.
- Try to have a normal, relaxed conversation.
- Answer the examiner's questions as fully as you can.
- Be spontaneous; make what you say interesting.

### Part Two (4 minutes)

- There are two phases to this part of the test.
- You talk about the photograph(s) that the examiner shows you.
- Listen to the examiner's instructions carefully.
- First of all, you will be asked to talk about one aspect of the photograph(s) for one minute.
- Then you'll be given a specific task based on the photograph(s) which lasts about three minutes.

In both phases of Part Two:

- you talk to your partner, not to the examiner.
- pick up on your partner's ideas.
- agree and disagree politely.
- have a natural conversation with your partner.

### Part Three (12 minutes)

This part of the test also has two phases.

In phase one:

- you talk alone for two minutes on a given topic.
- use the three points on the prompt card to help you.
- take your time and structure what you say.
- try to keep your listeners interested.
- be ready to answer a question about your talk from your partner or the examiner when you've finished.
- listen carefully to your partner's talk; you will need to ask a him/her a question about it at the end.

In phase two:

- the examiner asks both of you questions on a theme related to the topic of your talks.
- the idea is to generate discussion, so develop the ideas that are introduced.
- pick up on what your partner says and add your own ideas.

## UNIT 10 *The Road Ahead*

### REMEMBER

- Say what you think; don't wait to be asked.
- Make the conversation interesting for the examiner.
- Try to speak naturally and talk to the examiner or your partner, not to the picture or text.
- Try to develop the topic by introducing new ideas, telling anecdotes, giving examples, etc.
- Smile, and try not to look too nervous!

**2** Here is an example Part Two task.

1  First, look at picture A on page 211. Talk to your partner about how you think the person in the picture is feeling and why he is in this situation. You have about one minute for this.

2  Now look at all the pictures. They all show people under pressure. Talk together about the pressures each person faces, say how typical these are of modern society and then decide which form of pressure is potentially the most and least damaging. You have about three minutes for this.

**3** Here is an example Part Three task.

1  Now talk on your own for about two minutes. Look at the question on the card and say what you think. There are some ideas on the card to use if you like. Remember to listen to your partner's talk and be ready to ask and answer questions after each talk.

**STUDENT A**

*It's a small world and it's getting smaller every day.* Do you agree with this comment?

- language barriers
- role of international companies
- development of technology

**STUDENT B**

To what extent do you think modern life is more stressful than life was hundreds of years ago?

- work and leisure
- speed of communications
- social pressures

2  Now talk together on the same theme for about four minutes. Here are some further questions to discuss.

- How do you think the world will change in the next century?
- How much choice do we have regarding the type of lifestyle we lead?
- How easy is it to drop out of society? What problems does this cause?

The Road Ahead **UNIT 10**

A

B

C

D

211

# UNIT 10 The Road Ahead

## EXAM PRACTICE 10

**1** For questions **1–10**, read the text below. Use the words given in **capitals** at the end of some of the lines to form a word that fits in the space in the same line. There is an example at the beginning (**0**).

### Airspaces

Powered flight is (**0**) *undoubtedly* to be counted as one of the wonders of the modern world, and the world it inhabits, both literally and (**1**) _____ , is the subject of an eclectic and thought-provoking book by David Pascoe (**2**) _____ simply 'Airspaces'. Aviation, however, is full of contradictions. The construction of a new airport, or the (**3**) _____ of an existing one, has the potential to bring employment and (**4**) _____ to a region. But, at the same time, airports are voracious users of land and ruin the lives of those who have the (**5**) _____ to live directly under the flight path. Similarly, although they are the least environmentally-friendly form of transport, aircraft open up far-flung destinations to all sorts of people for whom long-distance travel suddenly becomes a viable (**6**) _____ as airlines compete to provide services and prices fall. Aircraft also (**7**) _____ the transportation of goods around the world, increasing choice and (**8**) _____ prices for consumers, whilst simultaneously providing new markets in otherwise (**9**) _____ places for producers. Yet, at the same time, they contribute to the process of (**10**) _____ which many people feel is robbing some parts of the world of their intrinsic character and individuality.

**DOUBT**

**METAPHOR**

**TITLE**

**EXPAND**

**PROSPER**

**FORTUNE**

**PROPOSE**

**FACILITY**

**LOW**

**FEASIBLE**

**GLOBAL**

**2** Read the text again and answer the following short-answer questions.

1. Which word from the text is used metaphorically to suggest that airports are in some ways greedy places?

2. Which phrase from the text reinforces the idea of 'long-distance travel'? (lines 11–12)

3. In your own words, explain what the writer means by the 'intrinsic character' of places. (line 18)

**3** For questions **1–6**, think of **one** word only which can be used appropriately in all three sentences.

**1** Working in the travel industry, the peak season really _____ it out of you.

Melanie really _____ after her mother when it comes to choosing holidays.

It _____ a lot of courage to go bungee jumping at her age.

**2** Frank is said to have learnt the _____ of rope-making during the period he spent working by the sea.

Before the holiday finishes, I'd like to visit a few shops selling local _____ goods.

The storm was gathering and the small _____ was tossed about on the waves as it entered the port.

**3** I wish the weather would brighten up a bit; it's so _____ at the moment.

The film has a tantalizing plot and is packed with action so that there's never a _____ moment.

It's not really a pain, more a sort of _____ ache.

**4** The new airport has the capacity to _____ 14 million passengers per year.

Always wear protective clothing when you _____ dangerous chemicals.

Sarah gave up her job because she couldn't _____ the level of responsibility expected of her.

**5** It seemed _____ that five minutes before the film was due to start, Tom was the only person in the cinema.

When he sat down, you couldn't help but notice that the professor was wearing _____ socks.

I don't really like sweet things much, but I do enjoy the _____ bar of chocolate.

**6** Walk down the _____ , go up a flight of stairs and you'll see the library on your right.

With the _____ of time, the events of that day began to fade in all their memories.

The students were told to pick a short _____ from the novel and analyse it for homework.

# UNIT 10 *The Road Ahead*

**4** For questions **1–10**, complete the second sentence so that it has a similar meaning to the first sentence, using the word given. **Do not change the word given.** You must use between **three** and **eight** words, including the word given.

1 Everyone has a great deal of respect for Mr Jones, the accountant.
   **highly**
   Mr Jones _____ accountant.

2 On long journeys with children, arguments are inevitable.
   **bound**
   There _____ children are taken on long journeys.

3 I only have to think of all those children and I get a headache.
   **thought**
   The mere _____ to give me a headache.

4 The demand for guidebooks has been rising steadily this year.
   **rise**
   There _____ for guidebooks this year.

5 For some reason, we never considered renting a car in Hawaii.
   **occurred**
   For some reason, _____ car in Hawaii.

6 'Please, please, don't tell my mother what you've seen,' Marie said to Darren.
   **pleaded**
   Marie _____ what he had seen.

7 Although it seemed trivial, Denise wished she'd reported the incident.
   **regretted**
   Trivial _____ reporting the incident.

8 You won't get to see the match unless you book a seat beforehand.
   **advance**
   Only _____ you get to see the match.

9 James persuaded his friends to join him on a camping holiday.
   **talked**
   James _____ a camping holiday.

10 Sue couldn't explain how she'd come to mislay her keys.
   **loss**
   Sue _____ her keys came to be mislaid.

# Help with writing

■1 When the examiners read the writing tasks you produce in the exam, they award a mark out of five for each task. The examiners are looking for the following things in your work:

**Content.** What you write has to be relevant to the task set. In both Part One and Part Two, the question will tell you the points you need to address in your answer. Remember that you get no marks for introducing material which is irrelevant to the task. You are expected to produce your own ideas, expressed in your own words, within the given context.

**Appropriacy of register and format.** Each of the text types requires you to write in a style appropriate to the context and target reader and to lay out your work accordingly. An article, for example, will use a different type of language to a report and will be presented in a different way.

**Organization and cohesion.** The division of the piece of writing into sentences and paragraphs, and the way that these are linked together, are important aspects to consider. A piece of writing which is badly organized and difficult to read may not communicate the intended ideas successfully.

**Target reader.** Each task defines the target reader and the examiners will be looking at how successful the piece of writing is in communicating relevant ideas to that person or group of people.

**Length.** The examination questions tell you how many words to write. If you write too little, then you will lose some of the marks. If you write too much, then only the first part of your answer will be assessed. However, it is not a good idea to waste too much time in the exam counting the words. Practise timing your writing when you are preparing so that you get a feel for what is the right length of answer and how best to organize your time.

**Handwriting.** Poor handwriting, spelling errors and faulty punctuation are not specifically penalized. But the examiners will reduce the mark if these areas are so bad that they make it difficult to understand what has been written.

■2 Look at these tasks written by students preparing to take the Proficiency examination. For each one decide whether:

- the correct text type has been produced with appropriate layout;
- all content points have been addressed;
- the style of writing is appropriate to the context and the target reader;
- the piece of writing has been well organized;
- there is a good range of expression and vocabulary;
- all parts are relevant and clear;
- the piece of writing is of the required length;
- the desired effect on the target reader has been achieved.

What mark out of five would you give each piece of writing?

N.B. These are real students' tasks which contain errors. They are not models for you to copy.

When you have thought about each piece of writing, read the examiner's mark and comments.

The Writing task which the three students have chosen is:

An international student magazine has invited entries for a writing competition entitled 'An Unexpected Pleasure'. Write an article as an entry for the competition describing an occasion which turned out to be more enjoyable than you expected.

---

*Sometimes life can hold so many surprises we have never dreamed of that make us feel really happy. It happened to me when I was fourteen years old. Christmas was coming and I was so sad that I wanted to go somewhere else other than stay with my parents and my brothers and sisters. The reason I was feeling so depressed was because for the second time my sister was not coming to spend Christmas with us. The year before she had been working during her holidays because her employer had had a car accident and had been forced to stay in bed for two months. But, this year was different, there was no apparent reason for her not coming for Christmas.*

*Strange as it might have seen, nobody appeared to be really sad about that, I was the only one feeling unhappy. I was the youngest and she was my eldest sister who had brought me up until the age of nine. I loved her as much as I loved my mother and that was why I was feeling so empty and lonely, though I had my parents and brothers next to me. Anyway, Christmas night came and we were all getting together for dinner. Suddenly, we heard a horn of a car, which was parked right outside our door. My mother ordered me to go and see who it was. I couldn't believe my eyes when I saw my sister getting out of the taxi and running to me with her arms open. I embraced her for a long time with my eyes full of tears with so much joy.*

*After having a wonderful meal, now with a complete family, it was time to open the presents. I could not have asked for a better present than having my so loved sister next to me. But what an expected pleasure when she told me to go to my bedroom where I found a brand-new mountain bicycle. Everthing was like a dream that had just became true when I least expected. My sister took me by surprise and offered me the best present in the world that I had wished for so long.*

*There could be nobody in the world happier than me.*

---

## ARTICLE 1

The candidate has not really described 'an unexpected pleasure' but rather 'a pleasant surprise', so the topic has not been well developed. The details are confusing – for example the sudden appearance of the bicycle – and the reader cannot be sure what constitutes 'the best present': the bicycle or the sister's presence.

There are no serious basic errors, although there is some awkward phrasing (e.g. 'next to me', 'we were all getting together', 'a horn of a car', 'with her arms open') and verbs are not always used correctly (e.g. 'as it might have seen' and 'I had wished for so long').

This piece of writing is not at Proficiency standard and gets a mark of 2/5.

> *At the age of thirteen when my most of my friends would ski as well as if they were born with skis on their feet I didn't find it interesting and had no intention to learn it. When the announcement of a two-week course came I wasn't delighted or happy like most of my classmates were, not at all. I was frightened by the idea of standing on top of a steep hill, freezing, shirvery and then move downwards faster than I can walk. If it wasn't for the fact that the course was compulury I would've never taken part in it.*
>
> *I had to admit that there is no way I can avoid going. It was time to pack all things I needed. As I didn't have the necessary equippment I was forced to borrow it from my relatives; skiies from my cousin, shoes from uncle who passed away a year before and windproof, but not waterproof clothes, I inherited from my grandfather. I didn't have very good impression when looking at myself in a mirror. I reminded myself of a combination of an Eskymo and homeless with all the different kinds of clothes. I didn't feel enthusiastic at all.*
>
> *It was the first day in the mountains and from the very first moment I didn't like it there. I didn't feel well about myself, I had no experience, I didn't like sking and I wasn't happy about the idea of feeling cold. As soon as we climbed up the hill I realized that from the top it looks much steeper than from the bottom, which filled me with the image of myself falling down every two feet. First thing first, in order to find out how well we could ski the instructor asked us to show him our skills so he could divide us into groups. When I was to show what I can do, the instructor wasn't impress at all. I was fell every time I started moving forward. Being placed into the last and lowest group didn't make me feel any better and the only thing I could think of, while watching more skillful classmates having a good time, was to go home.*
>
> *As the first week was the worse I could ever have, the second was the best. Things started getting better when ran into a group of local kids of my age. They were spending every day skiing and playing around and were willing to teach me in more enjoyable way than my instructor. My skills improved within a few days and at the end of the course I was able to ski as well as my classmates thanks to my new friends.*

## ARTICLE 2

The candidate has understood the question and developed the topic appropriately, but inadequacies in the language make this an unsatisfactory treatment of the task. There is a good attempt at description and the article is well organized and paragraphed.

There are spelling mistakes (e.g. 'shirvery', 'compulury', 'equippment'), problems with verbs (e.g. 'I can avoid going', 'when I was to show', 'was to go home'), problems with articles (e.g. 'all things', 'in more enoyable way'), awkward word order (e.g. 'I would've never taken part') and verb tenses are not always correctly used (e.g. 'they were spending every day').

The reader would probably enjoy this article and understand the writer's experience, but the language is not of Proficiency standard yet. The mark given is 2/5.

It was last year about this time, just before Christmas when I received the invitation from my old school. A reunion of our class which I had completely forgot about. The date had been set 10 years ago, when we finished school.

I didn't really feel like going. What is there to say with people that you haven't seen for ten years? Anyway with those that I really wanted to, I kept a contact through these years. We would meet occasionally for drinks or dinner we would call each other evey now and then. But did I need to meet 150 or so people that I haven't seen for ten years? and even when we were meeting everyday at school, we weren't close! I decided not to go. Two days before the event, my then best friend Maria called me. She wanted to ask me if I was going and tell me that she was really looking forward seeing me again. I reluctantly answered that I was going. I remembered all the fun we used to have together and suddenly I felt that I had really missed her. So, I did go. The party was in the ballroom of a very nice hotel. At the door was the welcoming committee. I remembered one of them Anna whom I hadn't seen for almost ten years, she came towards me to welcome me and then we went inside together. The hall was full, but I couldn't see anyone I really knew well enough. I heard someone calling my name. It was Maria. I went to her table where the rest of the old friends were. It was so nice we were just laughing and talking and remembering the old times.

There were so many things that I had forgotten over the years. Parties, cheeting on the test, diching school, excursions, old loves. After we had a few drinks we started dancing under the same old songs, that we used to hear when we were at school, I even danced and talked to people that I've never talked to at school. Eventually, I left about 2 am. I had such a good time that night. We exchanged phone numbers with a few of my old friends and decided to keep in touch and not to get lost again until the next reunion.

It is true unexpected pleasures are the best, and those that you never forget.

## ARTICLE 3

The writer has explained why she did not expect to enjoy the reunion, described what happened and shown that it did indeed prove to be 'an unexpected pleasure'. The article is well organized, although there are some problems with punctuation.

The meaning is always quite clear, but there are a number of errors of different kinds: with verb forms and tenses (e.g. 'I had forgot' , 'I haven't seen', 'we were meeting'), with prepositions (e.g. 'to say with people' and 'under the same old songs'), with spelling (e.g. 'cheeting' and 'diching'), with the use of articles (e.g. 'kept a contact') and with inappropriately used vocabulary (e.g. 'not to get lost again'). There is an adequate range of structures and some evidence of stylistic devices – varied sentence length and rhetorical questions are effectively used.

The article achieves the desired effect on the reader, and is a satisfactory attempt at the task. The piece is awarded a mark of 3/5.

Macmillan Education
Between Towns Road, Oxford OX4 3PP
A division of Macmillan Publishers Limited
Companies and representatives throughout the world

ISBN 0 333 97436 0
ISBN 0 333 97431 X (Greek edition)

Text © Nick Kenny 2002
Design and illustration © Macmillan Publishers Limited 2002

First published 2002

All rights reserved; no part of this publication may be reproduced, stored in a retrieval system, transmitted in any form, or by any means, electronic, mechanical, photocopying, recording, or otherwise, without the prior written permission of the publishers.

Designed by Artistix
Illustrated by Paul Beebee, Hardlines, Kath Walker

**Acknowledgements**

The authors would like to thank Edith Boreham, Nikos Demenopoulos, Cristina Forosetto, Lynn Gold, Tomas Helsus, Chrisa Kalamara, Barbara Lewis, Kondylia Michou, Clive Nightingale, Filomena Pinto Fernandes, Eleni Psoma, Sergio Rodriguez, Bertrand Steinmetz, Ian Tolley, Fanny Tsironi and Sotiria Vamvakidou for their help and advice. Special thanks to my editor Helen Holwill and to Debi Hughes for researching the photographs.

The authors and publishers would like to thank the following for permission to reproduce copyright material:
Independent Newspapers for adapted extracts from 'Crisis in a Sesame Bun' by Paul Vallely (*The Independent*, 27.3.96) and 'Afraid to open wide'? by Sandra Alexander (*The Independent*, 17.9.96); R. Twining & Co Ltd for material from their publicity leaflet *The Legend of Tea Drinking*; Express Newspapers Ltd for adapted extracts from 'Deep-fried coronary' by Jonathan Miller (*Sunday Express Magazine*, 25.8.96); The Geographical Magazine for material from 'A rare animal' by Trevor Lawson (*Geographical Magazine April*, 1995); Express Newspapers Ltd for extracts from a feature article by John Ingham (*The Express*, 4.3.97); News International Newspapers Ltd for extracts from 'The Horse's Tale' by Rachel Campbell-Johnston (*The Sunday Times Magazine*, 21.6.97) © Times Newspapers Ltd 1997; The Guardian Newspapers Ltd for extracts from 'Suspect is blue, large and hairy' by Martin Wainwright (*The Guardian*, 16.4.96), 'Two beers please' by Dolly Dhingra (*The Guardian*, 19.2.01), 'Mind your language' by Bill Saunders (*The Guardian*, 18.3.96) © The Guardian; Penny Cottee for extracts from 'Think before you send' (*The Guardian Office Hours supplement*, 14.1.00); Express Newspapers Ltd for extracts from 'Secrets of the office password' by Edward Black (*The Express* 23.6.01); Independent Newspapers for extracts from 'The joy of reading leaves men on the shelf' by Marianne Macdonald and Michael Streeter (*The Independent*, 2.1.97); Express Newspapers Ltd for extracts from 'Brief Conceit' by Wendy Vaizey (*Sunday Express Magazine*, 14.10.01), 'How do you row?' by Maria Trkulja and Oliver James (*Sunday Express Magazine*, 25.2.96), an article by Joseph O'Connor (*Sunday Express Magazine*, 23.07.00); Macmillan, London, UK for an extract from *How to argue and win every time* by Gerry Spence; Independent Newspapers for extracts from 'They don't make them like they used to' by Dominic Lutyens (*The Independent Weekend*, 9.3.96); News International Newspapers Ltd for extracts from 'The everyday prodigy' by Sue Fox (*The Times Magazine*, 10.03.01), 'Can you make a Genius' by Joe Joseph (*The Times*, 14.06.01) © Times Newspapers Ltd; Independent Newspapers for extracts from 'Gene Genius?' by Hugh Aldersey-Williams (*The Independent on Sunday*, 10.01.99); Time Out Group for use of material from 'Street Fighter' film review and 'Fortnight Club' comedy review (*Time Out* No. 1293, 31.5.95); City Life Magazine for an extract from 'The Rivals' play review (*City Life* No. 299, 21.1.96); HarperCollins Publishers Ltd for extracts from 'Music and the Mind' from *Origins and Collective functions* by Antony Storr; Cambridge University Press for an extracts from *Working with words: A Guide to Teaching and Learning Vocabulary* © 1986 by Ruth Gairns and Stuart Redman; Telegraph Group Limited for extracts from 'Sixth sense helps to watch your back' by Robert Matthews (*The Sunday Telegraph*, 14.4.96) © Telegraph Group Limited (1996); New Scientist for extracts from 'Dead Letter' (*New Scientist*, 15.5.00); The Economist Newspaper Limited for extracts from 'Machines with minds of their own' (*The Economist Technology Quarterly*, 24.3.01) © The Economist Newspaper Limited,

London (2001); Nicholas Foulkes for 'Minimalism' (*Financial Times Weekend*, 24.02.01); Roger Scruton for 'Winter warmer' (*The Business Magazine, Financial Times Weekend*, 23.12.00); Lucinda Bredin for 'How to live with your own Cézanne' (*The Sunday Telegraph Review*, 11.2.96); Telegraph Group Limited for extracts from 'The naffing of Constable' by John McEwen (*Sunday Telegraph Review*, 28.07.01) © Telegraph Group Limited (2001); David Higham Associates on behalf of Penelope Lively for an extract from *Next to Nature, Art*, published by Random House; Lynn Macritchie for extracts from 'Experiments overshadow video stars' (*Financial Times Weekend*, 28.7.01); Geoffrey Wansell for extracts from 'Looking Ruff' (*The Business Magazine, Financial Times Weekend*, 11.11.00); Financial Times for extracts from 'Postcards from the cutting edge' (*The Lux Column – How to Spend It Magazine*, September 2001); Steven Rose for an extract from *The Making of Memory* (Bantam Press); New Scientist for extracts from 'Strolling by numbers' by Hazel Muir (*New Scientist*, 5.7.97); The Guardian Newspapers Ltd for extracts from 'Bohemia hosts alienated tribe' by William Booth (*The Guardian*, 12.3.96) © The Guardian; New Scientist for extracts from 'Lies, Damn Lies and Statistics' (*New Scientist* 15.9.01); Random House Group Limited and Sheil Land Associates Ltd on behalf of John Humphrys for an Extract from *Devil's Advocate* by John Humphrys published by Hutchinson (1999); Royal Brompton and Harefield NHS Trust for an extract from an Operations Engineer advertisement and Syngeta (formerly Zeneca Agrochemicals) for an extract from a Formulation Chemist advertisement (*New Scientist*, 20.9.97); Independent Newspapers for extracts from 'When Caruso Met Giacomo Puccini' by Nancy Caldwell Sorel (*The Independent Magazine*, 17.2.96); Express Newspapers Ltd for extracts from 'Does Mummy Know Best?' (*Sunday Express Expresso Magazine*, 3.3.96); Independent Newspapers for extracts from 'Who Loves the Firm Today?' by Jack O'Sullivan (*The Independent*, 8.8.96); Metro for extracts from 'Why stress has turned work into a real chore' by Suzanne Stevenson (*Metro Magazine*, 12.06.01); Independent Newspapers for extracts from 'A sticky Business' by Rosalinde Sharp (*The Independent Magazine Section*, 20.4.96); Financial Times for extracts from 'Antartica's Ancient Mariner' by Bill Glenton (*Financial Times Weekend Travel*, 4.6.00); Ned Denny for extracts from 'Ski posters' (*Financial Times How to Spend it Magazine*, January 2001); Atlantic Syndication Partners for extracts from 'The Thrill of it all' by Alistair Scott (*Daily Mail*, 19.01.01); Nicholas Roe for extracts from 'How I lied my way to the top' (*The Sunday Telegraph*, 24.3.96); Independent Newspapers for extracts from 'Stress? It's as old as the hills' by Yvette Cooper (*The Independent*, 8.5.96); David Baker for extracts from 'Is it a bird, is it a shark?' (*Financial Times Weekend*, 14.07.01).

The author and publishers would like to thank the following for permission to reproduce their material:
Abode p144(t); Advertising Archive pp150(tl, bl, br); Alamy/Peter Bowater p7(mr); All Sport p160; Ancient Art and Architecture p122; Arcaid p144(b); Anthony Blake Photo Library pp1(tr, bl, bm, br, ml, tl); Camera Press p131(br); Corbis pp149, 7(tr), 42(tr), 131, 131(tr, br), 193; Haddon Davies/ Macmillan pp150(tr), 188; Derain, Andre, *Harbour of Westminster* © ADAGP Paris and DACS London p136(t); Empics p7(m); J. Friers p63(tl); Getty Images pp22(tr), 42(bl), 43(tr, br), 57, 63(br, bl), 73, 151, 170(mr, br), 193(tr), 206(a), 211(b, c, d); Impact Photos pp106, 107, 170(bl); Image Bank pp13, 42(bl), 161(t), 162, 193; Independent Newspaper/Edwards Sykes p116; Lebrecht Music Collection pp89, 95, 97; Mary Evans Picture Library pp26; D.J Mills and Co p182; Ronald Grant pp84, 87; Macmillan p58; Mondrian, *Piet Tableau No 1*, Mondrian/Holtzman Trust, 90 Beeldrecht, Amsterdam, Holland and DACS London p136(r); A Painter p137; Popperfoto pp6, 22(l), 27; Frank Spooner pp22(t), 24; Stone pp1(mr), 7(b, tl)22(b), 68, 116(m), 170(t), 195; Sunday Times/Jason Bell p161(b); Superstock (Chen, Tsing Fang, *The Awaking Gypsy*) p136(m); Topham p62; World Pictures p131(tl)

Commissioned photography by: Chris Honeywell p148(tr) and p188.

Whilst every effort has been made to locate the owners of copyright, in some cases this has been unsuccessful. The publishers apologize for any omission of original sources and would be pleased to make the necessary arrangements at the first opportunity.

Printed and bound in Spain by Edelvives

2006 2005 2004 2003 2002
10 9 8 7 6 5 4 3 2